EXPLORATIONS IN SOCIOLOGY
British Sociological Association conference

Sami Zubaida (editor)	1	Race and Racism
Richard Brown (editor)	2	Knowledge, Education and Cultural Change
Paul Rock and Mary McIntosh (editors)	3	Deviance and Social Control
Emanuel de Kadt and Gavin Williams (editors)	4	Sociology and Development
Frank Parkin (editor)	5	*The Social Analysis of Class Structure*
Diana Leonard Barker and Sheila Allen (editors)	6	*Sexual Division and Society: Process and Change*
Diana Leonard Barker and Sheila Allen (editors)	7	*Dependence and Exploitation in Work and Marriage*
Richard Scase (editor)	8	*Industrial Society: Class, Cleavage and Control*
Robert Dingwall, Christian Heath, Margaret Reid and Margaret Stacey (editors)	9	*Health Care and Health Knowledge*
Robert Dingwall, Christian Heath, Margaret Reid and Margaret Stacey (editors)	10	*Health and the Division of Labour*
Gary Littlejohn, Barry Smart, John Wakeford and Nira Yuval-Davis (editors)	11	*Power and the State*
Michèle Barrett, Philip Corrigan, Annette Kuhn and Janet Wolff (editors)	12	*Ideology and Cultural Production*
Bob Fryer, Allan Hunt, Doreen MacBarnet and Bert Moorhouse (editors)	13	*Law, State and Society*
Philip Abrams, Rosemary Deem, Janet Finch and Paul Rock (editors)	14	*Practice and Progress: British Sociology 1950–1980*
Graham Day, Lesley Caldwell, Karen Jones, David Robbins and Hilary Rose (editors)	15	*Diversity and Decomposition in the Labour Market*
David Robbins, Lesley Caldwell, Graham Day, Karen Jones and Hilary Rose (editors)	16	*Rethinking Social Inequality*
Eva Gamarnikow, David Morgan, June Purvis and Daphne Taylorson (editors)	17	*The Public and the Private*
Eva Gamarnikow, David Morgan, June Purvis and Daphne Taylorson (editors)	18	*Gender, Class and Work*
*Gareth Rees, Janet Bujra, Paul Littlewood, Howard Newby and Teresa L. Rees (editors)	19	*Political Action and Social Identity: Class, Locality and Ideology*
*Howard Newby, Janet Bujra, Paul Littlewood, Gareth Rees, Teresa L. Rees (editors)	20	*Restructuring Capital: Recession and Reorganization in Industrial Society*
*Sheila Allen, Kate Purcell, Alan Waton and Stephen Wood (editors)	21	*The Experience of Unemployment*
*Kate Purcell, Stephen Wood, Alan Waton and Sheila Allen (editors)	22	*The Changing Experience of Employment: Restructuring and Recession*
*Jalna Hanmer and Mary Maynard (editors)	23	*Women, Violence and Social Control*
*Colin Creighton and Martin Shaw (editors)	24	*The Sociology of War and Peace*
*Alan Bryman, Bill Bytheway, Patricia Allatt and Teresa Keil (editors)	25	*Rethinking the Life Cycle*

*Patricia Allatt, Teresa Keil, Alan Bryman and Bill Bytheway (editors)	26	*Women and the Life Cycle*
*Ian Varcoe, Maureen McNeil and Steven Yearley (editors)	27	*Deciphering Science and Technology*
*Maureen McNeil, Ian Varcoe and Steven Yearley (editors)	28	*The New Reproductive Technologies*
David McCrone, Stephen Kendrick and Pat Straw (editors)	29	*The Making of Scotland*
*Stephen Kendrick, Pat Straw and David McCrone (editors)	30	*Interpreting the Past, Understanding the Present*
*Lynn Jamieson and Helen Corr (editors)	31	*State, Private Life and Political Change*
*Helen Corr and Lynn Jamieson (editors)	32	*Politics of Everyday Life: Continuity and Change in Work and the Family*
*Geoff Payne and Malcolm Cross (editors)	33	*Sociology in Action: Applications and Opportunities for the 1990s*
*Pamela Abbott and Claire Wallace (editors)	34	*Gender, Power and Sexuality*
*Robert Reiner and Malcolm Cross (editors)	35	*Beyond Law and Order: Criminal Justice Policy and Politics into the 1990s*
Pamela Abbott and Geoff Payne (editors)	36	*New Directions in the Sociology of Health and Illness*
Claire Wallace and Malcolm Cross (editors)	37	*Youth in Transition: The Sociology of Youth and Youth Policy*
Malcolm Cross and Geoff Payne (editors)	38	*Social Inequality and the Enterprise Culture: Towards a New Sociology of Work*

**Published by Macmillan*

Series Standing Order

If you would like to receive future titles in this series as they are published, you can make use of our standing order facility. To place a standing order please contact your bookseller or, in case of difficulty, write to us at the address below with your name and address and the name of the series. Please state with which title you wish to begin your standing order. (If you live outside the UK we may not have the rights for your area, in which case we will forward your order to the publisher concerned.)

Standing Order Service, Macmillan Distribution Ltd, Houndmills, Basingstoke, Hampshire, RG21 2XS, England.

Gender, Power and Sexuality

Edited by
Pamela Abbott
Principal Lecturer in Sociology and Social Policy
Polytechnic South West, Plymouth

and
Claire Wallace
Lecturer in Applied Social Science
University of Lancaster

© British Sociological Association 1991

All rights reserved. No reproduction, copy or transmission
of this publication may be made without written permission.

No paragraph of this publication may be reproduced, copied or
transmitted save with written permission or in accordance with
the provisions of the Copyright, Designs and Patents Act 1988,
or under the terms of any licence permitting limited copying
issued by the Copyright Licensing Agency, 33–4 Alfred Place,
London WC1E 7DP.

Any person who does any unauthorised act in relation to
this publication may be liable to criminal prosecution and
civil claims for damages.

First published 1991

Published by
MACMILLAN ACADEMIC AND PROFESSIONAL LTD
Houndmills, Basingstoke, Hampshire RG21 2XS
and London
Companies and representatives
throughout the world

Typeset by
Footnote Graphics, Warminster, Wiltshire

Printed in Hong Kong

British Library Cataloguing in Publication Data
Gender, power and sexuality.—(Explorations in
sociology v.34)
1. Society. Role of women. Feminist theories
I. Abbott, Pamela *1947–*   II. Wallace, Claire *1956–*   III.
Series
305.4201
ISBN 0–333–54277–0 (hardcover)
ISBN 0–333–54278–9 (paperback)

Contents

List of Tables		vii
Notes on the Contributors		viii
Introduction		xi
1	Women's Oppression in the World and in Ourselves: A Fresh Look at Feminism and Psychoanalysis *Caroline New*	1
2	Women and Citizenship: The Insane, the Insolvent and the Inanimate? *Yvonne Summers*	19
3	Money and Power in Marriage *Jan Pahl*	41
4	Governing by Gender? School Governing Bodies after the Education Reform Act *Rosemary Deem*	58
5	Human-Centred Systems ... Women-Centred Systems? Gender Divisions and Office Computer Systems Design *Eileen Green, Jenny Owen, Den Pain and Isabella Stone*	77
6	Young Women, Sexual Harassment and Heterosexuality: Violence, Power Relations and Mixed-Sex Schooling *Jacqui Halson*	97
7	Gender Issues in Inter-Agency Relations: Police, Probation and Social Services *Alice Sampson, David Smith, Geoffrey Pearson, Harry Blagg and Paul Stubbs*	114
8	Policing 'Domestic Violence' *Susan Edwards*	133

9 Penetrating Woman's Bodies: The Problem of Law
  and Medical Technology
  Carol Smart 157

Bibliography 176

Author Index 193

Subject Index 197

List of Tables

2.1	Comparison between British and Swedish rates of universal child allowances	31
3.1	Control of finances by total household income	44
3.2	Control of finances by employment pattern	45
3.3	Employment pattern by dominance in decision-making	48
3.4	Control of finances by dominance in decision-making	48
3.5	Marital happiness by control of finances	56
4.1	Case-study school governing bodies' membership by gender, July 1989	67
8.1	Evaluating police policy on domestic incidents – Holloway	152
8.2	Evaluating police policy on domestic incidents – Hounslow	153

Notes on the Contributors

Harry Blagg is a Lecturer in Social Policy at Lancaster University and Director of the University's Child Policy Research Centre. He is co-author of *Crime, Penal Policy and Social Work* (1989) and *Child Sexual Abuse: Listening, Hearing and Validating the Experiences of Children* (1989). He is currently carrying out research on sexual abuse inquiry work.

Rosemary Deem is a Senior Lecturer in Education at the Open University. From 1981 until May 1989 she was a county councillor in Buckinghamshire; she is also an experienced school governor. Much of her work has been in the area of gender and education (*Women and Schooling*, 1978; (ed.) *Schooling for Women*, 1980; (ed.) *Coeducation Reconsidered* 1984) and the sociology of leisure (*All Work and No Play*, 1986; *Work, Unemployment and Leisure*, 1988). Since October 1988, she has been conducting research on school governing bodies in two LEAs. This is a joint project being carried out with Dr K. J. Brehony of the University of Reading.

Susan Edwards has been working in the area of criminology and sociology of law since 1975. She is author of *Female Sexuality and the Law* (1981), *Women on Trial* (1984), and editor of *Gender, Sex and the Law* (1985) and *Policing and Domestic Violence* (1989). She teaches socio-legal studies and criminology at the University of Buckingham and trains police officers and magistrates in the UK.

Eileen Green has co-directed the Human-Centred Office Systems Project at Sheffield City Polytechnic since 1987. Previous research includes projects on mothers in paid work, and gender and leisure. She teaches sociology and women's studies and since 1988 has been Director of Sheffield Polytechnic's Centre for Women's Studies.

Jacqui Halson is a Lecturer in Sociology at the University of Kent at Canterbury, teaching 'deviance' and research methods. She has previously lectured at Coventry Polytechnic and taught in Adult and Further Education in Coventry and Leeds. She is currently writing up a doctoral thesis on *Gendered Subjectivity: Coercion and Resistance*.

Notes on the Contributors

Caroline New is co-author, with Miriam David, of *For the Children's Sake* (Penguin, 1985) and is at present working on a thesis/book about mental health, psychotherapy and politics, based at the School of Advanced Urban Studies, University of Bristol.

Jenny Owen has been working with the Human-Centred Office Systems Project at Sheffield Polytechnic since 1985, as a research student until 1988, and now as a research associate. Before joining the project she worked for nine years in adult education and community work, primarily with women. She has two children.

Jan Pahl is Director of Research at the National Institute for Social Work. Her previous publications include *Private Violence and Public Policy* and *Money and Marriage*. Her current research programme includes studies of maternity care and of services for mentally ill and mentally handicapped people.

Den Pain has co-directed the Human-Centred Office Systems Project at Sheffield City Polytechnic since 1984. He also teaches computer studies, economics and business studies, with major responsibilities for systems development. Prior to joining the Polytechnic he worked as a computer programmer and project manager for a software company.

Geoffrey Pearson is Wates Professor of Social Work in the University of London, at Goldsmiths College. He has previously worked at University College Cardiff, the University of Bradford and Middlesex Polytechnic. He is the author of *Deviant Imagination* (1983) and *The New Heroin Users* (1987).

Alice Sampson is a former Visiting Research Fellow at Middlesex Polytechnic, and at present a Research Officer at the Home Office Crime Prevention Unit.

Carol Smart is a Senior Lecturer in Sociology at the University of Warwick. She was formerly the director of the National Council for One Parent Families. Her publications include *Feminism and the Power of Law*, *The Ties that Bind* and *Woman, Crime and Criminology*. She is co-author of *Ideologies of Welfare* with Allan Cochrane and John Clarke, and co-editor of *Child Custody and the Politics of Gender*, *Women in Law*, and *Women, Sexuality and Social Control*.

Notes on the Contributors

David Smith is a Lecturer in Social Work at the University of Lancaster. He is co-author of *Out of Care* (1980) and *Crime, Penal Policy and Social Work* (1989). He has published a number of articles on social work and criminal justice, and at present is doing research on social work in prisons.

Isabella Stone worked as a Research Associate for the Human-Centred Office Systems Project at Sheffield City Polytechnic from 1988 to 1989. Her previous research work was undertaken in the area of women's employment and equal opportunities policies, primarily in the public sector. The report of the research she carried out in 1986 for the Equal Opportunities Commission was published in 1988 by HMSO. She is currently employed by a major metropolitan local authority on policy development in the area of equal opportunities and social inequality.

Paul Stubbs is a Visiting Research Fellow at Lancaster University.

Yvonne Summers is a postgraduate student in the Department of Social and Political Studies at the University of Cambridge. Her thesis concerns the implications of family policy approaches on the social citizenship of women in Britain and Sweden.

Introduction

In a recent collection of readings on power edited by Stephen Lukes (1986), a number of classical discussions of power are brought together. Each seeks a definition of power in different ways – as domination, as legitimate authority, as a product of class or state relations, as an act of will, and so on. The authors also search for the places in which power is to be seen in its operation – in governments, in Cabinets, in organisations, in courtrooms, to name but a few. Nowhere, however, is there any discussion of gender relations in terms of power. In the classical discussions, power is more often seen as a product of public institutions such as the state and the economy rather than of private institutions such as the family and interpersonal relations. Yet if we are considering gender and power, our attention is directed towards these more 'private' institutions, and their relations to the more public institutions of power.

It could be argued, perhaps, that male/female relations can be taken as an example of power as defined in the 'classical' discussions, but to do so ignores the fact that patriarchy is a fundamental structuring institution in society rather than simply another example of a kind of power. Patriarchal power – domination by men – has been one of the most fundamental structuring devices of all societies, and the kinds of explanation usually advanced to explain power relations are not adequate to encompass it. When discussing the granting of political power through citizenship since the eighteenth century, we have to note that this did not include women. Women can be office-holders and sit on governing bodies, as Rosemary Deem's research shows (chapter 4, this volume), and yet be silenced and ignored. Women can hold positions of responsibility equal to those held by men – in the police, for example – and still be diminished through sexual harassment. Women can earn their living in the market-place and yet still be subordinated within the family. The courts can be used to 'protect' women, but do so by defining them as at the mercy of their hormones or their unreliable bodies. Within the family women hold power over children and dependent relatives, but this also needs to be set within the context of a patriarchal power which serves to define family relations. We need to understand the interpenetration of public and private domains in order to make full sense of all this.

Why do men hold power? We reject the explanation that is simply because they are physically stronger. Rather, we need to look at how power enables men to define situations, to define what is 'real' – even within sociology, so that patriarchal power is not even seen as a main issue. The ways in which women are defined away or portrayed in particular ways through legal or medical discourse are examples of the diffusion of power which we need to unravel: for example, the ways in which they are not even defined as potential citizens, the ways in which they are defined in terms of their bodies or their sexuality, and the ways in which the skills which they possess are not considered to be of any importance.

This volume is a selection of papers around a common theme which were prepared for the April 1989 Annual Conference of the British Sociological Association, *Sociology in Action*, held in Plymouth. They are all concerned with issues of gender, power and/or sexuality. They are written from different feminist perspectives and have different areas of concern, but they all focus on the subordination of women in contemporary British society, in the home, at school, in the workplace and in the legal system. The papers explore the various diffusions and complexities of power in relation to gender. However, they are not dealing with issues of concern only to women, but issues that need to be made central to sociology and of importance to society as a whole. If we can understand the ways in which power is structured and the ways in which it affects women, the possibility emerges of challenging it more effectively. Many of the papers in this collection not only describe power but also illustrate ways in which women resist it and ways in which it could be resisted more effectively in the future. Contributions to this volume illustrate that women are controlled by lack of access to economic resources and to positions of formal power, but also in a range of other ways which involve sexuality – the ways in which they are defined as sexual beings and, deriving from these, the ways in which they are the victims of sexual abuse. Sexuality emerges repeatedly as the instrument by which power over women is maintained and exercised because it serves to define them in particular ways.

Feminists start from the view that women are oppressed and that the oppression is primary. Women's freedom of action is limited by the power of men – because men possess more economic, cultural and social resources than women. The traditional emphasis in mainstream sociology has been on the state, the economy and other public institutions as the main sources of oppression. Power and oppression in 'private' institutions such as the family and in interpersonal relationships in both the public and the private spheres have been ignored or marginalised. Feminists have pointed out that the personal is political – i.e. that it is active agents who 'do the oppressing' and that it is necessary to give credence to women's concrete experiences of oppression – ones occurring in personal everyday events – as well as those at the collective and the institutional level. We need to recognise that men and women, oppressors and oppressed, confront one another in their everyday lives, in the home, at school, at work, in the courts, and so on.

The contributions to this volume not only document the ways in which women are subject to patriarchal power, but they also illustrate the ways in which women can challenge this. On the basis of their own experience and from their own position, women can challenge patriarchal ideology and discourses that construct women as different from and inferior to men. Men's power rests not on biological fact, but on the ways in which they have constituted the production of knowledge and become arbiters of truth. It is this also that women have to challenge and reveal as construction, not eternal truth.

PAMELA ABBOTT
CLAIRE WALLACE

1 Women's Oppression in the World and in Ourselves: A Fresh Look at Feminism and Psychoanalysis

Caroline New

INTRODUCTION: CONSCIOUSNESS-RAISING AND PSYCHOANALYSIS

Consciousness-raising has played the unifying role in the second great wave of feminism that the struggle for the vote played in the first wave. Women had been sharing feelings and experiences 'since language was invented – but what was new was that they were now drawing political conclusions from their personal experiences' (Coote and Campbell, 1987, p. 5). What had seemed individual turned out to be general, what had seemed psychological turned out to be the result of social organisation, what had seemed acceptable turned out to be outrageous. This meant that things could be changed that had seemed like facts of nature. The motor of change was consciousness; the enemy, lack of awareness. Inevitably the women's movement at first saw psychoanalysis as one of the bulwarks of patriarchy, as a distracting, disempowering route to conservatism.

Freud was a patriarch, and looked the part. His misogyny was blatant, extraordinary, delivered in the bland, professorial tones of the lecture hall.

> Modesty, which is regarded as *par excellence* a characteristic of women ... was, in our opinion, originally designed to hide the deficiency in their genitals ... People say that women contributed but little to the discoveries and inventions of civilisation, but perhaps after all they did discover one technical process, that of plaiting and weaving. If this is so, one is tempted to guess at the unconscious motive at the back of this achievement. Nature herself might be regarded as having provided

a model for imitation, by causing pubic hair to grow at the period of sexual maturity so as to veil the genitals. The step that remained to be taken was to attach the hairs permanently together, whereas in the body they are fixed in the skin and only tangled with one another. (Freud, 1955e, p. 132)

He offered the female analysts around him the age-old message, which in terms of his theory might have been a sting in the tail:

psychoanalysis ... does not try to describe what women are ... but it investigates the way in which women develop out of children with their bisexual disposition ... several excellent women analysts have begun to work on the problem. A special piquancy has been lent to the discussion of this subject by the question of the difference between the sexes; for, whenever a comparison was made which seemed to be unfavourable to their sex, the ladies were able to express a suspicion that we, the men analysts, have never overcome certain deep-rooted prejudices against the feminine ... On the other hand, on the basis of bisexuality, we found it easy to avoid any impoliteness. We had only to say 'This does not apply to you. You are an exception, in this respect you are more masculine than feminine.' (Freud 1955e, p. 116)

It is easy to see that psychoanalysis, the study of the unconscious mind, would lack appeal to a group of women who were discovering the very real power of deliberately changing a conscious viewpoint. It echoed women's experience of being told that what they saw and felt and heard happening was not, in fact, the case. In 1897 Freud had retreated from his 'trauma theory' of neurosis, and developed the theory of infantile sexuality and fantasied wish fulfilment. (Freud, 1955c, p. 370). Thus Freud turned from a view of the relationship between parent and child as involving asymmetry of power which is sometimes abused, to a view in which seduction, when it does happen, is disturbing for the child precisely because its fulfils forbidden desires. This shift puts psychoanalysis on a collision course with feminism. The emphasis on the child's sexuality in cases of incest is reminiscent of the emphasis on the woman's sexuality and her response in cases of rape.

The actual power structure of psychoanalysis, and the notion of the client as 'patient' (i.e., as pathologised), was also an obstacle for feminists. Most psychoanalysts were male, and it seemed that they were setting themselves up against women as experts on the reality of women's lives. Such relationships had become anathema to those many women whose conception of feminism was to question all such asymmetries of power.

All oppressed groups have their experience dismissed as imaginary, exceptional or exaggerated. This is an integral part of the oppression itself, and an inevitable one, since all those with an interest in the status quo (or simply frightened of change) will defend a viewpoint which minimises or denies the oppression (cf. Miller, 1978, p. 8). To become conscious of your oppression, to decide to resist it, involves rejecting certain dominant viewpoints. The corollary of this is twofold. On the one hand there is inevitable loss, in this case loss perhaps of parents, husband or other loved men and women whose disapproval has now to be faced. The sense of loss is often denied to avoid the pain of its recognition. On the other hand the radical often secretly fears that her new viewpoint is wrong. To set oneself against society and to be wrong is akin to being mad, and the very possibility awakens fear of the mental health system – itself an important dimension of women's oppression. This possibility, too, has to be denied. On several counts the new Women's Liberation Movement (WLM) had reason to suspect and dislike psychoanalysis, not only because of Freud's misogyny and the use of the concept of 'penis-envy' to dismiss women's claims for equality, not only because of ideological objections to its hierarchical structure and treatment methods, but also because of its suspected power to uncover and threaten necessary defences. It was denounced or dismissed. (See, for example, Millett, 1971, p. 178; Friedan, 1963, p. 103.)

Initially, because of the unacceptability of psychoanalysis, feminists turned to psychology and sociology for explanatory models of gender differentiation, for insight into what Denise Riley calls 'socialised biology' (Riley, 1983, p. 40). The enduring classic is, of course, role theory, about which but a couple of relevant points can be made here. A role is a set of expected behaviours that is in some way internalised so that the role-occupant feels that behaving in these ways is simply self-expression. But in that case how can gender identity survive behaving 'out of role'? Women or men who swap roles in the nuclear family, say, still remain quite sure of their sex, while many people of both sexes who follow conventional roles secretly feel unfeminine or unmasculine. The concept of role always suggests a removable mask over a true face. This fits some situations well: we do, sometimes, consciously play parts, dress for them, adjust our speech to produce the desired impact – the 'good mother', the 'reliable employee', the 'repentant defendant'. But for gender roles we'd be hard put to find our 'true selves'. The mask is fused to the skin, yet we squirm uncomfortably inside it. Just when the mechanisms become mysterious and we could do with an explanatory concept, 'role' illuminates nothing.

Social learning theory usually incorporates the concept of role, and tries to explain how socially expected behaviour is brought about and eventually 'learnt'. The use of the word 'learnt' is odd here, because we are not talking about acquiring competence, nor simply about acquiring the habit of behaving in this way, rather than another way, in certain situations. We are talking about learning to feel responsible for keeping everybody happy and harmonious, or learning to prefer Cindy dolls to Action Men, not just learning how to use a microwave. In the 'social learning' account, certain sorts of behaviour are punished and others, presumably, rewarded. Of course, this does happen, and it is important. However, while social learning theory can plausibly account for a lot of behaviour, it has more trouble accounting for how we *feel*. There is a difference between the girl who wants to play with boys but abstains because of social pressure, and the girl who does not have the slightest (conscious) desire to do so. If the former will, in the course of time, become the latter, the mechanism has yet to be explained. To move from behaviour to feeling, social learning theory, cognitive-developmental theory and role theory all depend on at least one psycho-dynamic concept: that of identification. Identification is more than imitation and implies some psycho-dynamic model of the mind.

Social learning theory has trouble explaining both conformity and non-conformity. It over-explains conformity to role. As Sayers points out, many women and men 'feel free to be both masculine and feminine in their behaviour' (Sayers, 1986, p. 28). How is this possible, in the face of the social armoury of positive and negative reinforcement? On the other hand, nonconformity itself is problematic. Women whose behaviour is autonomous and 'androgynous' often struggle against urges to look after everyone, especially men. It is not so much the role which has persisted, as the feeling. A stronger point could be made. People do contravene gender roles, but they do not always or even usually 'feel free' about it. They contravene them *although* they feel bad. A common example would be feminists refusing to shave their legs, yet disliking the appearance of the hairy legs they might find attractive on a man. If they don't like their legs hairy, why not shave them? Usually people contravene roles, despite discomfort, because they feel bad when they *obey* role expectations too. It is this dynamic aspect, this inner conflict, which social learning theory cannot deal with, and this realisation has been one factor in the current resurgence of feminist interest in psychoanalysis.

Feminists' return to interest in psychoanalysis also sprang from the felt inadequacies of consciousness-raising:

> we began to perceive the limitations of consciousness-raising groups ... Changing our own behaviour and feelings was ... sometimes excruciatingly difficult ... we believed women should be independent, not possessive or insecure, but these beliefs did not lead to habitual emotional responses ... A second difficulty ... was that precisely because the consciousness-raising groups were so emotionally charged ... feelings between members in the groups were often not handled very well. Feelings of envy, competition, anger and love emerged and were so powerful that the groups sometimes could not cope with them. Women in these groups had to ask: 'How do we change what is so deeply rooted in us? How can I change how I feel? How can I understand what is going on at an unconscious level?' (Eichenbaum and Orbach, 1985, p. 11)

The feelings of envy and competition between women were hard to handle for women who had taken refuge in the warmth and security of sisterhood. It became clear that the women's movement could not provide a warm interior, a refuge from the raging of patriarchy. As in Eichenbaum and Orbach's earlier title, the outside was inside and the inside out. Although the sentimentalising of sisterhood still persists, it has been increasingly challenged, by working-class women, by Jews, by black women, and through the resulting struggles the women's movement has become less united, less homogeneous, intellectually richer and wider in scope. These changes do not mean the conflicts of interest, disagreements and negative feelings between women are somehow more real or more permanent than love and solidarity between women. They do indicate that understanding sexual difference and gender differentiation is a political priority, so that our political aims are grounded in reality and we develop tools to handle the conflicts between us.

PSYCHOANALYSIS AND FEMINISM: ONE MEETING BETWEEN THEM

Thinking along these lines, some feminist activists and theorists have turned to psychoanalysis in search of solid foundations for their political practice. Others become patients in the hope that exploring their unconscious fantasies would reveal the source of self-sabotage and allow them to overcome it. In a parallel movement, a few therapists also turned to psychoanalysis (see, for example, Eichenbaum and Orbach, 1985, p. 13). They were not attracted by psychoanalytic claims to liberate women from the psychic reverberations of sexist society, for it made no such claims. The attraction was, rather, its apparent insight into the roots of conservatism in sexual politics. However, there is but a step between explaining the inevitability of conservatism and espousing it. Knowledge is power, but it is not yet clear whether any of the various schools of psychoanalysis give us the theoretical tools to frame new and realistic strategies and tactics in the struggle against the structure of male domination, or whether they disarm us by concluding that the feminist project is inherently utopian.

Which feminist project? I'm not talking here about 'revolutionary feminist' separatism, which has its own brand of biological essentialism unthreatened by psychoanalysis (for example Daly, 1979). I am referring to the strands in both radical and socialist feminism which aim to eliminate any institutionalised sexual division of labour beyond giving birth and breastfeeding. This means assuming that men can mother and women fight. If so, the psychological differences between men and women can only be creations of their life experiences, including the physical sensations that are sex-linked, but which get their significance, and even their quality as sensations, from their place in the human culture within which they are experienced. This strand of feminism, that challenges all gender-based restrictions, also rejects any clinical assumptions that 'mental health' is attainable for women without falling foul of social expectations around gender. It agrees with psychoanalysis that sexuality is constructed and that social pressure plays a major role in determining adults' sexual orientation, but does not draw the mysterious conclusion that heterosexuality is the only acceptable outcome. It seeks to change the family, not only by private struggles around childcare and sexuality, but also by

> the construction of campaigns to change the family at different levels and in different ways; social policy, income maintenance, child care provision, obstetric practices ... Unless the family *is* radically changed (not abolished) I do not see how we can develop different child rearing practices in which a sexual identity is constructed that gives more conscious and creative control to the child than s/he currently enjoys, and which is not so hysterically obsessed with one particular form of difference. (Wilson, 1981)

Is such a project possible? We need to know – the answer may well affect the way we decide to spend our time. Like Elizabeth Wilson in the article quoted above, I feel there is a new feminist orthodoxy which has stopped asking whether psychoanalytic theories are *valid*: whether they are consistent, whether the evidence for them holds water, whether they account for known phenomena. The sheer beauty and fascination of psychoanalytic accounts can have a hypnotic effect, so that their inconsistency with feminism goes unremarked. And then, by the same token, the validity of feminism and its political project remains unchallenged. In the pages that follow I look very briefly at some major schools of psychoanalysis and focus on how their accounts of gender differentiation mesh or clash with the stand of feminism described above.

FREUD

Freud's account begins, of course, with bisexuality. Boy and girl begin with similar drives and potential for experiencing suckling, being kept clean and being toilet-trained as pleasurable. Both are active and passive. Freud rejected the equation of 'active' with masculine and 'passive' with feminine (though he regularly fell into it, for example when he unequivocally assumes the female part in heterosexual intercourse is passive). Gender differentiation occurs at the phallic stage, as a result of what seems a contingent series of events. The girl sees the boy's penis and perceives her clitoris as inferior (both sexes are ignorant of the vagina at this stage). She eventually realises that her mother, too, is without a penis, and that for both of them this is a permanent state of affairs. Disillusioned, she gives up masturbating. She turns against her mother: the specific complaint of not having a penis now added to the list of failings that all infants consciously or unconsciously lay at mother's door. She turns to her father, hoping for his love, his penis (to attach to herself or to take into herself) or his (preferably male) child. For the boy, on the other hand, the sight of the girl's penis-less state lends plausibility to castration threats. It confirms him in his heterosexual object choice, since to be loved by his father entails castration. But in his fear of his father's anger, he renounces his desire for his mother and internalises the prohibition against incest, setting up the super-ego as an internalised father (Freud, 1955e).

Many things could be said about this story, and many of them have already been said. In one crucial way it seems compatible with feminism, since it is an account of the *construction* of gender on the basis of original bisexuality. Together with the understanding of psychic conflict made possible by the concept of the unconscious mind, the idea of bisexuality enabled Freud to explain women's *submission* to male-dominated society (in terms of the female Oedipus complex) without making women's *resistance* (persistence of the 'masculine') incomprehensible (Sayers, 1981, p. 100).

However, as an account of the *social* construction of gender, Freud's is unusual. The mechanisms which bring about obedience to the incest taboo, and (usually) the choice of heterosexual adult love objects, are presented in terms of universal 'natural' human reactions to the sight of the female genitals and the realisation that the lack of a penis is permanent. The superiority of the penis is presented as obvious, common sense; an anatomical rather than a social fact. In this sense the account is highly determinist, and anatomy plays the determining role.

What if the boy or girl never see the genitals of the other sex? Ann Oakley (1981, p. 99) cites a whole series of studies that claim to show that gender identity and development are independent of knowledge of, or sight of, genitals:

> Physical sex differences are not the most salient determinant of gender identity for children (it is not irrelevant that blind children develop stable gender identities – Person, 1974). Identification with a parental model is not, apparently, the most powerful force establishing gender differences. Most persuasive of all, children regard themselves as feminine or masculine at an age at which Freud has them still in a state of ignorance. (Oakley, 1981, p. 100)

Reading these pages of Oakley's, it is easy to see why psychoanalysis and sociology sometimes pass like ships in the night. Freud's statements *sound* like empirical ones, so that some difference in psycho-sexual development might be expected if the posited happenings did not occur in individual instances. But in fact, they are not really this sort of statement at all. This is clear for castration threats, where Freud remarks that their absence will not affect the basic course of development, for 'children construct this danger for themselves out of the slightest hints, which will never be wanting' (1955a, p. 8). Writing of a four-year-old whose infantile neurosis he analysed in retrospect, Freud said:

There is no doubt whatever that at this time his father was turning into the terrifying figure that threatened him with castration ... At this point the boy has to fit himself into a phylogenetic schema, and he did so, although his personal experiences may not have agreed with it. The threats or hints of castration which he had come across had, on the contrary, emanated from women, but this could not hold up the final result for long. In spite of everything it was his father from whom in the end he came to fear castration. (1955d, p. 86)

Freud thought that the unconscious contained memories from human prehistory, including the guilt for the original murder of the father by his sons (1955b, p. 158). He believed this notion of 'psychical continuity' from generation to generation was essential to explain social development. Phylogenesis, though confined to footnotes in most of Freud's works, plays the role of a second line of defence for the theory. From that point of view sociological investigation into the prevalence of the nuclear family is irrelevant to establishing the validity of the Oedipus complex. Knowledge of gender has certain pre-given unconscious meaning, and should itself trigger the appropriate responses. Yet in the main text Freud emphasises the profound effect on the child of seeing the parents in intercourse, and realising the mother has no penis, as if it were the actual sight which was crucial for gender development. Freud's anatomical determinism is clearly incompatible with feminism, but feminism need not tremble. The status of these events is unclear to Freud himself (see his discussion in 'An Infantile Neurosis', 1955d, Section V) and his followers have clarified them in one way or another.

THE LACANIAN DEVELOPMENT

Juliet Mitchell and other feminist Lacanians offer a certain reading of Freud which substitutes patriarchal society and the Symbolic for phylogenesis as the methodological *deus ex machina* (Mitchell, 1974, p. 402). Certainly it makes a lot more sense to assume that it is a relationship of the penis to the phallus, symbol of power, that determines the boy's and the girl's reactions to her lack. In Mitchell's useful account of Freud's thought (weakened by her tendency to cover up its inconsistencies), she stresses that Freud is not *prescribing* the girl's move to adult womanhood as her repression of active clitoral sexuality, but *describing* what happens in patriarchal society. Freud begins the analysis of patriarchy, without which it cannot be overthrown: 'That Freud's account comes out pessimistic is not so much an index of his reactionary spirit as of the condition of women' (p. 362).

Like Freud, Lacanians begin with bisexuality. Mitchell describes how the concept develops during Freud's work, moving

> from being a simple postulate of a sort of infantile unisex, to being a complete notion of the oscillations and imbalance of a person's mental androgyny . . . the subject is still resolving the precise point of the place he occupies in the world, in terms of his (and her) wish for it not to be the feminine place, which is the only, and ever-present, alternative to where anyone really wants to be – in the male position within the patriarchal human order. (1974, p. 51)

> At first both sexes want to take the place of both the mother and the father, but as they cannot take *both* places, each sex has to learn to repress the characteristics of the other sex. But both, as they learn to speak and live within society, want to take the father's place, and *only the boy will one day be allowed to do so.* (1974, p. 404)

Yet the boy cannot 'have' the phallus any more than the girl can. In settling for being a little boy, who cannot have his mother as his father has her, the boy is accepting symbolic castration, submission to the law of the father.

Lacan does not let us forget that gender differentiation takes place in language and culture, which exist prior to the individual, and which encompass and transcend the micro-social events of the family. His approach should not be confused with the sort of sociological explanation offered by Clara Thompson and, later, Karen Horney (Miller, 1973). In their view the penis is envied because of its association with various powers and privileges. In this account upbringing could have an effect. In a family of strong and self-determining women, the effects of penis envy might be mitigated despite male domination in the wider society. But the power of the Symbolic is beyond such contingencies. It is impossible not to envy the penis, because language itself thinks those thoughts. Such determinism is inevitably conservative. The woman is, not biologically but culturally, the eternal other. Her biology is how we recognise her, but her place, or her exile, is eternally ready-made. Society is *in essence* patriarchal, because it is men who exchange women, and not vice versa. This is in itself no index of inferiority or superiority, Mitchell writes: 'Nevertheless this primary sexual division is an important indicator of difference and a difference that may well be historically exploited to establish a system of deference' (1974, p. 372). There is no theoretical reason why women should not exchange men, she cites Levi-Strauss as admitting, but they never do, and this feature is definitional of human society. Social structure, language and the rest of culture are founded on this patriarchal base. The incompatibility with feminism seems clear.

How, Sayers asks, can Mitchell explain herself and other feminists, if 'women repress in early childhood the desire to accede to the place accorded men in patriarchy'? (Sayers, 1986, p. 89). In the classical Freudian account the answer is clear: repression is not always successful. In the Lacanian account the question has new poignancy: how is it possible for feminism even to be *thought*, if the law of the Father is by definition all-encompassing? Mitchell has an answer: the material basis for the exchange of women and for the incest taboo no longer exists in late capitalism. There is now a contradiction between 'the internalised law of patriarchal human order described by Freud as the Oedipus complex', and the actual forms of the nuclear family and the organisation of work (Mitchell, 1974, p. 413). This contradiction has made women's oppression visible, and now (incomprehensibly, in the light of previous arguments) puts the overthrow of patriarchy on the agenda for the first time in human history and prehistory. So Mitchell advocates Cultural Revolution, and, with a sudden move into voluntarism, finding 'some other expression of the entry into culture than the implications for the unconscious of the exchange of women' (1974, p. 415). Gallop criticises this attempt from a Lacanian perspective. Human beings, subject to the unconscious, are fated not be rational, she says. They cannot 'insist on the birth' of new structures in the unconscious (Gallop, 1982, p. 13). 'It is not patriarchal culture, but the biologistic reduction of the Law of the Dead Father to the rule of the actual, living male that must be struggled against' (Gallop, 1982, p. 14).

This attempt to drive a wedge between phallus and penis, to assert the possibility of patriarchy without male domination, fails to obscure the incompatibility of Lacanianism and feminism.

The theories of Freud and Lacan looked as if they might provide a theoretical basis for feminism only because they were misrepresented. These are not accounts of the social construction of gender in any ordinary sense of 'social', for in both stories gender differentiation is *impervious* to social change – its construction along predictable lines is characteristic of human societies in general, not of particular historical human societies. This does not, of course, mean that Freud and Lacan have not made real discoveries, nor even that they are wrong – but it does shift the terrain of the debate. A closer look at bisexuality – which seems a hopeful concept from a feminist point of view – shows that its psychoanalytic versions are fraught with the sort of difficulties inherent in the term 'androgyny'. The masculine and feminine characteristics united in both terms come to us by courtesy of a sexist society, and their amalgamation tends to obscure the processes of their construction. The very word 'bisexuality' suggest an *original* dualism which I think is simply projected back from our adult gendered selves. Try as he might, Freud continued to think of activity as masculine and passivity as feminine – the yet-to-be-constructed genders are present in his schema from the beginning. The dilemma for girls was to give up being 'masculine' – i.e. autonomous, strong and assertive, as well as clitoral sexuality. Women's 'masculinity' – the extent to which they remain in possession of qualities which all adults need to be able to function well – has been something psychoanalysts have felt bound to explain, only because of the acceptance of the conventional stereotype in the first place.

RECTIFYING THE BIAS – JONES AND HORNEY

Ernest Jones, Karen Horney, Melanie Klein and others criticised Freud's notion of bisexuality as ignoring femininity. They saw themselves as rectifying his bias when they argued that woman was born rather than made, and rejected the idea of the phallic stage in which the little girl, with her clitoral sexuality, was 'a little man'. Little girls had vaginal sensations, they claimed, and were *inherently* heterosexual. Horney did not see penis envy as the result of a blow to female narcissism, but as a regressive flight from womanhood, brought about by unconscious Oedipal fantasies of vaginal damage through intercourse with the father (Horney, 1973a, 1977b). Although Horney increasingly saw the oppression of women as an additional factor in penis envy, her idea of mental health for women was that they stop comparing themselves with men. This 'different but equal' view, rooted in a notion of gender as biologically based, does have supporters in the women's movement, but it is certainly incompatible with the feminism I have described.

MELANIE KLEIN

Melanie Klein is a theorist of great importance in Britain, but comparatively unknown across the Atlantic. Perhaps because Kleinean theory is not readily usable to explain the oppression of women, it has been relatively neglected by feminists. As Sayers says:

> her general focus on internal reality [is] at the cost of losing sight of the extent to which this reality is conditioned by external social reality ... Klein's instinct-based account of psychology ... does not take sufficient account of the way social factors like sex inequality shape women's psychology, and their psychological resistance to the inequality. (Sayers, 1986, p. 62–3).

Where feminists use Klein it tends to be to explain hatred, envy and competition of and between women in terms of infants' feelings towards their mothers (e.g. Dinnerstein, 1987; Bower, 1986).

Klein believed that both boys and girls have innate knowledge of the penis and the vagina. Unlike Freud's concept of *drives* which could have various aims and objects, the tighter Kleinean concept of *instinct* has built-in object and aim: 'Instincts by definition are object-seeking. The experience of an instinct in the mental apparatus is connected with the phantasy of an object appropriate to the instinct' (Segal, 1984, p. 2, and cf. Robinson, 1984, pp. 178–9).

When genital desires appear during the first year of life, still mingled with oral, urethral and anal libido, for the boy they 'imply the search for an opening in which to insert his penis' (Klein, 1988, p. 409) and for the girl 'correspondingly prepare the desire to receive her father's penis into her vagina' (ibid.). It sounds as if Klein conceives gender as simply given by sex, and heterosexuality as instinctually given. But such is not the case. In fact, gender does not play a central part in Kleinean theory. The processes of introjection, projection, splitting and all the defence mechanisms of the infantile ego operate irrespective of gender. (Using these concepts, feminists have been criticised for projecting women's destructive urges onto men, and refusing to recognise our own sadistic impulses (Bower, 1986).) Envy is an early and an inescapable emotion, experienced by the young baby in relation to the breast, because this source of life and good experiences makes her or him feel bad by comparison. Later, each sex will envy the biology of the other. In infancy, the penis is an alternative object of oral desire for both boy and girl. The move to the penis happens in response to frustration with the breast, but is not a once for all event, since 'the inevitable disappointment in the new relation reinforces the pullback to the first object' (Klein, 1988, p. 408). Similarly, heterosexual object choice 'is never completely final ... accompanying the classical positive Oedipus complex, we shall always find in a repressed symbolised form its counterpart, the negative Oedipus complex' (Segal, 1984, p. 99).

Indeed, the negative Oedipal complex, in which the child fantasises itself as being of the other sex and desires the same-sex parent, plays a crucial role in Klein's account of development. Knowledge wins out over phantasy in determining eventual sexual orientation (when it *is* heterosexual), because 'A growing reality sense brings with it the perception of the infant's own sex, and helps towards a partial renunciation of homosexual desires and an acceptance of whichever sex the child is' (Segal, 1984, p. 98).

It seems as though Klein combines Freud's account of the construction of gender on the basis of an original bisexuality with an essentialist conception comparable to Horney's. However, Klein's account is less determinist in terms of outcomes than Freud's. Penis envy in girls is secondary: a defence against the frustrations, anxiety and guilt experienced in the positive Oedipus position, rather than a reaction to a blow to her narcissism. Freud saw women as taking one of three paths. They could remain masculine, at great social cost, become feminine at great personal cost, or reject sexuality altogether and become ill. Klein sees more potential for integration. The girl's admiration for her father (and his penis) and her identification with him in which she imagines herself as male, can coexist with her *feminine* internalisation of his penis as the object of her heterosexual desire (Klein, 1988, p. 414).

From a feminist point of view, the difficulty with Klein's account is its resolutely asocial nature. Women's oppression is not needed to account for women's feelings of powerlessness or anger – the dualism of the life and death instincts, the inevitable frustrations of infancy can do that. On the other hand, the persistence of strong infantile feelings can be used (as by Dinnerstein, 1981) to explain the oppression of women. Social structure is almost redundant. But this means that Klein treats society (especially the nuclear family) as a given; a position that impoverishes her theory and robs it of radical possibilities.

FEMINIST OBJECT-RELATIONS THEORY

The disunity of psychoanalysis is starkly visible when we contrast Lacanianism with feminist object-relations theory, the other school of psychoanalysis associated with Fairbairn, Guntrip and others and developed in their own ways by such feminist therapists as Eichenbaum and Orbach, founders of the Women's Therapy Centres in London and New York. For them 'femininity is part of a girl's experience from birth and not something that comes about at the Oedipal stage' (1985, p. 31). Unlike Freud and Lacan, they are clear that there is no pre-social period in the life of a human being. As Riley puts it, life is not a progression from the biological to the social (1983, p. 33). Even in the womb, the infant has a place in society, and the process through which s/he becomes a conscious participant in social relations begins at birth.

The infant has a place in society, but that place depends on its sex, unknown to the baby, but known to the mother. In this account the baby's responses are circumscribed or powerless, while the mother's carry the full explanatory weight. Experiencing the boy as different from her, she does not merge with him as much as with the little girl. The mother of a son 'sees someone who is quite other, for whom she can imagine a whole world of differing possibilities. But she knows that her daughter will follow her own footsteps' (Riley, 1983, p. 41). With a son 'the difference in sex and gender helps her to be more aware of her own boundaries . . . with a daughter . . . the boundaries are blurred. When she looks at her . . . she sees mirror images of her own experience of being mothered' (Riley, 1983, p. 61).

Her daughter's dependence reawakens buried feelings of neediness, a 'little girl' part of herself which her own mother could not listen to and which social expectations for women have obliged her to repress. The mother then behaves to the little girl in terms of a 'push-pull dynamic', responding appropriately and lovingly when she is able to see her as a separate person, and at other times with the fear and anger she directs towards her inner 'little girl'.

The inconsistency of girls' mothering creates difficulties for their separation and individuation. Just because the daughter is female, the mother unconsciously turns to her 'to make up the loss of her own maternal nurturance and satisfy her continued yearnings . . . As the daughter learns her role as nurturer, *her first child is her mother*' (Riley, 1983, p. 57).

The Oedipus complex is not the crucial level of gender differentiation for Eichenbaum and Orbach. They see the father as representing a welcome escape from the relationship with the mother, because of his clear separateness and the way he stands in for an impersonal world. As Frosch points out (1987, p. 186), the mother is central even in the turn to the father, who confirms and embodies the differences and similarities which have already been unconsciously communicated by the mother's different treatment of boy and girl.

As adults, women have low self-esteem, and feel inadequate and lacking:

> They feel there is a disjuncture between the way they show themselves and are seen to be adults in the world, and their internal experience of insecurity and uncertainty. They worry that if people could see through them they would discover the frequently frightened, nervous and angry little girl inside who is not at all sure where she does belong in relation to others. (Eichenbaum and Orbach, 1987, p. 54)

Women who come for therapy often describe themselves as making relationships in order to feel they have some identity, and as staying in unsatisfactory relationships because they fear a loss of self if they leave them.

Eichenbaum and Orbach try to situate the mother-daughter couple in society. They see the mother as operating within 'excruciating parameters. The oppressed mother must negotiate her relationship with her daughter around and within the fact of her own subordination' (1987, p. 59). She passes on to her daughter, consciously and unconsciously, the information that women are subordinate. It seems as if the role of contingencies in Eichenbaum and Orbach's account offers a lever for social change. Whereas for Lacanians more strong female characters in children's books, for instance, could make no difference to women's built-in marginality, such changes ought to bear some sort of fruit in this less rigid scenario. However, their theory is more determinist than it seemed at first sight. While women mother, the very fact that mother and girl are of the same gender makes successful separation impossible, while it is 'easier for boys to separate from mother, not only because they have father to identify with but also because they can hope to grow up and have another woman to nurture them' (Ernst, 1987, p. 98).

In this case the prospects for feminism are gloomy while women mother women, and the prospects for changing *that* are, as Sayers points out in relation to Chodorow, almost ruled out by the theory itself (Sayers, 1986, p. 75). The cycle of deprivation will roll inexorably on, only slightly chipped by a few women's achievement of separation through remothering in feminist therapy.

Certainly mothers have feelings about their children's gender which affect how they treat them. But they have feelings about many other things as well. I know a white woman with four black children who told me she loved them 'because they are not like me'. Gender was secondary to this other sense of difference. An upwardly-mobile mother may feel that there are possibilities open to her daughter which were not available to her as a child; she may have feelings of difference, of envy and so on. One woman I know decided that her daughter was like her male partner, despite her gender. The phenomena Eichenbaum and Orbach draw attention to are certainly of great importance in working out the relationship between the external and the internal, but that relationship is more complex than they suggest.

It is true that women do, on the whole, have more problems experiencing themselves as separate, autonomous people than men do. Yet mothers also identify with sons, and look to their baby boys for solicitude and nurturance, as well as to their baby girls. Mothers indicate to their sons, as well as to their daughters, that they cannot always tolerate their dependence, and require them to 'develop an acceptable self' in order to be loved. As adults, men and women defend themselves against similar bad feelings, but the socially available means of defence are different for each gender. If women typically feel inadequate and incomplete, men tend to be one step further removed from allowing themselves to feel these feelings. Being the agent of oppression does not encourage mental health any more than being its target; women are not sicker than men, and by suggesting they are, Eichenbaum and Orbach are uncritically repeating a myth which is used to scapegoat woman.

QUESTIONS AND CHALLENGES

This brief review shows the problems involved in enlisting psychoanalysis as a theoretical foundation for feminism. All the schools reviewed (which are typical in this respect), explain the development of gendered subjectivity in ways which seem to rule out a feminist future. According to Frosch, the political relevance of psychoanalysis lies in its potential to link the level of subjectivity with that of social structure, and to theorise the relationship between them. The late Freud, Klein and other object relations theorists make 'object relations and hence social events central aspects of development. From here it is a short step to an elaborated account of how the politics of the external world enter into the mind of the individual' (Frosch, 1987, p. 37).

I think psychoanalysis has not yet taken this 'short step', and that this has limited its contribution to our understanding of women's oppression and liberation.

The shortcomings of the accounts outlined above are not unique to psychoanalysis. As Ros Coward says:

> theoretical explanations of sexual relations are hopelessly polarised between essentialist and deterministic explanations. (Coward, 1983, p. 6)

> Under the theoretical division between individual and society, sexual behaviour has been consigned to the realm of the individual ... [but] sex cannot be consigned to the realm of the individual, [and] the division between individual and society is purely conceptual. It ... must be displaced if we are to develop an understanding of how sexual division can be the basis for oppressive relations. (ibid., p. 262)

A tall order. But clearly psychoanalysis is just as liable as role theory, social learning theory and so on to baulk at these philosophical jumps. Ros Coward seems to be suggesting that the terms of the problem are themselves doomed. On similar lines Burniston, Mort and Weedon (1978) argue that the basic project of psychoanalysis – 'to understand the process of constitution of sexed subjectivity' – is philosophically flawed because it is approached ahistorically (p. 126). There is no general answer to the question of how we become female and male that can explain women's subordination, and to expect one is already to *assume* that the basis of this subordination is universal and unaffected by historical development. Such an argument has implications for the terrain of psychoanalysis which there is no room to explore here. Nor can this paper attempt to tease out the philosophical, historical and political roots of psychoanalytic conservatism. Whatever these may be, we cannot ignore or wish away the current theoretical inconsistency between feminism and psychoanalysis. To move forward, feminists need to challenge psychoanalysis at the level of theory, and to accept the challenge psychoanalysis offers *us*. This involves defining our political aims, identifying the assumptions about human nature and society we are implicitly making, evaluating these assumptions and, in particular, assessing the validity of a psychoanalytic critique.

2 Women and Citizenship: The Insane, the Insolvent and the Inanimate?

Yvonne Summers

INTRODUCTION

Citizenship has been an essential concept in any discussion of the welfare state whether historical or contemporary. The New Right have recently attempted to give a new emphasis to what they have termed 'active citizenship'; the discerning participation of all members of society in the process of welfare provision. But citizenship has never applied equally to men and women. This re-examination of the terms begins with one of the best known theories of citizenship, that of T. H. Marshall, from the point of view of its relevancy to the experiences of women. I shall then go on to consider the ways in which Britain and Sweden deal with men's and women's social citizenship, and the effects of the so-called 'Scandinavian model' for women in those countries.

Some of Marshall's basic assumptions, understandable in the 1960s, have tended to be incorporated, unquestioned, into academic work in the 1980s. For example, Michael Mann recently stated that: 'Marshall's view of citizenship is essentially true – at least as a description of what has actually happened in Britain' (Mann, 1987, p. 340). In fact, Marshall's historical observations describe only the experience of men (Pateman, 1983, 1985).

Marshall's conception of citizenship rights and their development was first presented in the Marshall lectures given in Cambridge in 1949. His central concern was to examine the way in which the dynamic nature of a historical progression towards a position of full equal citizenship for all might interact with the inherent inequalities of a class society. He divided citizenship into three elements: civil, political and social, and charted their historical development, allocating what he described as: 'the formative period in the life of each to a different century – civil rights to the eighteenth, political rights to the nineteenth and social to the twentieth' (Marshall, 1963, p. 76). He then proceeds to qualify this rather rigid distinction by adding a degree of elasticity to the boundaries and an allowance for overlaps, but remaining apparently unaware that this time-scale is completely inappropriate to women's experiences. However, women merit very little attention throughout Marshall's discussion; the male experience is consistently assumed to be the definitive one, the norm.

In Marshall's view, the development of citizenship for all men consisted of 'the gradual addition of new rights to a status that already existed' (Marshall, 1963, p. 79) through the evolution of the Common Law, which Marshall conceived of as reflecting the 'common sense' of the judiciary. However, with respect to women, the Common Law, instead of adapting to allow the addition of further rights to the citizen's portfolio, was used to exclude women from any pretensions to citizenship. The judiciary, far from operating as the far-sighted and benevolent shepherds of progress, resisted every attempt by women to have the Common Law interpreted inclusively (O'Donovan and Szyzyczat, 1988).

Although citizenship has been divided into three separate elements, it is actually more sensible, at this point, to deal with civil and political citizenship simultaneously since, as far as women are concerned, the development or rather formal acknowledgement of both sets of rights followed similar paths and was dependent on the same controversial point: the resistance to the definition of women as 'persons'.

Civil rights, as defined by Marshall, consist of those rights which facilitate the exercise of individual freedom, for example 'liberty of the person, freedom of speech, thought and faith, the right to own property and to conclude valid contracts and the right to justice', while those of political citizenship concern 'the right to participate in an exercise of political power, as a member of a body invested with political authority or as an elector of the members of such a body' (Marshall, 1963, p. 74). But as far as women are concerned, the formative period in the establishment of these rights was not the eighteenth century for civil citizenship nor was it the nineteenth century in the case of women's political rights. It was not until the early twentieth century after considerable campaigns by feminists that the Franchise Act and the Qualification of Women Act 1918 recognised women as citizens with political rights, by allowing women over thirty to vote for Parliament, and in 1919 the Sex Discrimination Removal Act finally legalised women's entry to the public sphere of civil society. Thus in the mid-nineteenth century, when Marshall claims that 'civil rights had come to man's estate' (p. 77), the political rights of women were held to be encompassed and represented by their male kin while their rights to exercise what we now view as basic civil liberties were being disputed in the courts as they fought to be recognised as 'persons'.

Perhaps the best way to illustrate the implication for women of their inadequate citizenship is to look at what Marshall saw as one of the fundamental civil rights in the economic sphere: the right to work, or more precisely, 'the right to follow the occupation of one's choice, in the place of one's choice, subject only to legitimate demands for preliminary technical training' (Marshall, 1963, p. 77). Marshall argues that in the case of restrictions on the location and types of employment open to particular men, the flexibility of the Common Law and the changing attitudes of society as a whole, reflected by the legal profession, allowed changes in custom and practice to come about relatively quickly and painlessly. This was certainly not the case for women. Of course the experiences of women with respect to paid employment varied considerably according to, among other things, social class, but in essence the problem in every case can be brought back to the perception of women as possessing deficient citizenship status. In the case of middle-class women this can be seen in the attempts by women to enter the professions and the efforts of men to keep them out, while for working-class women, who could not be excluded from the labour market for obvious reasons of economic expediency, similar preconceptions are recognisable in the implementation of protective legislation.

One of the most celebrated cases of middle-class women turning to the law for recognition of their civil citizenship rights concerns the admission, in 1869, of Sophia Jex-Blake and six other women to the Edinburgh medical school. Having been admitted to classes, held separately from their male colleagues, the seven were subsequently thrown out because they refused to give an undertaking that they would not demand degrees if they reached the required standard in examinations. Understandably, they resorted to the law in the hope of having their 'universal' rights recognised. However, the result in this case, as in so many others of its type, was not validation of the women's status as 'equal citizens' or 'qualified persons' but was rather seized upon by the judiciary as an opportunity to restate and reinforce the dominant perception of women's place in society: 'Without embarrassment or apology, the judges painted a picture of women as being too delicate and refined to undertake public function, and accordingly classified them legally alongside the insane, the insolvent, and even in one case alongside the inanimate' (Sachs and Wilson, 1978, p. 6). (See Sachs and Wilson, 1978; O'Donovan and Szyzyczat, 1988; or Atkins and Hoggett, 1984, for other examples.)

Thus people certified as insane as well as those individuals poor enough and desperate enough to resort to the workhouse were among those who were not considered capable of dealing with the rights and duties of citizenship. In one case the presiding judges declared that the election to public office of a woman was like the election of a dead man or an inanimate thing; in other words, 'a mere nullity' (Sachs and Wilson, 1978, p. 27).

The concern of upper-class men and, most influentially, the judiciary for the delicacy and refinement of women, so threatened by the demands of public office, did not appear to extend to the working class, and as industrialisation and the development of capitalism enforced the separation of home and workplace, hundreds of thousands of women took up employment in the mines and factories of industrial Britain, in order to earn the wages upon which the survival of their household often depended. However, by the mid-nineteenth century, a slightly belated, paternalistic concern began to manifest itself among the Victorian bourgeoisie with regard to the moral welfare of working women and the effects on their children. The catalysts and consequences of sex-specific protective legislation are contentious issues which are impossible to explore here. It has been convincingly argued, however, that there was a concern for the moral, perhaps even more than for the physical, welfare of working-class women in industry, an attitude which seems to have echoes of the judicial concern for women wishing to enter the professions (Humphries, 1981).

However, if the picture of civil citizenship in the latter half of the nineteenth century was an unattractive one for single women, the situation for married women was that much worse since on marriage a husband could forcibly keep a wife in the house a whole century after it was illegal to do so to a slave (Sachs and Wilson, 1978). This was deemed to be justified since it was generally accepted that when a woman married, she simply ceased to exist as an individual. The extent of this assumption was put into words by William Blackstone in his *Commentaries on the Laws of England*, where he held that: 'By marriage, the husband and wife are one person in law: that is the very being or legal existence of the woman is suspended during the marriage, or incorporated and consolidated into that of the husband, under whose wing, protection and cover she performs everything' (Blackstone, 1974, p. 442). Consequently, a married woman had the right to exercise very few of those actions considered to constitute the civil element of citizenship. She could not make a contract and was therefore, in legal terms, incapable of taking part in business and, until the introduction of the 1857 Marriage and Divorce Act which allowed women to keep their own earnings, any money earned subsequent to her marriage automatically became the property of her husband. This made it virtually impossible for a woman to leave her husband or to support herself independently while her husband survived since any money or possessions she had owned on marriage now belonged to her husband and any money she managed to earn while married, her husband had the right to confiscate.

As mentioned earlier, the struggle for the recognition of the political citizenship of women was very much enmeshed with the parallel campaign for civil citizenship and was essentially dependent on the same point of contention, the inclusion or exclusion of women from the category of 'persons'. The story of the fight for the enfranchisement of women is possibly the best known and most widely covered of any period in women's history so there is no need to attempt a potted history here (see, for example, Strachey, 1928; Pankhurst, 1931; Fawcett, 1911, Billington-Greig, 1911; Spender, 1982; Liddington and Norris, 1978). What is interesting to note, however, is that, again, over a century after noted liberal philosophers such as James Mill had rejected the idea that the political interests of the community as a whole could be adequately protected by their rulers without 'representative' government because of what he presents as the 'grand governing law of human nature' – explicitly 'that all human beings desire to exercise power over their fellow creatures, and that if given the means to do so, they will use it without compunction so as to increase their own pleasures' (Okin, 1980, p. 201) – it was still considered possible, and indeed necessary, for the political interests of women to be adequately represented by their adult male relatives. It was not until 1928 that women gained the right to vote on the same basis as men, and the upper house of the so-called 'Mother of Parliaments' continued to restrict the political citizenship of women into the 1960s by refusing to allow female peers to take their seats.

Consideration of the third element, the social constituent of citizenship, is more complex since the parameters of the concept are very vague and even less directly influenced by legislation. Marshall defines it as 'the whole range from the right to a modicum of economic welfare and security to the right to share to the full in the social heritage and to live the life of a civilised being according to the standards prevailing in the society' (Marshall, 1963, p. 74). The final qualification about prevailing standards highlights the fact that social citizenship is a historically relative concept and so what is accepted as constituting the possession of social citizenship will vary through time according to the changes taking place in the surrounding society.

The main point is that despite the struggles for women to be accepted as equal citizens with men over the past 150 years, women are still *in practice* unable to participate equally with men in the economic, political and civil spheres because they are mainly responsible for childcare. If women are to become genuinely equal citizens this aspect of citizenship needs to be addressed from the point of view of social citizenship. It follows therefore that a welfare state committed to providing full citizenship rights for women needs also to make some provision to see that these are attainable.

The second part of this paper, then, takes the form of a discussion of some of the aspects of social citizenship in contemporary western industrial societies which are of particular relevance to women. Marshall tied each disparate element of citizenship to a particular institution of the modern state; civil rights were linked to the courts, political ones to Parliament and social rights he considered the responsibility of the welfare state. But the welfare state is not a homogeneous concept and its form and content tends to vary from country to country. Next, therefore, I will look briefly at how variations in the nature of the welfare state may affect both the content of social citizenship rights for women in particular countries and the resources provided to allow them to exercise those formal rights. Britain and Sweden are used here as representatives of the liberal/marginal welfare state and social democratic/universal welfare state types respectively. Both Britain and Sweden are formally committed to the equal citizenship of women and, in both cases, the state intervenes to a certain degree in an attempt to facilitate the achievement of this goal, but the issue under consideration here is the form taken by that commitment and what might be the most effective approach for the state to adopt.

The following part of the paper will therefore focus upon the extent to which childcare provision is used to enhance or inhibit women's full participation in economic and civic life. In order to understand, on a theoretical level, the differences between the British and Swedish systems, it may be useful to keep in mind a distinction recently restated by O'Donovan and Szyzyczak (1988) between 'equal treatment' and 'treatment as an equal'. The first of these is defined as 'the right to an equal distribution of some opportunity or resource or burden', while the latter is a more fundamental right 'to be treated with the same respect or concern as anyone else' (p. 6). The argument seems to be that if people's needs are different, then treating them as if they were all the same will do nothing to rectify any pre-existing inequalities. A brief examination of Britain and Sweden will illustrate how these different philosophies manifest themselves in politics.

FAMILY POLICY IN SWEDEN AND BRITAIN

It should perhaps be made clear at this point that the policies of Sweden discussed here compose only a fragment of a widely-encompassing, integrated system of social welfare which has been built up over a period of almost fifty years. It is impossible to understand any particular area of social policy in isolation from this system and the strong relations both between the state and individual citizens and between each of these individuals and the rest of the 'community' that this system has fostered. However, for present purposes, it is felt that the existing policies on parental leave, childcare provisions and child allowances are sufficient, at least, to demonstrate the type of approach favoured by the Swedish state. These policies began to acquire their present shape in the early sixties with the publication, in 1962, of a study by Dahlstrom, later translated into English as *The Changing Roles of Men and Women*, a book which is widely acknowledged to have been one of the major influences in the development of present-day policies. It contributed to Sweden's becoming, in 1968, the first country in the world to frame a government policy of achieving equality between the sexes by changing the roles of men as well as of women (Scott, 1982). Consequently, the 1970s saw a series of path-breaking changes in Sweden which indicated a commitment on the part of the state to a policy of intervention in an area which had previously been widely held to be outside the jurisdiction of the state: the family. Family policy in Britain is a much less explicit affair than it is in Sweden, primarily because of the very different attitudes or at least rhetorics concerning the 'private sphere' and state intervention which prevail in the governments of each country. The differences become obvious when we compare the official stance of the British government on statutory parental leave with the system in operation in Sweden. In May 1984, when asked about his policy towards parental leave for employees, the then Secretary of State for Employment, John Selwyn Gummer, replied as follows:

> The government believes that the family is the basic unit of our society and seeks to strengthen it and put a high value on the job of bringing up children. Parental leave can have a part to play in this. However, the Government believes that in the UK arrangements for parental leave and leave for family reasons are best dealt with through voluntary negotiations between employers and employees, rather than by creating a statutory entitlement to such leave. Legislation would increase the administrative burden on employers and tend to impair the climate for the maintenance of economic recovery by increasing costs and decreasing competitiveness, consequently damaging the employment prospects of those it seeks to assist. (Quoted in *Employment Gazette*, May, 1984)

This policy fits the Thatcher government's approach of allowing the 'free market' to decide how much, or how little, time they need allow their employees for family responsibilities. Although the government declines to intervene directly, its policies nevertheless embody a 'familial ideology' which sees the position of women as unpaid carers for children as the normal, natural and universal position for them to occupy within the family.

Parental Leave

The Swedish policy on parental leave is one of the twin pillars upon which Swedish family policy is built. Parental leave replaced the existing rights to maternity leave in 1974, and has been gradually extended to its present length of one year. As its name suggests, parental leave may be taken by either parent or they may split the allowance in any proportions they wish. A certain proportion of the leave may even be retained to allow one parent to work shorter hours over a longer period of time or to allow extended paid 'holidays' up till the child's fifth birthday. The first nine months of parental leave is paid at the rate of 90 per cent of usual earnings while the remaining three months are paid at a basic 'benefit' or 'guarantee rate' which, in 1988, stood at SEK 60 per day (approximately £6). If the person taking advantage of this leave was not in paid employment immediately previous to the birth, however, the 'benefit rate' is paid for the full twelve months. In addition, fathers are also entitled to ten days' leave at 90 per cent of pay at the time of the mother's confinement.

Alongside the introduction of parental leave in 1974 came an allowance for leave to take care of sick children. Again, this can be used by either parent and can also be taken if the child's regular childminder is ill. Since 1980, the allowance has stood at 60 days a year per child and applies to children under the age of twelve.

In Britain, statutory provisions allow for a period of maternity leave of no more than forty weeks, if the woman wishes to be sure of returning to her old job, or one which is not 'substantially less favourable in terms and conditions' than her old one. The period allowed for maternity leave stretches from the beginning of the 11th week before the baby is due (known as the EWC or 'expected week of confinement') to the end of the 29th week after the baby is born. Unfortunately, neither Statutory Maternity Pay (SMP), paid by employers, nor Maternity Allowance, paid by the Department of Social Security (DSS), covers anything like this length of time.

Statutory Maternity Pay or SMP is payable to full-time (over 16 hours per week) female workers who have been in continuous employment, usually with the same employer, for a period of at least six months and who earn enough to be paying Class 1 National Insurance contributions – that is, over £41 per week. The situation is more complex for part-time workers. This benefit is paid by employers regardless of whether or not the woman intends to return to work, and covers a maximum of 18 weeks. The benefit is payable at two different rates, according to length of service. If a woman has been working full-time (over 16 hours per week) for the same employers for at least two years, or part-time (8–16 hours per week) for five years, then she qualifies for the higher rate which equals 90 per cent of usual earnings. However, this only covers a period of six weeks, after which everyone is paid the standard rate which, in April 1988, stood at £34.25 per week.

For those women whose employment record does not qualify them for SMP, there is the alternative of Maternity Allowance (MA), which is paid by the DSS, but again the woman must have been employed or self-employed and paying standard rate National Insurance contributions for 26 weeks of the 52-week period preceding the

26th week of pregnancy (called the 'qualifying week'). As with SMP, this benefit is payable for a maximum of 18 weeks and the rate at present stands at £31.30 per week. Once entitlement to SMP or MA runs out, if a woman is still not fit to work she may be able to claim Statutory Sick Pay or Sickness Benefit for up to 168 days. Women who are classified as unemployed when they become pregnant have to follow a different route. They can continue to claim Unemployment Benefit (if their previous contributions entitle them to it) as long as they remain both available for and capable of work. Sickness Benefit then becomes payable for the period beginning six weeks before the EWC until two weeks after the birth.

The last form of financial support available for expectant parents through the welfare state are Maternity Payments, which recently replaced the universal Maternity Grants. These are available to expectant, or new, parents if one parent is getting Income Support or Family Credit. The payments amount to £85 for each baby expected (April 1988) but the total amount is reduced by any savings over £500 possessed by either parent.

Childcare

The second pillar of Swedish family policy is municipal childcare, a policy which has long enjoyed support across the political spectrum in Sweden. Unfortunately, the Social Democratic Government is, as yet, nowhere near its target of a place in municipal childcare for every child who needs one, but if we look at the figures available, the extent of the commitment to such a situation in the foreseeable future becomes clear.

Between 1951 and 1966, places in municipal childcare, which includes both day-care centres and family day care (child-minders) grew from 10 000 to 20 000. However it was not until the late sixties that women in Sweden really began to enter the labour market in force and the demand for childcare began to increase proportionately. From the mid-sixties to the mid-seventies, childcare places tripled but they still could not keep pace with demand. As of 1974, only 14 per cent of all pre-school children (that is children under seven) had a place in public day care and only 26 per cent of the children of working mothers had access to subsidised municipal childcare. However, priority was given to the children of single parents as well as children from 'disadvantaged' families, for example those considered to be living in overcrowded conditions.

There followed a period of rapid expansion, which did not seem to be affected by a period of non-socialist government between 1976 and 1982. By 1983, 40 per cent of all children under seven were in publicly-funded day care while the figure for children with both parents working or studying was 55 per cent. This expansion continued apace under the new majority SAP (Social Democratic Party) Government, with the figures rising to 47 per cent of all pre-school children in public day care by 1986 following a bill passed in 1985, with support from the Social Democrats, the Communists and the Liberals, resolving that by 1991 places should be available for all pre-school children over eighteen months in either day-care centres or family day care. This was felt to be a pretty tall order and some municipalities have expressed doubts about their ability to implement it within the deadline, given that the burden of finance falls fairly heavily on the municipalities themselves. However, at the present time, the situation nationally continues to improve with the most recent figures suggesting that 350 000 or 59 per cent of children under seven are covered by publicly-funded day-care arrangements. In the British context, what concerns us primarily is the availability of state-funded or state-subsidised day care which is flexible enough to allow both parents to go out to work full-time if they so wish. This is not the same issue as that recently discussed by the Commons Select Committee on Nursery Education, which led to a call for an expansion of provision for three- to five-year olds. As was pointed out by the Workplace Nurseries Campaign (*The Guardian,* 17 Jan. 1989), nursery education, which usually covers two or three hours in the morning during school terms, is very different from full-time day care and does very little to expand the opportunities of women with young children to enter the labour market on anything but the most restricted terms.

Between 1966 and 1983, there was a substantial rise in the number of Local Authority places for the education or day care of the under-fives from 276 000 to 612 000. However, given the increase in the number of children under five, this meant that only 17.5 per cent of these children have access to any type of state-funded childcare, with most of these being found in 'rising-five' classes for children about to start school (Walker, 1988, p. 223). Private schools, nurseries, playgroups and registered child-minders are estimated to provide another 623 000 places (*Social Trends 1985*, p. 45) but many of these places will be part-time and some children may attend more than one scheme while the vast majority of children under five in Britain and their parents have to rely completely on the 'private sphere' of family or friends to provide childcare if both parents want to, or have to, participate in the labour market. Ruggie (1984) has argued that the provision of childcare in Britain is characteristic of the state's 'liberal' approach to the provision of welfare in general in that its priority is to ameliorate the position of those disadvantaged by the market while maintaining the social relations which created the disadvantage and in fact producing a qualitative barrier between those receiving welfare, the welfare 'clientele', and the rest of society. Thus, public day care in Britain is reserved for the children of families which are experiencing some kind of breakdown, or for the children of parents whom poverty has 'forced' to work (in practice, usually single parents). In contrast to part-time public and private childcare – nurseries, nursery schools/classes or playgroups – day nurseries are argued to emphasise a 'caring' or 'custodial' role while the former tend more towards an educational policy. But across the board, British under-five provision tends to be justified on the grounds of the social needs of the child. Swedish childcare, on the other hand, is considered important to answer the needs not just of the children but also of the parents as individuals and of society as a whole.

Child Allowances

Child allowances have not enjoyed the same kind of high profile in Sweden as have childcare facilities. If the payments at present are more representative of the cost of bringing up children than those available in Britain this is largely due to the power of pressure group lobbies in Sweden. Child allowances replaced tax deduction for children in 1948. These payments are paid monthly to all mothers regardless of income and they are tax-free and so have no unwelcome marginal effects on household income. However, these allowances have never been indexed, unlike other welfare benefits, so that the failure to increase the value of the allowance in line with prices meant that between 1979 and 1984 alone, Child Allowances lost 25 per cent of its purchasing power. Due to pressure from various lobbies as well as from other political parties, the Social Democrats did increase the allowance by 45 per cent in 1985 and again in 1987, to a basic level of SEK 5820 per child per annum (approximately £529). Reports of poverty in large families also prompted the introduction, in 1987, of Child Allowance Supplement which means that the third child in a family receives an extra allowance equal to SEK 2910 while the fourth and subsequent children receive an amount equal to 160 per cent of the basic allowance. However, the government has resisted pressure to index the allowance against inflation, a situation which some Swedish commentators feel reflects the inferior status of this benefit in the hierarchy of Swedish welfare provision.

Child Benefit is one of the very few remaining universal benefits in Britain. Anyone responsible for a child aged up to sixteen is eligible, it is not means-tested or taxable and in the vast majority of cases it is paid to the mother. But these positive points are overshadowed by the fact that the rate of payment has remained frozen at £7.25 per child per week for the last two years and is fast becoming little more than an empty gesture towards redistribution of resources both in society – from families without children to those with – and within the family. This payment compares unfavourably with the Swedish system of child allowances where a Swedish family with one child would receive £152 per year more than a comparable British family while a family with four children in Sweden would be £1719 per year better off than its British counterparts.

British and Swedish rates of universal child allowances for families with up to four children are as shown in Table 2.1.

Table 2.1 Comparison between British and Swedish rates of universal child allowances

No. of children	Britain £ p.a.	Sweden SEK p.a.	£ equivalent*
1	377	5820	529
2	754	11640	1058
3	1131	20370	1852
4	1508	35520	3228

*Approximate figures (1 Swedish Kroner [SEK] is worth about 10p sterling).

IMPLICATIONS

What do the evident differences in approach and policy between Britain and Sweden actually mean in practice, as regards the social citizenship of women in these countries? How do the particular policies outlined above affect women's abilities to exercise their right to 'share to the full in the social heritage' and to enjoy 'a modicum of economic welfare and security'? First of all, it should perhaps be restated that the recognition of a formal right to something means very little without the resources to exercise that right. So the formal recognition of women's right to enter any sphere of the labour market is of limited value if the lack of a certain resource makes it impractical for many of them to make full use of that right. Thus the crux of the argument is that the Swedish system of universalistic, extended welfare provision is one which provides women with much more freedom to exercise their social citizenship rights than does the British system because it emphasises 'treatment as an equal' rather than according women 'equal treatment'.

This is manifested in a number of ways. The ability to actually secure for oneself a 'modicum of economic welfare and security' would seem to depend upon one's position with regard to both the labour market and the state. For example, when women take breaks from full-time employment, this tends to have a negative effect both on her lifetime earnings potential and on her opportunities for advancement in the relevant career structure. A system which makes it possible for women to have children while maintaining employment continuity, therefore, has considerable implications not only for the economic position of individual women but for the position of women in society as a whole in that it would be less difficult for women to attain positions of authority in a society which did not penalise them for having children by wiping out their seniority. This experience of continuous lifetime employment would seem to be becoming the norm in Sweden in the eighties. A study of female labour-force participation shows that, rather than the M-shaped curve which has characterised many Western European nations since the Second World War and which is still the pattern in Britain, the pattern of participation of Swedish women now follows approximately the inverted-U shape that is typical of male participation rates (see Paukert, 1984; Organisation for Economic Co-operation and Development 1988), as women are able to take advantage of state-provided childcare to maintain continuity of employment.

But is the state in Sweden merely taking over some of the responsibilities encompassed in women's dual role as mother and wage-earner or are its policies actually having any effect upon the way that domestic responsibilities are distributed within the family? One indication that the latter may be the case is found in the most recent figures on the sharing of parental leave.

The scheme did not have a particularly auspicious beginning. In the first year after its introduction, only 2 per cent of fathers made any use of their new-found right at all. In 1976 this rose to 7 per cent, in 1978 to 11 per cent and in 1979 12 per cent of fathers took paid leave to look after their infant children. The movement into the eighties would seem to have had a significant effect on male attitudes to shared childcare because between 1979 and 1981, the percentage of men taking parental leave almost doubled to 22 per cent and in 1988 this was holding steady with about one father in five taking advantage of his right to parental leave.

On the face of it, these figures would seem to indicate a positive, if gradual, improvement in direct male commitment to shared childcare. However, if we look more closely, we find that, although the actual numbers of men playing a part in the care of their children have been steadily rising, the proportion of the possible leave that they actually use has remained remarkably constant at an average of around 30 to 40 days. In the eighties, this has tended towards the 40 mark with a high in 1981 of 47 days for men compared with 265 days for women. But in 1988 the average was back down to 41 days. On the other hand, if we look at the distribution of time taken to look after sick children, we find a much more equal division between the sexes than is the case with parental leave. According to the limited information available, in 1985 2.2 million days were taken by men while women used 2.89 million days.

Given this type of data, the next obvious thing to ask is: who are the men and women who are sharing the care of their new-born or sick children? Information on this subject is extremely scarce but a recent government survey (SOU (Swedish Central Government Publications Office), 1985) suggests that women who work in the private sector are more likely to share parental leave, whether fully or partly, with their partner than women employed in the public sector (26 per cent compared with 22 per cent), while for men the reverse was true; men in the public sector were much more likely to share parental leave than fathers employed in private firms or self-employed (31 per cent compared with only 19 per cent). These data support the findings of an earlier study carried out by Leiulfsrud and Woodward of thirty cross-class families (families where the male and female partners were in different social classes) in Stockholm (Leiulfsrud and Woodward, 1987). One of their findings was that in cross-class families, the partner with the working-class job was most likely to stay at home with a sick child, regardless of sex. When this didn't occur the explanation was most likely to be found in whether the working-class partner was employed in the public or private sector. The proposed explanation was that the person in a working-class job was more likely to be carrying out the type of routine tasks which could be most easily be taken over by someone else if they were absent. On the other hand, it was felt that employers in the public sector might be more amenable to requests for leave than those in the private sector. Leiulfsrud and Woodward also found that, in the case of what they called 'non-traditional cross-class families' – that is those families where the woman occupied a higher occupational position than her partner – the division of household tasks other than childcare also tended to be less inegalitarian than in other types of household. However, in practical terms, what this meant was that fewer of these women were doing more than 75 per cent of the housework.

One of the most interesting aspects of these findings, however, is that they seem to suggest the possibility of a reversal of the causal link between domestic responsibilities and labour market participation which has been analysed in several other studies. Siltanen (1986) among others has suggested that the form of labour market participation adopted by women in Britain is strongly influenced by their domestic commitments. Completing the circle, the above evidence seems to suggest that in Sweden domestic responsibilities and their distribution in the family are also affected by experiences and position in the labour market.

It can be argued, then, that Swedish family policy as part of an integrated system of labour market and welfare policies operates to expand the opportunities for women to escape from the vicious circle which dictates that women are primarily responsible for childcare and the necessity of structuring paid employment around the constraints that this entails. However, it has recently been proposed that citizenship need not always be mediated through the labour market. One of the major themes of the earlier work of Helga Hernes (1987) was the creation by the Scandinavian welfare state of a new form of citizenship which is particularly accessible to women; that of the 'welfare-citizen'.

Hernes has adopted the concept of citizenship as a way of focusing attention upon a particular set of developments which she identifies as crucial in unravelling the complexities of the relations between women and the modern state, especially in its welfare mode. She interprets recent changes in Scandinavia not as heralding a move towards the long-awaited financial and legal independence of women, but rather a shift in the locus of women's dependence from the private to the public sphere. This means that although women are becoming less dependent upon individual husbands or partners as breadwinners, they now have a similarly dependent relationship with what Hernes characterises as a largely 'paternalistic' state. According to Hernes, women's interaction with the state takes place under three distinguishable guises: as employees, as clients and as citizens. Men also interact with the state wearing each of these hats, but women are intrinsically more dependent on the state because of the type of activities which have become part and parcel of the state's responsibilities in the post-war period, in other words the *verstaatlichung* of the reproductive sphere. In Hernes' subsequent writings (1988a, 1988b) it becomes clear that the 'citizen' role is the pivotal one in that, to a significant extent, the nature of the other two roles is seen as being determined by the way in which men and women relate to the state as citizens. Her interpretation suggests that traditionally, the ideal conceptualisation of a citizen under social democracy has been that of the largely male 'worker-citizen' where: 'HIS rights, identities and participation patterns were determined by HIS ties to the labour market and by the web of associations as well as corporate structures which has grown up around these ties' (Hernes, 1988a, p. 213).

However, with the advent in the post-war period of a second wave of welfare development, women are argued to have been mobilised as citizens through the welfare state in much the same way that men were earlier mobilised through the labour market. So we have a situation where the possibilities of state/citizen interaction have expanded but where women tend to have more direct contact with the state whereas male citizens are more likely to have their dealings with the state mediated through the labour market and usually also through large 'buffer' organisations such as trade unions. This difference carries through into the other two roles demarcated by Hernes of employees and clients, in that women are more likely to be employed in the public sector and they also constitute a disproportionate number of welfare state claimants.

So, under this interpretation, women are included in the category of citizen but they are defined primarily as 'welfare-citizens' rather than 'worker-citizens': in Hernes' typology, it seems, an inferior basis of incorporation.

This three-way division of women's role in contemporary society is repeated in Birte Siim's work but she reconceptualises the categories as workers, mothers and citizens. Within the citizenship role, she appears to accept Hernes' distinction between women as 'welfare-citizens' but argues that women's relationship to the state as employees must be seen as qualitatively different to their rather weaker position as clients. Siim also questions Hernes' assumption that women's dependence on the state is, of itself, a bad thing. Hernes hinges her negative attitude towards women's increased dependence on the state on which she calls the 'tutelary' nature of that state as far as women are concerned. In her opinion, the welfare states in Scandinavia are still institutions where men are the decision-makers while women are merely the objects of those decisions; the recipients of welfare. Hernes holds on to this image despite quite significant increases in the representation of women in the Scandinavian parliaments and in regional and local councils in the last two decades because of what she identifies as a transferral of power in Scandinavian societies from the official, democratically elected political positions to non-elected bodies in the corporate sector. This shift is argued to be extremely disadvantageous in terms of the empowerment of women because of the vastly under-representative nature of these bodies. Two factors contribute to this situation; firstly the elitist nature of recruitment onto those bodies which wield power whereby the majority of people chosen to sit on such corporate boards or committees have reached senior positions in either the private or the public sector. This, of course, militates against the inclusion of women who are still under-represented in positions of authority. The second factor which contributes to women's weak voice in the corporate sector is the exclusion from these corporate bodies of many women's interest groups which are not considered to command enough authority to warrant their inclusion. It is, therefore, on the basis of women's lack of control over the state that Hernes condemns their dependence upon its benevolence. This is consistent with her argument elsewhere that advances in citizenship must consist of two complementary elements where improvements in material conditions must be matched by the extension of participatory control. These conclusions again find echoes in Siim's work (see Siim, 1987). However, Siim later argues that it is necessary to consider separately the two questions of women's dependence upon the state and their under-representation in the decision-making structures of the state. Her contention would seem to be that it is primarily the existence of the latter state of affairs that makes the former situation unacceptable.

Both Siim and Mary Ruggie (1988) argue that the needs of women as a discrete group have tended to be subsumed under the needs of the working class as a whole. To express it more directly, women have been considered as workers first and women second, if at all. Ruggie goes on to use this contention as a justification for her hypothesis that the 'Scandinavian model' has reached the limits of its effectiveness as far as the specific needs of women are concerned. She explains that one of the goals of the labour movement is equal treatment for all workers, and since the majority of women are organised through trade unions rather than women's organisations, this had led to a situation where the existing structure cannot cope with problems which specifically disadvantage women. Women have, admittedly, benefitted from many of the policies adopted by the labour movement, and in some cases disproportionately so. For example, the policy of wage solidarity aimed at narrowing income differentials had considerable impact on female wages since women tend to be concentrated in low-paid occupations. On the other hand however, sex-segregation has remained prevalent in the Swedish labour market, a phenomenon which has a depressing effect on the overall level of female wages. This is one of a number of reasons, along with women's higher representation in non-socialist unions and the increasing number of women in part-time employment, why equal pay seems no more within reach now than it did ten or twenty years ago.

So, has the 'Scandinavian model' reached its limits as far as women are concerned? The indications are by no means unequivocal. To deal first of all with Ruggie's argument that the needs of women have been sacrificed in favour of relating to the labour forces as an ungendered whole: this suggests an approach closer to O'Donovan's definition of 'equal treatment' rather than 'treatment as an equal' which was earlier argued to characterise at least the Swedish approach to social policy. This is at odds with the Swedish government's explicit aim of achieving equality by changing the societal roles of both men and women (Scott, 1982) nor does it square with the numerous policies which have recognised the particular difficulties that women face and attempted to resolve them, for example publicly-funded day care, leave for both parents to look after sick children and the numerous training schemes designed to encourage men and women to enter non-traditional areas of employment.

In the second place, it could be argued that some of the findings cited earlier may provide a counterbalance to the negative aspects of the Swedish approach as identified by Ruggie. The continuing high level of sex-segregation in the Swedish labour market is a problem that must be attacked at its root, part of which lies in the assumptions which go along with the maintenance of traditional sex-roles within the family. But it is in precisely this area that the state is committed to having an effect, and where some earlier studies suggest changes are taking place (Haas, 1981, 1982 and 1986; Leiulfsrud and Woodward, 1987). Ruggie's theory also discounts the suggestions coming out of Hernes' and Siim's work and particularly that of Drude Dahlerup (1988) that the possibilities offered to women by the 'Scandinavian model' are expanding beyond the confines of the labour market with their increased participation in formal and informal political structures and their widening involvement in negotiating the terms of their relations with the state as consumers, workers, mothers and taxpayers. All of these would appear to provide alternative channels through which women can, and are, attacking the limitations of the 'traditional Swedish approach to social and political action on behalf of women' (Ruggie, 1988, p. 182). This is not to suggest that Ruggie is necessarily mistaken in her analysis of the historical approach to women's problems or in her conclusion that crucial problems have resisted this approach. It is merely to propose that possibilities for the future are more complex and optimistic than she implies.

The work of the other two women discussed above has been vital to an understanding of the development of new aspects of the relationship between women and the state in Scandinavia. However, it is my proposal that there are certain areas where a re-examination might point to a more positive interpretation of recent developments.

First, as is implied in Siim's work, Hernes' dualistic division between men as 'worker-citizens' and women as 'welfare-citizens' tends to underplay the fact that women as state employees can also be defined as 'worker-citizens', based on the argument that in terms of power resources and the possibility of interest mediation, such women may have more in common with male state employees than with women as welfare state clients (although obviously these two female roles are not mutually exclusive). It is also essential to note that many of the family or social policies discussed above, enacted by this 'paternalistic' state, have indeed made it easier for women to expand their role as 'worker-citizens' in many ways, in either the private or the public sphere.

Hernes also neglects to mention that due to the universalistic nature of the Scandinavian welfare states and their emphasis on changing the sex-roles of both men and women, men also have considerable interaction with the welfare state as clients. This must surely have had some effect upon the content of and popular conception of the 'worker-citizen' role, and perhaps the continued use of the static term 'worker-citizen' has obscured the changes or variations in the relationship it has been used to denote.

Moving to the second point I wish to discuss, the problem identified by Hernes as a shift in the locus of decisive power in Scandinavia from parliamentary to corporate bodies is evidently a matter of considerable importance and one which may well have negative implications for democracy in these countries, especially given the particular problem of the under-representation of women in these areas. However, as Hernes herself has pointed out, there is a great deal of difference between women having a little power and having no power at all. As far as women's representation in parliamentary political bodies is concerned, Drude Dahlerup (1988) has documented the impressive increase which has taken place in the past ten to fifteen years and has presented several possibilities of positive changes that this increase presents. She lists six specific areas where her research has indicated that the advent of women as a large minority in politics may have a positive impact. These include reactions to women politicians, the eficiency of women politicians, the tone of political culture, the nature of the political discourse in terms of putting the positions of women firmly on the political agenda, and finally changes in concrete policy and in the empowerment of women.

The last two are bracketed together because they are particularly interdependent and have, arguably, the most immediate impact on the lives of ordinary women outside the political arena. It is argued here that although we cannot expect the achievement of a 'critical' mass of women in politics to set off an inevitable and irreversible chain reaction, it is evident that the little power that women have gained should not be ignored or undervalued but exploited in order to both limit and counteract the increasing power of the less democratic corporate sector. For example, legislation enacted in Norway in 1973, requiring that all organisations put up both a male and female candidate for every post on a corporate committee, has been remarkably successful in increasing female representation in this area. This must suggest possibilities for the women in other Scandinavian parliaments, even allowing for variations and contingencies in their own political systems.

Another potentially productive area for the mobilisation of all women activists whether corporate, parliamentary or 'movement', must be around the extension of the recruitment base of these corporate committees to include women's organisations. On a longer-term basis, changes facilitating women's continuous participation in the workforce may mean that the chances of finding women in elite positions ready and willing to be co-opted into decision-making bodies will improve as the next generation of Scandinavian women enjoy the benefits of an uninterrupted employment pattern and a more flexible labour market.

In conclusion, there is no question that it is essential for women to have participatory control over the state in order to avoid a purely passive 'client' role. However, it must be kept in mind that the situation of increased dependence on state provision of welfare resources should not necessarily be deplored. The implications of this development must be analysed quite separately from the fact of women's under-representation in decision-making elites. Indeed, to take this argument one step further, it is argued here that the welfare state systems in Scandinavia and the policies emanating from these institutions must be carefully evaluated in terms of their positive implications for the empowerment of ordinary women and the enhancement of their opportunities to exercise their social citizenship rights, before these policies are labelled as aspects of a system of 'public patriarchy' or 'a new kind of male domination'.

One final point about the transformative potential of citizenship is worth mentioning. As mentioned at the beginning of the essay, the term has come back into the political vocabulary through the New Right's adoption of the idea of the 'active citizen' might prove to be to neo-liberalism what the 'free and equal individual' was to liberal capitalism in earlier centuries. In other words, just as the concept of the 'free and equal individual' was used to create the conditions necessary for the development of capitalism but then began to challenge the very foundations of the system which had created it by encouraging expectations of 'real' equality and freedom, so might the 'active citizen' turn against its creator by encouraging people to demand the concrete rights behind the rhetorical sham. This might lead to an expectation of an effective input into the decision-making process – a demand which goes against the rapid and seemingly inexorable process of centralisation of power which has been so predominant a feature of the last decade in Britain.

3 Money and Power in Marriage
Jan Pahl

The aim in this chapter is to examine the relationship between money and power in marriage and to explore the ideological foundations of particular financial arrangements. Previous research has focused on the relationship between earnings and power, that is, on the association between a person's financial contribution to the household and his or her power within it. Here the focus moves to the intra-household economy and to its links with intra-household power. What happens to the link between money and power as money passes from earners to spenders? An increasingly large proportion of couples pool their money, either in a common kitty or in a joint bank account. Is this sharing of money associated with a sharing of power, or does the apparent togetherness mask continuing inequality? The connection between power and ideology is a familiar one. But what is the connection between ideologies about family life and the relative power of men and women within marriage? Can ideology exacerbate structural inequalities between husband and wife, or alternatively, mitigate the effects of inequality in earning capacity? In attempting to answer some of these questions, I shall draw on my own study of the control and allocation of money within marriage (Pahl, 1989).

THE STUDY

The main aim of the study was to gain a better knowledge of patterns of financial management within households and to investigate the significance of different allocative systems for individual members of households. Ideally the study would have included a variety of household types, living in several different parts of Britain. However, time and money were both limited, so the research focused on a random sample of married couples with at least one child under sixteen and was carried out in three different parts of Kent from 1982 to 1983 (Pahl, 1989).

Husband and wife were interviewed first together and then separately, and interviews were completed with 102 couples. The small number of respondents means that it would be rash to claim that they were representative of a wider population of families. However, in many respects the study couples had characteristics which one would have hoped to see in a representative sample. At the time 48 per cent of married women with children in Britain were in employment, while the proportion in the sample was 50 per cent. In Britain as a whole 88 per cent of married men with children were employed, while the proportion among the men who took part in the study was exactly the same (Office of Population Censuses and Surveys, 1984). Nearly three quarters of the couples owned their own homes, a proportion very similar to the figure for married couples in England as a whole (Department of the Environment, 1981). In terms of social class and of the ownership of consumer durables the study couples were again similar to the total population of households with children in Britain at the time. All the women were in receipt of Child Benefit, since all had at least one child under sixteen, and all the men who were not in employment received either Unemployment Benefit, Invalidity Benefit or Supplementary Benefit (now Income Support). Thus every individual who took part in the study had some form of income, whether as wages, salary or social security benefit.

FOUR PATTERNS OF CONTROL

There are many different criteria which might be used to create a classification of household financial arrangements. However, this analysis focused on the extent to which income was pooled and on the control of the pool, if there was one. The existence of joint and separate bank accounts offered a relatively objective way in which to assess the jointness or otherwise of a couple's financial arrangements. Having a joint bank account suggested some degree of pooling, so couples with a joint account were divided from those without.

Next the couples were sorted according to the wife's answer to the question 'Who really controls the money that comes into this house?' The possible answers to this question were 'wife', 'husband' and 'both'. However, where 'both' were said to control finances, the analysis showed that husbands were likely to be responsible for paying major bills, checking the bank statement and making financial decisions. So couples where 'both' controlled the money had finance arrangements which most closely resembled those where husbands controlled finances. In the analysis which follows 'both' and 'husband' have been combined in order to reduce the number of categories. Support for the choice of the wife's answer came from the interviewers, who at the end of the joint interview noted discreetly which partner had been the most authoritative in talking about money. A very significant correlation existed between the husband appearing authoritative in the joint interview and his being described by his wife in her separate interview as controlling the money: conversely wives who appeared authoritative were likely to control the money.

Sorting the couples in this way produced four categories. The first category contained couples where there was a joint bank account and where the wife described herself as controlling the money. There were 27 of these and they were described as 'wife-controlled pooling'. Among these couples it was usually the wife who paid the bills for rates, fuel, telephone, insurance and mortgage or rent. In the majority of cases, neither partner had a separate bank account and all finances were handled from the joint account.

The second category was described as 'husband-controlled pooling'. This contained couples where there was a joint bank account, but where the wife considered either that the husband controlled the finances or that they were jointly controlled. There were 39 couples in this category. Among this group husbands were typically responsible for the bills for rates, fuel, telephone, insurance and for paying the mortgage or rent.

Lack of a joint account implied one of two things. Either the couples were paid in cash and were too poor ever to need a bank, or one or both partners rejected the idea of a joint account. The third category contained couples where there was no joint account and where the wife considered that control was in the husband's hands or was joint. There were 22 couples in this category, which was described as 'husband-controlled'. Typically the husband had his own personal bank account and he was responsible for all the main bills.

Finally, there was a small group where there was no joint bank account and the wife considered that she controlled the finances. This category contained 14 couples and was described as 'wife-controlled'. These couples typically had no bank accounts at all and operated in cash, with the wife controlling and managing the finances and taking responsibility for the major bills.

Wife control of finances was particularly common in low-income, working-class households where neither partner had any qualifications. Wife control was associated with the payment of wages in cash and with the absence of any bank accounts. Typically the wife also managed the money, paying for food and for rent, fuel, insurance and so on, while the husband had a set sum for his personal spending money. Thus in many respects wife control was synonymous with wife management.

Husband control was associated with relatively high income levels, as Table 3.1 shows. Typically these couples had a set amount of housekeeping money, which was given by the husband to the wife as an allowance: she paid for food and daily living expenses, while he paid the main bills. Most of these couples kept their money separate and when this was the case the wife's wages typically went on housekeeping, while the husband was responsible for larger bills. Husband control was characteristic of couples where the husband was the main or sole earner.

Table 3.1 Control of finances by total household income

	Household income		
	Low Under £100	Medium £100–£174	High £175 and over
Wife control	5	7	2
Wife-controlled pooling	2	16	9
Husband-controlled pooling	2	18	19
Husband control	1	9	12
Total number	10	50	42

There were interesting differences between wife-controlled pooling and husband-controlled pooling. As Table 3.1 shows, wife-controlled pooling was associated with medium-income levels, while husband-controlled pooling was more typical of higher-income levels. Table 3.2 shows that wife-controlled pooling was associated with the employment of both partners; when only the husband was in employment he was likely to control the pool. The more the wife contributed to the household income the more likely it was that she would control household finances; this effect was particularly marked among pooling couples. Where wives' earnings were 30 per cent or more of their husbands' earnings, wives were twice as likely as husbands to control the pool; where wives had no earnings, husbands were three times more likely than wives to control the pool.

The effect of social class was also particularly marked among

Table 3.2 Control of finances by employment pattern

	Both employed	Wife only	Husband only	Neither employed
Wife control	5	—	5	4
Wife-controlled pooling	19	—	7	1
Husband-controlled pooling	17	—	19	3
Husband control	9	1	9	3
Total number	50	1	40	11

pooling couples, especially where the husband and wife were of different classes. Where the husband was classified as middle-class and the wife as working-class, the husband always controlled the pool, or joint account. Where the wife was middle-class and the husband working-class, she controlled the pool in all but one instance. The same pattern occurred for qualifications. If one partner had more qualifications than the other he or she was likely to control finances; where both partners had gained some qualifications after leaving school there was a tendency for the husband to control finances.

To sum up this section, then, where a wife controls finances she will usually also be responsible for money management; where the husband controls finances he will usually delegate parts of the money management to his wife. Thus where a wife controls finances she will usually be responsible for paying the main bills and for making sure that ends meet, as well as for buying food and day-to-day necessities. Where a husband controls finances he will typically delegate to his wife the responsibility for housekeeping expenses, sometimes giving her a housekeeping allowance for this purpose. Marriages where the wife controls the money and the husband manages it are rare. There were no examples of this pattern in the study sample, nor were there examples of the small number of marriages where the husband both controls and manages the money. Evidence from other studies suggests that in these circumstances there is likely to be extreme inequality between husband and wife and deprivation on the part of the wife and children (Pahl, 1980; Homer, Leonard and Taylor, 1985; Wilson, 1987).

POWER AND DECISION-MAKING

What are the connections between power in the financial domain and power in marriage more generally? There is an enormous body of literature on power in marriage and on the difficulty of defining exactly what the concept means in this context. There is not space to discuss this literature here, nor is there any need since there have been several comprehensive surveys of the field (Safilios Rothschild, 1970; Cromwell and Olsen, 1975; Scanzoni, 1979; McDonald, 1980). In attempting to measure power empirically most researchers have used information about which partner makes specific decisions. This approach has been criticised for giving the same weight to decisions of different importance, for neglecting the processes which precede making a decision, and for ignoring the structural inequalities between men and women (Gillespie, 1972; Edgell, 1980). Nevertheless the great majority of those who have investigated the determinants of power in marriage have used the making of decisions as a measure; my study followed in that tradition, inadequate though it may be as a way of assessing so elusive a concept as power.

Each interview ended by listing various decisions and asking whether each was likely to be made by the husband alone, the husband in consultation with his wife, both partners together, the wife in consultation with her husband, or the wife alone. The decisions which were presented were: organising finances; buying a car; buying consumer goods such as a washing machine; what to do at Christmas; where to go on holiday; deciding something to do with the husband's job; deciding something to do with the wife's job. Given five possible answers to each of seven different decisions it was possible to create a score which ran in theory from 7, if a husband decided everything alone, to 35 if a wife decided everything alone. A score of 21 implied equality between husband and wife in decision-making and occurred either because all the answers were 'we decide together' or because the husband's greater power in one decision was balanced by the wife's in another. A score of over 21 meant that the wife played a dominant role in decision-making, while a score of less than 21 meant that the husband was dominant. The separate interviews meant that there was one decision-making score for the wife and another for the husband.

It was interesting to see that the husbands' answers to this question did not correlate closely with the wives'. Only 48 out of the 102 couples agreed about which partner was dominant in decision making. This result, which has been observed by other researchers, underlines the danger of studying marriage through the eyes of one partner; it is also a reminder of the differences between 'her' marriage and 'his' marriage. In the analysis which follows the answers given by husband and wife have been combined to produce a joint decision-making score.

The analysis provided confirmation that the questions about decision-making did indeed measure something which might be described as power. There were statistically significant correlations between the decision-making score and two other key measures of power in marriage. These were, first, the interviewers' assessment of which partner spoke most authoritatively in the joint interview, and second, the wives' answers to the question, 'Who really controls the money in this household?' It was interesting to see that the husband's assessment of who controlled the money correlated poorly with decision-making. Perhaps husbands took the business of being interviewed less seriously, or perhaps they were simply less aware of the realities of power in marriage? At all events this finding provided support for the decision to use the wife's assessment of who controlled the money in constructing the typology of control of finances.

Husbands were more likely to be dominant in decision-making than were wives. This was so whether the answers used were those of the wife or of the husband. In about half of the couples the husband was defined as dominant, while the rest of the sample were divided between equality and wife-dominance in decision-making. Combining the answers given by husband and wife produced a larger number of couples who appeared to be equal in decision-making, but husbands still dominated.

Previous research on decision-making in marriage has suggested that the partner with the larger income is likely to play a more dominant part in decision-making and that wives are likely to have greater decision-making power if they are in paid employment rather than working at home; older wives are likely to be more dominant in decision-making, partly because they are more likely to be in paid work. This study offered an opportunity to explore the economic inequality between husbands and wives, not just in terms of how much each partner earned, but also in terms of who controlled and managed money within the household: is the same true inside the household? Does power in decision-making remain with the partner who earns the money or does it pass to the partner who controls or manages finances?

The results confirmed the link between inequality outside the household and inequality in decision-making within the household. Husbands were more likely to dominate decision-making where the

Table 3.3 Employment pattern by dominance in decision-making

Employment	Dominant partner in decision-making		
	Husband	Both equally	Wife
Both employed	17	19	14
Wife only	—	1	—
Husband only	22	15	3
Neither employed	6	3	2
Total number	45	38	19

wife did not have a job, as Table 3.3 shows; conversely wives who were dominant in decision-making were usually in paid employment. Other analysis, not presented here, showed that younger women and those with small children were less likely to dominate in decision-making than older women. Equality in decision-making seemed to be associated with couples being in their thirties, with having the house in their joint names as opposed to in his name alone, and with both partners having stayed on at school after the leaving age and having acquired post-school qualifications.

Though Table 3.3 is interesting it is only marginally statistically significant according to conventional tests ($p < 0.08$). On the other hand Table 3.4 is highly significant ($p < 0.01$). Until this point in the argument it has not seemed appropriate to lay great stress on tests of significance because of the small numbers involved. However, the contrast between these two Tables is important. It seems as if power, as measured by dominance in decision-making, was associated more strongly with the control of finances *within* the household than it was with factors external to the house, such as income or employment pattern.

Table 3.4 Control of finances by dominance in decision-making

Control of finances	Dominant partner in decision-making		
	Husband	Both equally	Wife
Wife control	6	5	3
Wife-controlled pooling	6	10	11
Husband-controlled pooling	21	16	2
Husband control	12	7	3
Total number	45	38	19

Table 3.4 shows that where wives had power in terms of decision-making it was likely that the couple would operate the system called wife-controlled pooling; this means that the couple had a joint account and that the wife controlled the couple's finances. Where the husband dominated decision-making it is likely that financial arrangements would be either husband-controlled pooling or husband control; that is, the husband controlled finances, whether or not the couple had a joint account. Equality in decision-making was associated with having a joint account. Taken together Tables 3.3 and 3.4 suggest that very poor couples, where neither partner is in employment, are associated with quite high levels of husband-dominance; the fact that wives controlled finances in these households was not necessarily associated with the wife being dominant in decision-making. In poor households controlling money is a chore and not a source of power (Pahl, 1983).

However, the anomalies in the results of the study provoked many questions. Though wives who were in paid employment were more likely to control finances and play a dominant part in decision-making, this was not always the case. On the other hand, some non-earning wives controlled finances and took an equal share in making decisions. Most striking of all, in the one instance where the wife was the sole earner it was the husband who controlled finances, as Table 3.2 shows. In attempting to understand these variations from the norm it was necessary to explore the ideological nature of the discourse when individuals talked about their financial arrangements.

IDEOLOGY AND MONEY IN MARRIAGE

The term ideology is essentially concerned with the sets of ideas held by individuals and groups, ideas which are rooted in the social and economic circumstances which shape people's lives. An ideology is a coherent system of beliefs and attitudes which serves to make sense of reality and to shape social action. In any one society at any one time the conflict between ideologies is likely to be concealed by the creation of what Therborn has called a 'discursive order', or dominant ideology: 'The construction of a discursive order in a particular society is the historical outcome of struggles waged by social forces at crucial moments of contradiction and crisis' (Therborn, 1980, p. 82). A discursive order affirms the ideologies of the most powerful groups in society, while devaluing and excluding competing ideologies.

The concept of 'the family' is itself a powerful ideological construct, containing within it assumptions about the nature of relationships between men and women, between children and parents and between other members of the same kin group. Morgan has pointed to the need for more work on the ideologies which surround the notion of 'the family' and especially on 'the process whereby the link between family, marriage and inequality is obscured or ignored in favour of a model of marriage which emphasises the interpersonal and the relational as against the economic' (Morgan, 1985, p. 103). Studies of couples where the woman rather than the man is the chief earner show the force of the ideologies surrounding the conjugal contract. Female breadwinners somehow have to compensate their husbands for the loss of status. Stamp found that breadwinning wives held back from exercising as much power as they might, given their financial contribution, and that they tended to involve their husbands in financial responsibility (Stamp, 1985, p. 22). Hunt described how a husband who chose to swap roles with his wife and be financially supported by her still maintained a strong bargaining position with regard to housework, because of ideological support for housework being her rather than his responsibility (Hunt, 1978 and 1980). McRae investigated the allocation of money in families where the wife was of higher social class than the husband. She found that the tensions to which this gave rise were often resolved by treating all income as joint funds: thus an ideology of equality, as expressed in financial arrangements, concealed the reality of economic inequality (McRae, 1987, p. 121).

The one couple in my sample where the wife was the breadwinner also dealt with this situation by pooling all their money. Mrs Hedger was a farmworker; Mr Hedger had lost his job as a driver when he was injured in an accident two years earlier and was in receipt of Invalidity Benefit. Mr Hedger paid the rent and did the daily shopping, the cleaning and weekday cooking while Mrs Hedger was responsible for the other bills and for weekend shopping and cooking. He described what happened before his accident:

> I used to pay the wife housekeeping money and the rest I'd have in my pocket to spend how I liked. Five years ago I used to spend £10 to £15 per night, four or five nights per week. But now I can't – and I can't say I miss it.

Mrs Hedger also described the changes in their financial arrangements

> He used to give me housekeeping and out of that I had to pay all the bills, rent, food and so on. It didn't work because I never had enough money left. If I was short I could ask for extra, but I tried to manage. When I started work we started putting it together.

In answer to the question 'Who would you say really controls the money that comes into this household?', she said,

> He does: he has all the money. I come home and hand him my pay packet – like a fool! Then he hands me back money for food for the weekend and bits for myself. I don't think people believe I hand my pay packet over. Most of the time it's the woman what controls the money, but in our position with him not working it's been reversed. With him being at home all day he has to do most of the shopping.

When asked what the advantages of this system were for him, he said,

> It's done me good, to be honest – it's taken a lot of responsibility off the wife and drawn me more into the family and the running of the family.

These quotations illustrate the complicated negotiation which occurs when ideology and reality do not coincide. When Mr Hedger was the breadwinner he delegated the work of managing the money to his wife and kept back a substantial sum for his personal use; his wife managed whatever amount he had decided to give her. When their positions changed she did not become a breadwinner in the sense that he had been. Control remained with him and he took over the management of most of their income; this gave him the feeling of being 'drawn more into the family'. It is as though, if he had been neither the breadwinner nor the controller of finances, he would have had no part in the life of the family: that is to say, a subordinate role would not have seemed like any role at all.

The three case-studies which follow are all concerned with couples where the husband was the sole earner; all had young children and in each case the wife had given up a relatively well-paid job when the first child was born. Though these three women were in very similar economic positions, their access to financial resources within the household varied greatly. The first couple had a joint account, into which the husband's income was paid; he controlled finances by controlling his wife's access to the joint account. The second couple also had a joint account but in this case it was controlled by the wife and spent by her as she thought fit. The third couple had no joint account; the husband controlled finances and had his own personal account from which he gave his wife an allowance to buy food. These three very different financial arrangements reflected profound ideological differences between the couples, and particularly between the three husbands concerned.

Strong religious beliefs dominated the lives of Mr and Mrs Church and were expressed in their financial arrangements, which were classified as 'husband-controlled pooling'. They had a joint account, out of which Mr Church paid all the bills, while Mrs Church used the Child Benefit for their four children as daily housekeeping money. If she ran short she could draw money from their joint account, but she always let her husband know if she had done this and it was a rare occurrence. When asked why they organised their finances as they did, he said:

> Because the biblical principle is that the man is the head of the home and it relieves my wife from these emotional pressures. I would take the strain off those things and pressures which God didn't intend her to carry. [The advantages?] It helps me to be a man and it helps my wife to be a woman.

He saw financial control as shared, but she considered that he controlled finances. Her comments contain within them echoes of conflicting ideologies:

> Because we're Christians we feel that the man should have the responsibility. We feel that the man is the head of the home from the point of view of care and responsibility – and authority when necessary. There's some couples where the woman is more capable. But as a basic principle it's a good one, we feel.

When asked 'Have you and your husband always done things this way?' she stopped speaking as a couple, in the first person plural, and began speaking as an individual, but with some hesitation:

> I found it hard initially – thinking that the man's going to do it all, sort of thing. From being single to doing things together. Pete thought it was right for the man to do it, and it worked out alright. But when you've been independent, it seemed a bit hard, sort of thing.

After his interview had ended, and while his wife was still being interviewed in the next room, Mr Church commented that for him women were created from Adam's rib and as such were 'weaker vessels'. There seemed some disparity between this ideology and the reality, in which his wife was feeding six people on £23.40 per week, a feat that was described by her husband as 'marvellous: I don't know how she does it'.

By contrast Mr and Mrs Appleyard's financial arrangements were classified as 'wife-controlled pooling'. Mr Appleyard's salary as managing director of a local business was paid into their joint account. His wife had given up her job as a secretary when their two sons were born, but both agreed that she controlled the family finances: she paid the main bills and she checked the joint account when the bank statement came. When asked why they arranged their finances in this way, Mr Appleyard referred back to the start of the marriage:

> So that we were totally open with each other. I trust her implicitly and she trusts me. I couldn't see that there was any other way. Eventually I was going to be the only one earning. I couldn't keep it all to myself, that wouldn't be a very fair deal. Basically what we have we share.

When she was asked the same question Mrs Appleyard's reply reflected the same ideology of togetherness and equality:

> When we were married we wanted to do everything together. We were both working then, but it just carried on. [Does it bother you not having an income of your own?] No. I always have access to our income. I don't feel dependent because I work quite hard for it. If it wasn't for the children I would be out to work anyway.

After this interview was over the interviewers commented that some of the questions 'seemed a bit silly' when a couple so obviously regarded their money as a common pool on which both partners could draw. This comment raises an issue which posed fundamental problems for the study. It proved very difficult to design a questionnaire which would be equally appropriate in situations of consensus and of conflict. The final case-study describes a couple where husband and wife led very separate lives and where there were high levels of conflict.

Mr and Mrs Cox owned a small fruit farm and she had given up her job as a health visitor to look after their two young children. Mr Cox had a business account for the farm, from which he gave his wife £60 per week, for food, petrol and things for the children; he also had a personal current account and a deposit account for larger farm expenditure. Their financial arrangements were classified as 'husband control', that is, there was no joint account and he controlled finances. When asked what she would feel about having a joint account Mrs Cox said:

> Impossible – because he is self-employed. I think he ought to get us a joint account but that's totally against farming religion. I don't like the system, but it's something I've got used to. When I was earning I used to save my money and he used to give me a set allowance to buy food etc. It just seemed to carry on from those days.

Mr Cox claimed that he had never thought about having a joint account. When asked why they organised their finances as they did, he found the question puzzling:

> I don't know really: it just seemed easier to have a set amount each week. You get through more money if you keep writing cheques. [The advantages?] I spend less money this way.

At a later stage in the interview Mr Cox commented that most of his friends gave their wives a housekeeping allowance, which suggests that Mrs Cox was correct in identifying this as characteristic of farming families. When asked 'Do you feel you need to justify to your wife/husband spending money on some of the things you buy?', Mr Cox answered 'No', but Mrs Cox said,

> He'll ask – so I feel I have to justify myself. Like the house, he thinks that's his domain. I went out and bought some wallpaper for the kids' room. He didn't like that at all because I did it without his permission and knowledge.

She found it difficult not having any money of her own:

> Because I had it before and I miss it. My housekeeping isn't for me: it is to run the house and the children, not for me. I've always had my own money up to the time I was married. I don't like being dependent. I'm always going on about it and it causes arguments.

These comments illustrate neatly the workings of patriarchy as both ideology and practice. Structural inequality in the labour market was compounded by assumptions about the husband's right to control financial matters and to spend autonomously, a right so taken for granted that he had never really thought about it before the interview. As far as the wife was concerned, the dominant ideology, which she called 'farming religion', assumed that she would defer to the earner, would use his money for the house and children and would accept that because her work was unpaid she had no right to any money herself. An alternative ideology expresses itself in her resentment and recognition of loss.

Studies of violence in marriage have described a pattern in which an ideology of male dominance is expressed both in physical abuse of the wife and in male control of the couple's money. The Dobashes, in their study of battered women, found that 'the majority of the disputes that preceded the violence focused on the husband's jealousy of his wife, differing expectations regarding the wife's domestic duties and the allocation of money' (Dobash and Dobash, 1980, p. 98). In her study of *Hidden Violence* Evason made important links between wife abuse on the one hand and the ideological construction of marriage on the other hand, with particular emphasis on financial arrangements within marriage (Evason, 1982). She distinguished three models of money management; these were, first, shared management, second the allowance system, in which the husband gave his wife a regular sum for housekeeping, and a third model in which the husband controlled and managed finances, allocating money to his wife if and when he saw fit to do so. Violent husbands were more likely to adopt the third model and less likely to use shared management than were non-violent husbands. Evason ended by identifying the financial dependence of married women as an important part of the pattern of structured constraints which keeps women within violent marriages (Evason, 1982, p. 76; see also Ayers and Lambertz, 1986).

Despite the continuation of extreme male dominance in some marriages the evidence suggests that, on the whole, the last twenty years have seen an increase in the prevalence of shared management of money. Studies carried out in the 1950s and 1960s tended to find the majority of couples divided between wife management and the allowance system and relatively few couples pooling their money (Zweig, 1961; Gorer, 1971; Land, 1969). Most studies carried out in the 1980s have shown much larger proportions of couples sharing the management of finances. To some extent this probably reflects the spread of joint bank accounts, but it seems also to represent a real change in ideology, since not all those with bank accounts have joint accounts.

MONEY AND HAPPINESS IN MARRIAGE

Sooner or later all researchers on this topic are asked: 'Which is the best way of organising money in marriage?' 'Best' may be defined in terms of convenience, in terms of never getting into financial difficulties, or in terms of acceptability to one or both partners. However, many people are interested in knowing whether there is any association between happiness and specific financial arrangements. Questions about happiness in marriage are notoriously prone to bias: few people are willing to admit that their marriage is unsatisfactory, at least in response to a single question in a single interview. So in the interviews moderately unhappy people tended to say their marriage was 'average', and anyone who admitted to problems was likely to be quite unhappy; the answers on this topic were corroborated by the interviewers, who had watched the interaction between the couple in the joint interview.

Respondents were asked, 'Would you say that your marriage is very happy, happy, average, unhappy or very unhappy?' Those who described themselves as 'average' were grouped with those who were unhappy. Table 3.5 shows the results. In the sample as a whole only one sixth of couples felt that their marriage was unhappy, but where husbands controlled the money this proportion rose to a quarter of the men and two fifths of the women. We cannot be certain whether husband-control leads to unhappiness or whether marital discord provokes the husband into taking control of finances. However, there was a very signficant association between male control of money and marital unhappiness, which applied both to men and to women.

Happiness in marriage was also related to the extent to which couples saw responsibility for spending as separate or shared. When a couple considered that they had separate spheres of financial respon-

Table 3.5 Marital happiness by control of finances*

Marriage described as	Wife control	Wife-controlled pooling	Husband-controlled pooling	Husband control
Happy/very happy	13(13)	23(25)	37(35)	13(16)
Average/unhappy	1 (1)	4 (2)	2 (4)	9 (6)
Total number	14	27	39	22

*Wives' answers (husbands' answers in brackets)

sibility both husband and wife were less likely to say that their marriage was a happy one. 'Separateness' in financial matters was also associated with the husband controlling finances and having greater power in decision-making. The four case-studies all fell into this pattern. The Hedgers and the Appleyards considered that financial responsiblity was shared; the Churches and the Coxes saw it as separate, although Mr Cox added 'but we confer together', a comment which seemed to represent a nod in the direction of an alternative ideology of marital sharing.

CONCLUSION

How can we bring together the evidence about the complicated links between money, power and ideology? Having power in a marriage is associated both with contributing money to the household and also with controlling finances within it. However, ideology has the power either to mitigate or to exacerbate structural inequality. An ideology which stresses the sharing of resources serves to conceal the structurally weak position of those who do not earn; an ideology of separateness in financial matters strengthens the position of those who earn, by comparison with those who do not. The continuing influence of patriarchy is underlined by the fact that it seems much more acceptable for a woman than for a man to be economically powerless: whenever possible male powerlessness is concealed by the sharing of resources.

Though the dominant ideology seems to suggest that married couples share their incomes, the results of this study showed that the reality was rather different. Even among couples who pooled their resources in a joint account there were still substantial inequalities between husbands and wives. Patterns of financial inequality reflected not only the relative structural position of men and women, but also different ideologies about the nature of marriage. Households where there was no joint account, and where the husband controlled finances, were characterised by high levels of male dominance in decision-making and by greater marital unhappiness, especially for wives.

ACKNOWLEDGEMENT

The research reported in this paper was funded by the Economic and Social Research Council and the Joseph Rowntree Memorial Trust.

4 Governing by Gender? School Governing Bodies After the Education Reform Act

Rosemary Deem

INTRODUCTION

In this paper I am going to explore some of the ways in which gender relations influence the activities of school governing bodies. Many books and articles have been written about school governing bodies, but none of those writings emanating from Britain have taken the gender issues seriously. This is despite the fact that a recent National Foundation for Education Research (NFER) study of the 1988 recomposition of governing bodies pointed to an under-representation of women (Jefferies and Streatfield, 1989) and despite the Equal Opportunities Commission's findings that in 1988 a number of successful sex discrimination cases taken to industrial tribunals concerned unlawful discrimination by school governors (EOC, 1989). As I will show in this paper, gender issues do quite frequently surface in the activities of school governing bodies and it is hard to make sense of what is going on in those bodies, particulary in relation to their power dynamics, without using an analysis at least partially based on gender and power.

The research on which the paper is based is part of a four-year project begun in October 1988. What appears here has only the status of a preliminary report, since at the time of writing the research has three years still to run. The project is being undertaken by myself and Kevin Brehony, and is looking at fifteen school governing bodies in two shire county Local Education Authorities (LEAs). Although both authorities have made some gestures in the direction of equal opportunities policies, one in relation to employment and the other more widely, neither has prioritised gender within those policies. The fifteen schools whose governing bodies we are studying include both primary and secondary, with a variety of catchment areas ranging from affluent middle-class white areas of prosperous towns to predominantly urban working-class and Asian areas. In common with the governing bodies of all maintained state schools in England and Wales, which have been reformed under the twin impact of the 1986 and 1988 Education Acts, the fifteen in our study were established in the autumn of 1988, and their term of office will run until the summer of 1992. We are using a variety of methods, including non-participant observation of formal meetings and some informal ones, attendance at governor training sessions, questionnaires and interviews. There are currently some 251 governors in our study; the exact number varies from term to term as resignations occur and there is often a time lag in filling vacancies. One-third of our governors are female and eight per cent of the total sample are black or Asian. The sample is overwhelmingly white and middle-class.

The study of school governors might at first sight seem to have few attractions for a feminist researcher, since although a substantial minority of governors are women, governing schools in England and Wales is a male-shaped activity which until recently has been dominated by local politicians and headteachers. Although since the 1944 Education Act, lay governors have had oversight of the curriculum and school organisation, it is only in the 1980s that governors in most schools have begun to take on responsibilities which offer them more than symbolic power over the running of schools. The 1986 and 1988 Education Acts have added quite significantly to the responsibilities of governors as well as shifting the numerical balance of power from LEA nominees to elected parent governors and co-opted business or community governors. The 1988 Education Reform Act was described by its author Kenneth Baker when passing through the House of Commons as a piece of legislation which will 'create a new framework ... raise standards, extend choice and produce a better-educated Britain ... [and] give the consumers of education a central part in decision-making' (Hansard, 1 Dec. 1987, c. 771–2).

GOVERNING SCHOOLS 1944–86 – THE INVISIBLE WOMEN

The 1944 Education Act supposedly established a partnership between teachers, central government and local education authorities, although this was never an evenly balanced distribution of power and responsibilities (Bogdanor, 1979). Although many ordinary teachers in the post-1944 'partnership' were women, the power structure which shaped the partnership was overwhelmingly male, consisting of male heads (except in primary and girls-only secondary schools), politicians, local authority officers and civil servants. Governors played little or no role in this partnership and nor did parents. The 'producers' of education were firmly in the driving seat. The 1944 Act also allowed for the establishment of lay governing bodies for state schools, although it was possible for one governing body to preside over all the schools in one LEA. Governing bodies were usually dominated by political party nominees and parents, for example, did not have to be represented at all. Lay governors in themselves were not new – in the 1880s there were lay managers for the state-funded elementary schools set up by School Boards. After 1944, which established free secondary education for all, LEAs oversaw the implementation of educational policy within the broad framework laid down by parliament, first the Ministry of Education and later (from 1964) the Department of Education and Science. Education was financed by a combination of local rates and money from central government. But during the period after 1944, teachers and heads gradually acquired the status of largely autonomous experts, to whom the running of schools could safely be left.

Given the structure of governing bodies, this autonomy was just as well. In 25 per cent of LEAs during the period 1965–9, all of their schools shared a single set of governors. In others, there was more than one governing body but it was not uncommon for all of them to meet in the council offices on the same night! Needless to say such meetings were brief in the extreme. Whether there were single LEA-wide or multiple governing bodies, their membership was often heavily dominated by politicians and sometimes their spouses (Bacon, 1978). The task was frequently undertaken for prestige reasons by those who often had little time to devote to the tasks of school governing. Therefore, as Bacon says, 'it was hardly surprising that many teachers viewed these often nominal lay bodies with a general cynicism and ... veiled contempt' (Bacon, 1978, p. 43). The producers of education, teachers and LEAs, held the reins of control and the consumers got no further, in most cases, than the role of interested observers watching the producer horses parade.

During the 1970s some authorities, like Sheffield, tried to develop a more representative system of school government, with each school having its own governing body. Although political nominees remained, elected representatives from parents, teachers, non-teaching staff and community and voluntary groups were also part of each board of governors (Bacon, 1978). But whilst Bacon's study tells us about the middle-class domination of the Sheffield boards, it says little or nothing about their gender composition. Gender appears in Bacon's book only in the guise of 'housewife'; professional and blue-collar workers were presumably ungendered. Nor does ethnicity get a mention. Only 2 per cent of fifty boards studied contained more than 40 per cent 'housewives' and nearly two-thirds of the boards had less than a fifth of their membership drawn from the 'housewife' category.

Until the eighties, notwithstanding the Sheffield example, most school governors in English and Welsh LEAs operated in a token and perfunctory manner, attending termly meetings, occasionally sitting on an appointments panel and visiting the school for formal occasions like sports days, prize givings and concerts. But by the mid-1970s concerns had already begun to be raised about the degree of teacher autonomy and the impact of this on educational standards. This was at least partly prompted by a *cause célèbre* about the 'progressive' regime and low standards of education allegedly provided at William Tyndale School in London (Dale, 1981). Questions were asked about how schools were run, the autonomy of heads to do what they wanted and the costs of education, most notably by the Black Papers (Cox and Boyson, 1975, 1977) which were the forerunners of many subsequent right-wing critiques of the state education system (Brehony, 1989). Such critiques and the aftermath of the Tyndale affair brought in their wake, by the late seventies, others who were also concerned about issues of accountability and the professional autonomy of teachers (Maclure and Becher, 1978; Lello, 1979).

In 1975 the Department of Education and Science (DES) had set up the Taylor Committee to examine the arrangements for governing schools. The Taylor Report (DES, 1977), whilst recommending that LEAs should continue to remain responsible for the overseeing of school government, suggested that much more power than previously should be delegated to governing bodies themselves. These would include establishing the aims of the school and the ways in which these were to be achieved, although the headteacher would retain ultimate control. Other powers would involve submitting annual estimates of school income and expenditure; consultation with the LEA over buildings and maintenance; joint responsibility with the LEA for appointments of heads and full responsibility for the appointment of other teachers. Ideally each school should have its own separate body, on which would sit equal numbers of LEA representatives, school staff, parents, pupils where appropriate and members of the local community. Yet although the Taylor Report was keen on the representation of different categories of governor (and although women were represented on the Committee itself), the report said nothing about the representation of different social groups like women and black people.

The Taylor recommendations were only partially incorporated into the 1980 Education Act, which tried to ensure that schools would usually have their own individual governing body. For maintained schools (i.e. not Church of England or Roman Catholic) a minimum of two parents and one teacher were added. This went little further than the changes that LEAs like Sheffield had already achieved. It did not extend the powers of governing bodies or radically alter their composition, although by setting up mechanisms requiring schools to publish exam results and provide 'Information for Parents' booklets, the Act did prepare the ground for what was to emerge under the 1986 Act (for example the annual report by governors to parents).

Although in the period after 1980, some governing bodies became much more involved in helping to support their schools than others, much of the research shows that governors generally continued to operate in an advisory and supporting capacity, in conjunction with headteachers (Kogan et al., 1984). Research still did not look seriously at the gender relations and issues raised by the changed composition of governing bodies. In particular it failed to explore the role played by those people, usually female, who became primary school governors mainly or partly because they already spent time in school helping with the pupils and other tasks. Such roles were not powerful in the sense of achieving change or telling teachers what to do, but they did give the parent governors concerned a much more informed knowledge of the school than that possessed by many co-opted and LEA governors, who had much less contact with their school. The research done on governing bodies and the running of schools prior to the 1986 Education Act also failed to consider whether governing bodies behaved differently when there were female chairs and female headteachers. A study of headteachers at work which could have illuminated this focused mainly on male heads (Hall, Mackay and Morgan, 1986). A major project on school governors by Kogan et al. (1984) did, however, suggest that primary school governing bodies (more likely to have female governors and female heads) behaved differently to secondary school governing bodies. However, this difference seems to have been confined to primary governors apparently having less knowledge about the aims of primary schools! It is then fair to say that we know little about the way in which gender and race dynamics affected governing bodies and their activities between 1944 and the late 1980s.

THE 1986 EDUCATION ACT

The 1986 Act changed the composition of governing bodies. The changes included increased parental representation, decreased LEA representation and increased co-opted membership (intended to bring wider community involvement, and more particularly people representing the business community). Only teacher governors and parent governors are elected positions, the latter by postal ballot. The 1986 Act also gave governors clearer powers than previously over staff appointments, the curriculum, ensuring that the education in their school is not politically biased, and the right to determine whether or not sex education takes place in their schools. From 1987 onwards all governing bodies had to write an annual report for parents in advance of an annual meeting between the governors and the parents of all pupils in the school. Initial research on attendance at the first round of meetings in 1987 (Earley, 1988) suggests a very low attendance at such meetings. Since these meetings often take place in the evenings many women might well experience difficulty in attending, especially if they have young children.

What was not included in the 1986 Act, somewhat surprisingly in view of the number of extra responsibilities given to governors and the emphasis on involving more parents and members of the wider community in governing schools, was anything requiring employers to allow employees who are governors paid time off work to carry out their tasks. This is especially significant for those (women, blacks and Asians, and many other working-class people) who are in poorly-paid and insecure jobs.

THE 1988 REFORM EDUCATION ACT

The Act may be seen as an attempt to 'do something' about education. The legislation is apparently more motivated by political ideology than any genuine concern for educational change (a critique of the Act is to be found in Flude and Hammer, 1989). The sheer number of changes required, the speed of their implementation, and the drastic shortage of teachers and resources seem to suggest a strategy which is either doomed to failure or which will lead to the end of a state education system as a major provider of schooling. The main features of the Act which are relevant to school governors are the National Curriculum, open enrolment, Local Management of Schools (LMS), the possibility of opting out and the policy on charging for education. Many of the innovations in the 1988 Act can only work with the help or at least the tacit consent of governors. Governors play a key role in making the initial decision to ballot parents on whether to apply to the Secretary of State to opt out of local authority control. Governors will have the responsibility of ensuring that their school's curriculum and assessment arrangements conform to the National Curriculum. They will have to work out a way of coping with open admissions policy and its implications for equal opportunities. The complex arrangements for charging for educational activities as set out in a DES circular in January 1989 have had to be turned into a workable policy by governors and heads.

The whole Local Management of Schools policy, in particular, will stand or fall by the ability and capacity of governors and schools to cope with the heavy responsibilities it will impose on them, including effective hiring and firing of staff. The increased autonomy of governing bodies will also make it harder for LEAs to enforce equal opportunities policies. But the running of schools will also be a huge task. Given that most women already have at least a dual role in employment and in the home, those who are also school governors, we can be sure, will hardly have time left to breathe! Some people have interpreted LMS as being mainly about finance. This in itself is problematic for women – although schoolgirls are showing increasing enthusiasm and aptitude for mathematics, this is a very recent trend and many adult women lack confidence in their ability to handle finance in the public domain – so that in our research governing bodies, although there are a few women involved, mostly accountants, finance subcommittees are largely being populated by male governors. But the actual implications of LMS go far beyond finance. Cooper and Lybrand's Report for the DES on LMS (Cooper and Lybrand, 1988) makes this point strongly: 'The changes require a new culture and philosophy of the organisation of education at the school level. They are more than purely financial' (Cooper and Lybrand,

1988, p. 5). It is the intention of the 1988 Education Act that this new culture and philosophy should be administered by the consumers rather than by the producers of education. What is particularly interesting for those of us whose concern is gender and power is how many women are amongst the new governors and how they will negotiate the maze of well-established male-dominated gender power relations which have held sway in many school governing bodies for a good many years.

THE PRODUCER–CONSUMER BATTLE – DO WOMEN COUNT?

Reshaping governing bodies is ostensibly supposed to be about transferring power from producers to consumers and about making schools more 'effective'. However we need to ask some searching questions about this transfer of power and its significance. Will the power transfer occur? After a year, many governing body decisions and subcommittees are still heavily influenced by male party political nominees (who are supposed to be on the producer side, although since many are business people, this seems problematic). Where LEA nominees are not still in powerful positions (or do not turn up to meetings frequently enough to exercise any power) it is mainly co-opted governors who are taking the centre stage. Is this notion of producers and consumers a helpful one? It is not always easy to see the dividing line – a teacher can also be a parent, a co-opted business person may be a former teacher – so that in practice the distinction does not necessarily mean a lot. In any case, logically the consumers of education are pupils, whom the 1986 Act specifically excludes from membership of governing bodies. Will the reshaping of governing bodies still exclude some categories of people from being governors? Our research suggests that it already has succeeded in excluding many people – women, working-class people of both sexes, blacks and Asians. Less than a quarter of each of the categories of LEA and co-opted governors in the study are women, although it is slightly higher – one-third – for minor authority (that is, district or parish council) representatives. Only a tiny fraction of those women LEA or co-opted governors are black or Asian. In our sample 40 per cent of parent governors are women, again mostly white. Parent governors, as the recent Leverhulme study has shown, are not always able to use their power effectively, are sometimes sidelined by other governors and have to struggle for recognition that their position is a legitimate one (Exeter Society, 1987; Golby, Brigley and Exeter Society, 1989). Women were most likely to be represented in our study in the teacher governor category (64 per cent) but there are no black women amongst them.

A not too dissimilar pattern of gender distribution to that in our study has been found in the Leverhulme study of parent governors based in Devon ('Governor power', 1988) although there more parent governors were women (57 per cent compared to 40 per cent, in our study) and there were slightly more female co-opted governors (a third as opposed to one quarter in ours). This may tell us as much about the relative social composition of Devon and our two LEAs (which are socially and ethnically more mixed and have a high percentage of modern medium- and large-size industries in their economy) as about greater efforts to attract women governors in Devon, although the latter cannot be ruled out. So far as we can tell, the Leverhulme Devon study only contained white governors.

Women and especially black women, then, do not seem to have been particularly drawn in by the reformed governing bodies. The consumer revolution has largely been a white male one. Nor is it the case that the consumers attracted by the reforms are necessarily representative of the schools on whose governing bodies they sit. Of course sometimes the social composition of governors reflects the social composition of the school's pupils; but where the latter is mainly working-class or has a high proportion of students from ethnic minority groups, this appears not to be the case. It is possible to see that the legislation itself is underpinned by ideological asumptions which themselves envisage women only as certain kinds of governors. Women are clearly invoked in the ideological construction of parent governors, since to do otherwise would be to lose sight of one of the central Thatcherite beliefs, that women are at the centre of the family and childcare (David and New, 1985). Furthermore, within the sphere of the household, it is acceptable to call women consumers. But they are largely excluded from that construction of co-opted governors which sees such governors as business people, since those to whom the appeal to be governors has been made are not those from amongst the ranks of small businesses where women are well represented but those who are in senior positions in large concerns, where women are still a tiny minority. Certainly women are well represented in the community, which is also part of the group from which co-opted governors may be drawn; but many secondary schools, including some of those in our sample, have tended to see business governors as of more use than community governors.

Table 4.1 shows the pattern of gender distribution of governors in our fifteen case-study schools. It is particularly evident that women are far more numerous in primary than secondary schools. Since there are far more women than men teachers in primary schools and since primary schools often have a female-like atmosphere, with many mothers (and far fewer fathers) acting as unpaid school helpers, this is not surprising. Perhaps women parent governors who develop confidence in their role will move on to secondary governing bodies as their children enter that sector.

Table 4.1 Case-study school governing bodies membership by gender, July 1989

School	Total govs.	Total fem. govs.	% fem. all govs	Fem. chair/ vice-chair
School E (Primary)#2	19	13	81	Ch
School F (Primary)	12	6	50	—
School A (Primary)#1	17	8	47	VC
School C (Primary)	16	6	37	Ch,VC
School J (Primary)#	16	6	37	VC
School O (Primary)	16	6	37	VC
School I (Primary)	11	4	36	Ch
School D (Primary)#1	18	6	33	—
School G (Secondary)	17	5	29	VC
School H (Secondary)	19	5	26	—
School K (Secondary)	19	5	26	—
School L (Secondary)	19	5	26	—
School N (Secondary)	17	4	23	—
School M (Secondary)	19	4	21	—
School B (Secondary)	16	3	19	—

Key # = woman head
   #1 = 1 female head from two (joint governing body of 2 schools)
   #2 = 2 female heads (joint governing body)

GOVERNING BY GENDER

Although little or nothing has been written about the relationship between gender and school governing bodies in England and Wales, a very interesting study of gender issues in the affairs of two primary

School Councils (the Australian equivalent of school governing bodies) in Australia has recently been published by Evans (1988). Evans suggests that something he terms a 'gender agenda' influences the life of the primary schools he studied, including the ways in which the School Councils of the two establishments operated. This gender agenda operates both for individuals and for groups. It does not operate in a vacuum however, but intersects with agendas based on other social divisions too – occupation, ethnicity, class. Evans writes: '*agendas* ... are areas of contestation, continuously being manipulated, shaped, defended or attacked by the people involved. However, the interests and motivations of the participants are not clearcut ... [they may be] ... rooted in the middle class, but ... divided along teacher–parent lines. Gender relationships help cement ... men ... together and separate them from the women' (Evans, 1988, pp. 41–2). This notion of intersecting interests is I think a useful one for looking at the power dynamics of governing bodies. That is because unlike in the household, for example, where gender relations are central to many aspects of the division of labour, in organisations like governing bodies gender relations are sometimes very salient indeed and at other times they are not at all relevant.

Women governors, especially those of different political persuasions, class and ethnic groups and representing different categories of producer and consumer do not necessarily ever see themselves as sharing gender solidarity. For example in secondary schools it is rare for women teacher governors and female parent governors to line up on a particular issue, nor do black and white women governors necessarily see eye to eye on particular matters. Insofar as women governors are united, it is often because men use patriarchal power against them as an (in male eyes) undifferentiated group, rather than because the women consciously think of themselves as sharing interests in common. Hence I am sure that most women governors in our study would deny vehemently that gender was at all relevant to their role as governors, even though our observation of meetings suggests that gender is sometimes very relevant. There are almost no avowedly feminist governors in our study either. However, some male governors, particularly if they are also united by other considerations like shared world views, political affiliation and similar occupations, clearly do consciously operate on the basis of shared gender solidarity, and do clearly exercise gender power as well as other forms of power in the governing body. However, for male governors too, their politics, their employment interests and their ethnicity may at times be far more significant in understanding the power relations within which they operate inside governing bodies than their gender. Nevertheless, gender relations do appear to have a quite significant, if largely unrecognised, impact on the power dynamics of governing bodies.

However, we also have to remember that governing bodies are locked into a complex set of interrelationships with other organisations, including not only schools but local authorities and increasingly local business and industry too, which also construct their own gender agendas. Women, of course, are increasingly well represented in the labour force of Britain but they are still far from numerous at higher levels, the levels from which many new co-opted governors have been drawn. So the education agendas of industry are intersected by class, ethnicity and gender considerations. This does not necessarily always mean white male interests are dominant – there are for example a number of Asian co-opted and parent governors who have business or commercial interests – but this is much more common than the obverse. In the political arena, local politics are still male-dominated although less so than parliamentary politics (Randall, 1988). Few senior education officers are women, although where LEAs provide clerks for governing bodies (and even where schools provide their own) these are usually women. National educational policy in the 1980s has also largely been constructed by men, although we should not forget the influence of Margaret Thatcher and Baroness Cox on that policy too (Cox played a key role in the sex education and political balance sections of the 1986 Act and the collective Christian worship aspect of the Reform Act). As we shall see, political experience in local government remains an important training ground for office-holders on governing bodies and the gender relations between the dominant governors and the subordinate clerks are also significant in the actions and activities of governing bodies.

POWER PLAY IN GOVERNING BODIES

Although it is clearly an intention of the new legislation that consumer governors should take over from producer governors, in several of our case-study governing bodies, a year into the life of the new governors, the LEA nominees and the headteachers have not yet handed over the reins of power to the consumer-oriented parent and co-opted governors. Some of this is to do with the relative inexperience (in relation to school governing bodies) of many co-opted and parent governors. The Leverhulme study (Golby, Brigley and Exeter Society, 1989) found that parent governors increased in confidence and power as their experience developed. Most of the governing bodies in our study have a reasonable number of continuing governors from the 1985–8 period and before. There is only one in which there are scarcely any previous governors and it is finding life a hard struggle. In the few governing bodies, parent governors have made a bid for power – usually by occupying the office of chair – and are successfully holding the politicians at bay. Many co-opted governors, despite the intentions of the DES that they should all be in place by 21 October 1988, came late in the day to their bodies and therefore stood little chance of being elected as chairs or vice-chairs, although several have taken over convening finance and marketing/Public Relations subcommittees. However, governing body chairs are subject to annual re-elections and given the much increased workload in the 1988/9 year, it may be that old hands will stand down or fail to be re-elected. Only three of our governing bodies are chaired by women (all three are parent governors) and all these are in primary schools. Only one secondary school even has a female vice-chair and none has a female chair. No black women are chairs or vice-chairs (there is only one black male chair).

Party politics do not always surface in governing body meetings despite the presence of party politicians – in some of the bodies we would be hard put to say what the political affiliations of LEA governors are, if we relied solely on what transpired in the meetings. However, there is a certain reluctance amongst some governors to admit that governing bodies are political at all, even with a small 'p'. The Leverhulme study noted this reluctance and dislike of party politics amongst some parent governors (Exeter Society, 1987). It is also evident amongst some experienced governors and governor pressure groups (Sallis, 1988). So far as our study is concerned, governing bodies are quite evidently concerned with the exercise of power and this has been exacerbated by the recent increase in what governors are responsible for overseeing in schools. Because governing body activities and interests are about the exercise of power and because in our society groups like women (even middle-class women) and blacks have little opportunity to hold or exercise power in the public sphere, it is not difficult to see that gender and race/ethnicity dynamics as well as class underlie the exercise of power within governing bodies.

Patriarchy and class are certainly evident in the ways governing bodies operate. Women, blacks and working-class governors of any gender and ethnicity have a hard time getting their point of view heard or their personal agendas listened to. Women speakers are frequently, as Spender (1982) has noted, ignored or interrupted by men and some of the female governors in our study appear completely in awe of what is happening and are therefore effectively 'silenced'. The most vocal women in most governing bodies are teacher governors, who base their power on access to professional teaching expertise and a handful of parent and LEA/minor authority governors. The remainder of the women governors, except for those who are chairs, are amongst the quietest governors on all the fifteen research governing bodies. This could have serious consequences for the future shape of state education, if the agendas and issues are dictated largely by white, middle-class men. In secondary schools such men are not only a large proportion of the governors but are also likely to be headteachers too. There are five ways in which gender relations seem to have been particularly influential in school governing bodies during the first year of our study. Who controls the tenor and direction of the meeting is one. Who speaks and who listens is another one. A third arises over governing body and clerking relationships. A fourth is to do with the construction of 'inadequate' mothers and teachers who are inadequate disciplinarians. A fifth arises over the timing of meetings and the ideological construction of the 'ideal' governor. There are of course many other potential ways in which gender may emerge; for example in debates over sex education, about how equal opportunities should be implemented in schools (this has in a year only surfaced once in one governing body) and in appointments panels and shortlisting discussions (we have not had the time or negotiated the access necessary to look at appointments, although they are undoubtedly a key issue).

The chair of a governing body occupies a key role in governing bodies, inside and outside the formal meetings. Preliminary analysis of our data suggests that only headteachers intervene in meetings more than chairs. As already noted, just three of our case-study governing bodies are chaired by women. This is not always a trouble-free role for men either but the women seem to have less tacit support from their male colleagues than male chairs can typically expect. Let's take one example of a primary school governing body chaired by a woman but where there is a male head. The woman was opposed by a male LEA nominee who is also a councillor and he and another male LEA governor do their best to make her life difficult, to the extent of whispering to themselves and others what they think should be happening, correcting her grasp of committee procedure and constantly suggesting courses of action which differ from what she has suggested. This behaviour is quite overtly sexist and is accompanied by muttered comments that support this view. Although male chairs may also on occasions be interrupted or corrected by other governors, that action is not based on gender or the exercise of patriarchal power. Nor is the reaction to female chairs just one about experienced governors being critical of inexperienced ones. Indeed, one of the male parent chairs in a primary school governing body is very inexperienced in chairing skills, whereas the female chairs all have, if not governing body chairing experience, then certainly other relevant experience of chairing meetings to draw on. Whereas inexperienced male chairs seem to get a lot of positive help and support from headteachers and other governors, women chairs seem less likely to get this wholehearted support from the whole governing body.

Who speaks and who listens is a major aspect of governing body meetings crucially influenced by gender, race and class as well as by category of governor. Our impression, yet to be confirmed by more detailed data analysis, is that on the whole parent governors speak less than other governors, that women speak less often than men, that working-class governors (there are very few of them anyway) speak less than middle-class ones and that black governors intervene less than white governors. But of course this may change as inexperienced governors gather more experience and gain confidence. To give one example, in one primary school, most of the silent governors are women parent governors, who feel that they should only voice opinions on things that directly concern them, such as passing on parental views about classes who are constantly taught only by supply teachers. Otherwise, they speak only if pressed to do so by other governors. In a second primary school the three Muslim governors say very little at all unless asked direct questions. There are several meetings we have attended (at both primary and secondary schools) where over three quarters of the meeting has been dominated by four or fewer male governors – typically the head, chair and LEA or co-opted governors – and few other people have spoken more than once or twice. We still have a lot more analysis to do on this aspect of governing body meetings but it does look as though certain governors, including many women, are silenced by a combination of gender power, class and lack of confidence.

Clerking is a major arena where gender relations come very much to the surface. This is partly at least because clerking and minute-taking are associated by many male governors, especially those with business and local authority political experience, with secretarial duties. That is, they are a low-status female activity undertaken mainly for male superiors by subordinates who play no other part in the proceedings (Pringle, 1988). In theory, clerks hold a lot of power – they decide agendas and the minutes provide an official account of the meeting. In practice agendas are largely determined by LEA education officers, heads and chairs of governors. Minutes are frequently challenged. There has been much concern in one LEA about the time taken for minutes to appear (the business analogy is frequently heard – at work we get minutes the next day/week – the association with secretaries is evident here) but governors, especially male ones, are usually horrified by the suggestion that one of them should take them instead. Taking minutes is low-status female work. Reading them is high-status male work. In one of our LEAs, governing bodies are clerked by people (usually women working part-time) provided by the authority, although local officers also sometimes attend meetings. In the other LEA, each school is given a financial allowance of so much per hour for so many hours clerking per year. Only one of our fifteen schools is regularly clerked by a man. In both LEAs only formal meetings are clerked. Because of the volume of business during 1988/9, much of it caused by the Reform Act, the LEA where money rather than clerks are provided has seen some governing bodies run out of money due to over-long meetings. In at least one instance where this happened the female clerk was offered flowers in lieu of money – it is hard to imagine this happening to a male clerk – perhaps he would have been offered a free round of golf instead? Because in the main (except on the relatively rare occasions where an education officer clerks the meeting) the female clerks are considered, rightly or wrongly, to have little knowledge of education or any other issue under consideration, they are 'seen and not heard'. They generally only speak when spoken to – scribbling down the meeting's procedures and keeping track of decisions is very time-consuming anyway. On the rare occasions where one of us has attended meetings clerked by a male education officer, there has been a much more deferential attitude displayed towards the clerk.

Sexism also arises in relation to governors' discussions about pupils, teachers and parents. Typically this occurs more often in the schools with predominantly working-class and Asian catchments.

First this happens when discussing teachers' capacity to discipline their pupils; questions are often raised about the ability of 'young girls' [sic] to control classes containing disruptive children (sometimes aged only six or seven years old). Female teacher governors are also clearly only listened to under sufferance by some male governors, whereas male teacher governors are invariably treated with respect even if their contribution is of no different quality to the interventions made by female teachers. Secondly gender (and ethnicity) arises in relation to the kind of pupils the school contains. Again this is most common in working-class schools. Where bad behaviour by pupils is an area of concern, it is not uncommon to hear derogatory references to 'working mothers' and 'inadequate' mothers who are seen to be responsible for the bad behaviour of unruly pupils or they involve oblique references to pupils' membership of ethnic minority groups; 'these children need more teachers' or 'these children require more support and resources' or 'what can you expect of these children?' Such comments are almost unknown in middle-class schools.

Finally, gender arises in connection with the amount of work governors have to do and when they meet. Governors, since the reforming of governing bodies, are under more pressure than ever to attend not only the termly formal meetings but also extra meetings, either of the whole governing body or of sub-groups dealing with things like finance, pupil matters and school visits. When extra meetings are suggested at one female chair's governing body, some governors pointedly say things like: 'Well, that time is fine for the ladies who look after the house but not for busy men like me.' Similar comments were made at another governing body chaired by a woman when it was suggested that two governors rather than one should try to visit the school each term. In general, meeting times at all the governing bodies are scarcely chosen for their ability to blend in with domestic commitments; for example the most popular times for formal meetings are either around four to five o'clock or seven o'clock, which are rather popular times also for children to come home from school or for households to eat their evening meals. The 'typical' governor is thus perceived to be one who has no domestic commitments, whose 'wife' is ready with a warming meal once the long meeting is over and who has enough spare time to read the endless papers which school governors these days have constantly to devour. Spare time, as studies of women and leisure have shown, is not something which lots of women have in vast amounts (Deem, 1986; Talbot and Wimbush, 1989). Given this situation it is amazing how many women do manage to find the time. From what we have seen so far however, in our research, it is not enough for women to be at governing bodies, they also need support and help if they are to undertake the task fully and in ways which are not bureaucratic and formalistic.

CONCLUSION

I hope I have shown in this paper that the study of school governing bodies is a worthwhile issue for feminists to study. Whilst it is undoubtedly the case that school governing operates very much within a patriarchal and middle-class framework, it is important to look at the role played by women in those governing bodies and at the gender and race/ethnicity dynamics of governor activities as well as the class dimension in order to reveal the experiences of women governors. The notion of a gender agenda is certainly evident in many governing body meetings and we hope to further develop this concept as our research progresses further. It will also be important to use our research findings to help support and educate women governors (and men governors too) in relation to equal opportunities policies and practices. Only in this way can we be sure that issues of anti-sexism and anti-racism will continue to be seen as valid concerns of schools.

The studying of school governing bodies at this conjuncture, in a sociologically informed way, is also, I would contend, vitally important if we are to retain a state education system which is fair and freely available to all children. Otherwise, there is the danger that what the state system will become is a rump provision for those whose parents cannot afford a private alternative. Whilst school governing bodies are far from representative of the population as a whole in their composition, their scope and activities will in future have a far more fundamental effect upon the education of children than they have had in the period since 1944. Not the least of the possible scenarios as Local Management of Schools is introduced is a gradual move to increasing privatisation of schooling (as school budgets get supplemented by private funds in schools where this is possible and feasible), with state-funded provision only for the most disadvantaged. Some commentators believe that vouchers are one hidden agenda of the Reform Act (Chitty and Lawson, 1988). The hidden class, race and gender agendas of educational policy and school governance are not ones that anyone who favours a liberal humanist approach to education should want willingly to accept. The recent educational legislation is not designed to improve schooling but to pit school against school and educational consumer against educational producer for the sake of an ideological hatred of the state education system as it has developed since 1944 (Deem, 1989). It has imposed an impossible workload at breakneck speed on teachers, schools, and governors. No comparable set of educational changes has been set in motion since the nineteenth century. Many aspects of our education system, including equal opportunities, need to be protected and we hope our research will show how governors who do not wholeheartedly support the Education Reform Act may be helped to resist its worst effects.

5 Human-Centred Systems ... Women-Centred Systems? Gender Divisions and Office Computer Systems Design

Eileen Green, Jenny Owen, Den Pain and Isabella Stone

INTRODUCTION

It is now well documented by both computer scientists and social scientists that *many* computer systems fail to meet their objectives (Mumford, 1985; Rosenbrock, 1982; Bell *et al.*, 1988). Not only do they fail within the areas of technical efficiency and cost-effectiveness but more importantly for our concerns, they also fail because the design methods employed focus on the technology more than on the needs of the people who use it. Typical problems encountered include work organisation and job design, quality of service, staff motivation and health and safety. What is now becoming clear is that in designing computer artifacts, not only are the tools themselves designed but also the social conditions for their human use. Isolation from other workers, strained backs and blurred vision are equally as important results of the design process as the functional efficiency of the machines themselves (Ehn, 1988).

An area less visible than the neglect of social and human factors is the neglect of the gender dimension to computer systems design. Unsurprisingly, traditional approaches which fail to consider humans also leave out a consideration of their gender (Bell *et al.*, 1988). However, it seems to be a problem inherited or shared by the majority of radical or human-centred approaches which have arisen as a challenge to this orthodoxy. Approaches which place the 'user' centre stage and seek to develop computer systems which protect or enhance the skills of workers tend towards androgyny at best and privileging male workers at worst (Cooley, 1980b; Ehn, 1988).

In this chapter, we critically analyse such approaches, concentrating instead upon women office-workers and their experience of the office computer systems design process. To do this we draw upon an empirical case-study being conducted within a research project funded by the Joint Committee of the British Economic and Social Research Council (ESRC) and Science and Engineering Research Council (SERC).

OFFICE COMPUTER SYSTEMS DESIGN

At the level of formal systems design methodologies, a rather ambiguous concern with 'user-involvement' forms part of the response to the inadequacies of computer systems identified above. 'Structured' systems analysis and design methods, for instance, emphasise 'a lot of interaction with the user', but do not specify whether the user is the manager who oversees a system in use, or the clerical worker who actually operates it. In fact the emphasis is on project control and productivity, and it is the manager who features in all the textbook examples of 'interaction with the user' (Learmouth and Burchett Management Systems, 1986). This approach has been criticised, within computer science, for implying a functionalist and deterministic view of organisations and human behaviour: structure and consensus are assumed to be the norm, while change and conflict are largely ignored. Such methods work, and are widely used, not because there is a lack of conflict among systems users, but because they can be imposed by the more powerful (managerial) users, whose interests they reflect (Land *et al.*, 1983; Jackson, 1982, 1985; Jayaranta, 1986).

Other methodologies do address the issue of user-involvement more thoroughly: 'Socio-Technical Systems' (Mumford, 1985) and 'Soft Systems' (Checkland, 1981) are examples. Neither, however, deals adequately with issues of power and conflict in the workplace. Mumford, for instance, assumes that the goals of increased job satisfaction and increased productivity can be pursued without conflict. While Checkland identifies the existence of different 'stakeholders' or sets of interests within an organisation, his response is a liberal and idealist one, concerned with securing the basis for these to be resolved through discussion among equals. In fact, neither of these two approaches has been used, or evaluated, very widely (Land et al., 1983). A survey conducted in data-processing departments in the UK, US and Europe found that it was rare for formal systems design methodologies to be strictly adhered to (Friedman, 1984, 1987). Instead there was a shift towards more flexible approaches to systems development, arising partly from both trade union and management pressure, and facilitated by the falling cost of hardware and the development of Fourth Generation Languages.

However, recent interdisciplinary design approaches – involving collaboration between social scientists and computer scientists – still tend to treat systems design methodologies as sets of techniques which are neutral and unrelated to any particular sets of interest within an organisation. (See, for example, Avison and Wood-Harper, 1986). The overriding concern is to involve users in order to avoid 'dysfunctional resistance' to computerisation (Hirschheim, 1985). In this sense, there is some similarity with the 'person–machine interface' concerns of 'Human–Computer Interaction' (HCI) research.

In contrast, labour process theory has provided a framework for a number of radical or 'human-centred' approaches to computer systems design. (Cooley, 1980a; Ehn and Kyng, 1987; Ehn, 1988; Greenbaum, 1987). Typically, such approaches have sought to develop computer systems which protect or enhance the skills of, and the exercise of control or discretion by, workers who conform to the ideal underlying Braverman's original deskilling thesis: craftsmen who possess not only skilled status, but also a high degree of union organisation and bargaining-power (Braverman, 1974). Cooley, for instance, discusses the experience of draughtsmen and engineering workers; Ehn et al. developed a collaborative project with craft printers and the Nordic Graphic Workers' Union. Two key issues are discussed in both examples:

(1) the importance of workers' skills, especially the tacit aspects, which cannot readily be reflected in conventionally-designed computer systems;
(2) the importance of the systems development process as an area in which crucial decisions are made concerning jobs and working conditions – decisions which cannot easily be tackled by unions whose new technology policies are limited to responses at the implementation stage.

Both initiatives have addressed issues of power and control in the workplace, and have related workplace experience to a wider concern with trade union and democratic rights: that is, within the terms of the relations between capital and labour. Neither the groups of workers involved, nor the analyses of skill or of workplace relations, reflect either women workers' experience or the existence of gender divisions.

Within Europe and Scandinavia, some recent research has begun to examine the issue of strategies available to women in relation to computer systems design. This work has included two main aspects. First, empirical accounts have been presented of innovative approaches to the active involvement of women workers in office systems design, emphasising the value of group-based or cooperative initiatives at the workplace level (Olerup et al., 1985; Vehvilainen, 1986). Second, a theoretical analysis has been initiated of the ways in which computer systems development methodologies reproduce gender-based dichotomies embedded in natural science traditions – for instance by according greater status to information about 'hard' quantifiable data and procedures than to workers' own accounts of office procedures and communications (Greenbaum, 1987).

However, these research initiatives remain fairly marginal. In the following section we review some of the probable reasons for this marginalisation, and made a preliminary assessment of the scope for incorporating a gender perspective into human-centred systems development approaches.

GENDER, TECHNOLOGY AND CLERICAL WORK

Within the framework of labour process theory, most women workers – including office workers – are not perceived as possessing the skills, the status or the levels of bargaining-power which would make them appropriate participants in 'human-centred' systems design initiatives. First, the clerical jobs done by women are perceived as particularly vulnerable during periods of computerisation and related restructuring. Second, clerical skills have historically been low-paid and low-status skills. And third, women's general lack of access to technological expertise is well documented.

We would argue, however for a critical reconsideration of these three points in the light of recent research on gender, office work and information technology.

The Vulnerability of Women's Jobs

Clearly information technology (IT) can be introduced into office work as part of a wider restructuring which does result in job losses and in worsening working conditions (Huws, 1982; West, 1982). However, neither the 'optimistic' forecasts of 10 years ago ('the paperless office'), nor the 'pessimistic' ones (large-scale job losses) have been fulfilled. Both may be seen as implying a degree of technological determinism, as well as attributing greater homogeneity and coherence to particular levels of management than in fact exist (Webster, 1988; Murray, 1987; Wood, 1982).

Clerical work remains a major area of women's employment: 'of all women in employment, 39 per cent are in the junior non-manual category, which typically means clerical work; women make up 71 per cent of this SEG' (Socio-Economic Group) (Walby, 1987, p. 7). Recent research also suggests that the technical skills and the working conditions which characterise many clerical jobs also make it a primary rather than a secondary labour market for women, thus revealing a simplistic and crude equation of women's work with 'peripheral' rather than 'core' employment (Dex, 1987; Walby, 1987). Clerical work is therefore an important and appropriate area in which to examine the positive strategies open to women regarding the design as well as the use of IT.

Women's Clerical Skills

Conventional systems design methodologies are based largely on the analysis and representation of formal data flows and formal relationships within an organisation. Clerical tasks are generally assumed to be largely routine, and to be an unproblematic area for computerisation. (See for example LBMS, 1986; Gane and Sarson, 1979; Hirschheim, 1985.)

Many social scientific analyses also view clerical work as either very vulnerable to deskilling and fragmentation, during periods of computerisation, or as 'already deskilled' prior to these (see, for example, Glenn and Feldberg, 1979).

Some recent research, however, suggests that in many contexts women's clerical skills are more complex than implied in either view, in three specific respects:

(1) In many clerical jobs, women combine a range of technical,

social and organisational skills which are not fully reflected in their job descriptions (Lie and Rasmussen, 1985; Gaskell, 1987; Murray, 1987).

(2) Important aspects of the social and organisational skills exercised by clerical workers are tacit, rather than formally articulated. As such they are easily overlooked by conventional systems design approaches, which therefore reproduce an incomplete picture of the clerical labour process. The resulting systems may both function imperfectly and contribute to increasingly stressful and degraded working conditions (Goodman and Perby, 1985; Lie and Rasmussen, 1985; Ehn, 1988).

(3) Gender divisions play an important part in the ways in which both clerical jobs and clerical skills are defined. For instance, there is a degree to which some employers rely on the organisational skills which women develop as 'household managers' (Davies and Rosser, 1986). The fact that women have had difficulty gaining formal reward or recognition for these skills is related both to the constraints women experience in balancing domestic and work responsibilities, and to the success with which men have organised to protect their own status and opportunities, both inside the workplace and in the family. The social and organisational skills developed by women are often rendered invisible by being perceived as 'natural' feminine attributes (Gaskell, 1987; Cockburn, 1985; Murray, 1987; Walby, 1986).

To summarise, then, the range and complexity of women's clerical skills is greater than implied in either the systems design or the social scientific models referred to above. In the office context, there is a variable degree of managerial dependence on these skills, although this remains largely unacknowledged.

Women's Lack of Access to Technological Expertise

Male dominance in most areas of scientific and technological activity is well documented and is particularly enduring in terms of the design of technological equipment and processes (Cockburn, 1985; Arnold and Faulkner, 1985; Easlea, 1981; Fox-Keller, 1985; McNeil, 1987).

However, research concerning office work itself indicates that many women clerical workers do express an interest in seeking improved opportunities in relation to IT. Their responses are not confined to perceptions of exclusion or insecurity, but are more complex. In surveys described by Wagner (1985) and by Liff (1988), for example, clerical workers described specific difficulties regarding computerisation such as increased stress and increased health and safety concerns; such workers also expressed satisfaction in relation to making use of new systems, and interest in developing further training or employment opportunities connected with computing. As Liff points out, however, it is important to be cautious about these positive reactions, as they may be relevant mainly in periods of transition (Liff, 1988).

In the case-study research presented in the next section, we make a preliminary assessment of the scope for women clerical workers to intervene in office computer systems design processes in a major UK local authority.

CASE-STUDY

The Local Authority Context

With a work-force of approximately 32 000, Northfield Council is by far the largest local employer. Around 7500 of its staff are employed in the Administrative, Professional, Technical and Clerical (APT and C) grades. The majority (60 per cent) of these staff are women, but women are concentrated in the lower-paid jobs. A 1984 Positive Action for Women project (unpublished) undertaken for the authority showed that 3500, or 80 per cent, of the 4500 women APT and C staff were on the four lowest clerical grades (Scales 1–4), whereas in the top 'Principal Officer' grades, 83 per cent of such posts were filled by men. The authority is therefore a very important employer of women clerical workers, as far as numbers are concerned, and the prevailing terms and conditions of local authority clerical employment have traditionally been both stable and relatively favourable compared with other sectors of female employment (Stone, 1988). For both these reasons, Northfield Council is a potentially important focus of attention for equal opportunities initiatives designed to improve the position of women clerical workers.

In Northfield, an entrenched Labour majority has been unchallenged for fifty years except for one brief one-year period. Until recent changes in legislation, there was a closed-shop union agreement, and there is still a high degree of support for trade union activity. In addition, during the 1980s, the authority established a number of radical equal opportunities and economic development initiatives.

These initiatives, however, are not clearly reflected in or related to, IT policy in the authority. Policy has been enforced through the Information Technology Panel, composed of councillors who have depended for advice upon the 'computing experts' located in Computer Services, and have lacked any coherent or credible basis on which to broaden the terms of discussion beyond the technical or financial details of departmental 'bids' (Pemberton, 1986). However, a more flexible approach has been developed recently by Computer Services in response to internal and external pressures, including the possibility of privatisation. In this climate, computerisation is perceived by some departmental managers as an increasingly important measure through which to sustain service provision within tight financial limits.

Current industrial relations practice in relation to new techology is directed by a detailed set of procedures regarding the introduction of new technology; this was agreed between the authority and the National Association of Local Government Officers (NALGO) in 1984, following a thirteen-week strike which involved 630 'key workers' throughout the authority. Amongst these were the 50 women data preparation staff in City Treasury. These women were also, coincidentally, the object of the Positive Action for Women study cited above, the report of which was presented to the Council during the strike. A combination of these two factors focused union and management attention on the appalling working conditions experienced by data preparation workers, conditions which were greatly improved after the strike. A programme of decentralisation was also initiated through which some data preparation staff moved to jobs in other departments which included both data entry and a range of clerical duties not based on Visual Display Units (VDU). Thus although NALGO policy remained (and remains) deliberately reactive in common with most British trade union new technology policies (see Williams and Mosely 1982; Williams 1987), the data preparation example also raised job design issues. These have since received further acknowledgment by NALGO officers, both at branch and at national level (see, for example, NALGO 1988).

To summarise, then, Northfield is a major, and thus far relatively stable, employer of women clerical workers. A potential framework exists, in the form of trade union agreements and equal opportunities policy, for gains to be made for these workers. However, in the area of IT, neither policy nor practice has explicitly addressed itself to such issues.

Study Circles: An Action-Based Case-Study

This case-study has involved us in devising and implementing a strategy which enables women clerical workers to become active in the process of systems development. Our approach derives from a similar base to the earlier 'human-centred' design innovations referred to above (Braverman, 1974; Cooley, 1980a), in that issues of skill and control are addressed from the point of view of the workers. It differs from those, however, in that we have addressed gender issues in an innovative way. More specifically, our approach recognises the issue of skill as problematic in relation to women clerical workers, and also acknowledges the importance of challenging women's exclusion from technological expertise and decision-making, in connection with computerisation.

The case-study began in 1987 when the research project approached the Council Libraries department with a view to undertaking an analysis of library workers' previous experience of the design and introduction of computer systems. Soon it became clear that the acquisition of a major new 'integrated' library computer system was under discussion and that this would have the potential for linking discrete areas of library work around a common data base. Interviews showed that there was some support in the department for a more active role by the research project in fostering clerical worker involvement in this process. As a result, we undertook a pilot group-work or 'Study Circle' project with six women clerical workers in 1987. Later that year, the department established a systems design team to plan the design and acquisition of the new system, and invited the research project to participate actively on this team as a result of the perceived success of our first Study Circle. Agreement was also reached for us to continue with our intervention with women clerical workers on the same basis as before. Our observations here are fairly preliminary, for two reasons. First, the work described addresses the earliest stages of planning and discussion regarding the proposed new system: at this point there was no final commitment to purchasing such a system, but only to reviewing in depth the possibilities and the implications. It seemed to us essential to examine the scope for clerical workers' involvement in these early stages, the outcome of which would necessarily shape future detailed decisions, including technical decisions. Second, the research carried out in 1987/8 was part of the first year of a three-year period of research, intended to analyse the experience of women clerical workers in the Libraries department throughout the computer systems design and implementation processes.

The Libraries department employs around 600 staff, of whom 88 per cent are women. The relatively few men employed are for the most part 'professional' librarians, and now predominate in the higher grades. In the 'non-professional' grades, the library assistants, women predominate; only five of the 395 such posts are held by men. The library assistants are the basic-grade clerical workers of the service, but their duties do vary somewhat from one worksite to another, and there are limited opportunities for advancement through three grade scales. The library assistant's job entails carrying out the basic clerical functions of a library. Specific duties include issuing, discharging, renewing and reserving books for borrowers; shelving, stock-checking and repairing books; and undertaking the clerical work surrounding the acquisition and cataloguing of new stock. They also assist the public in identifying sources of information and collect and collate information for public use, whilst maintaining records appropriate to all of these functions. In small branch libraries, the library assistant's role will include a considerable variety of tasks, whereas in the central cataloguing sections such duties are more routine and unvarying.

Management's openness to library assistant involvement in the selection of the new computer system stems from two sets of factors. First, in recent years there has been a shift in organisational emphasis towards a 'community-based' library service and away from a more traditional service, closely followed by a requirement for fairly radical thinking about the nature and structure of the service brought about by central government proposals for local government and the library service. The shifts in emphasis gave rise to an awareness on management's part that greater flexibility and commitment from staff was necessary. However, management also saw that this flexibility and commitment would not be forthcoming if the issues of low pay and lack of career advancement for women non-professional staff were not addressed. These concerns have been mirrored within the trade union branch and constituency, where, although still dominated by male 'professionals', issues of low pay and equal opportunities are seen as central, and efforts have been made to involve more women non-professionals as activists.

Second, there is a shared perception throughout the organisation that the last round of computerisation was a disaster both from the point of view of organisational efficiency and as regards the job satisfaction of staff at all levels. A root cause of this is seen to be the high-handed manner in which the systems design process took place, whereby one particular 'computer expert' made decisions about the system without consulting either the processional or non-professional staff who were to use it. The ability of the clerical staff to use this situation to their advantage is partly a result of the equal opportunities environment outlined above, and partly due to the kind of management disunity around information technology already described. There is an absence of an organisational IT strategy, with senior management displaying differing perceptions and levels of understanding of what such a strategy would look like. In addition, recent developments within library automation provide a wider range of options than were available in the past.

The intervention strategy which we have devised is based on the idea of cooperative or group-based methods of organisation around clerical work and systems design, developed by various researchers in Scandinavia (Gronfeldt and Kandrup, 1985; Ressner and Gunnarson, 1987; Vehvilainen, 1986). In these examples, group discussions, including 'Study Circles', were established as a method of involving workers in discussion about computerisation, and were used for three distinct purposes:

(1) *'consciousness-raising'*: group members were able to assess their own skills and work experience, in order to lay a confident and mutually-supportive basis for discussing new technology (cf. Vehvilainen, 1986);
(2) *a forum for discussion* of issues arising from the introduction, or proposed introduction, of computerised systems, for example, quality of work and of the service offered, training needs, health and safety problems (cf. Gronfeldt and Kandrup, 1985);
(3) *a way of taking part in the design process* either through workers being part of a design team (Ehn, 1988), or in much more small-scale examples, where the Study Circle equipped individual members to take advantage of opportunities for involvement if these became available (cf. Vehvilainen, 1986).

We felt it appropriate to adapt the Study Circle model for use in the library case-study because we could relate it directly to women clerical workers' experience of technology and, more specifically, to perceived areas of contradiction within that experience. First, we could relate it to the contradictory evidence for the vulnerability of women clerical workers' jobs to loss or deskilling as a result of technological developments. We could see that these jobs were inherently vulnerable because of the genuinely routine and labour-intensive nature of some of the work; but at the same time, evidence cited above strongly indicates that this picture is by no means clear-cut, especially in the public sector; women clerical workers cannot be simply viewed as peripheral and therefore easily dispensable. In addition, our own previous case-study work illustrated the central role of clerical workers even in systems design situations which are not expressly concerned with their own interests. These insights offered a basis for devising a method of intervention which draws on the strength of the women workers' position rather than its weakness.

Second, the method is built on our insights into the area of clerical workers' skills. Rather than assume that clerical workers' jobs are 'already deskilled', we perceive that both the lack of recognition given to traditionally female skills and the tacit nature of some of those skills have as much to do with the label 'unskilled' as they do with the nature of the work itself. Furthermore, the ability of male workers to organise around their skilled status to the detriment of women and, conversely, the constraints on women workers' ability to make equivalent gains for themselves, need to be taken into account in any strategy for improving women's bargaining position *vis-à-vis* technology. So an intervention strategy must be based on both 'revealing' clerical workers' real skills to themselves and within the formal decision-making arena, and on the necessity of overcoming the particular gender-based constraints operating against women organising in their own interests without support.

Last, our strategy is based on a recognition of the contradictory nature of the evidence about women's lack of access to technological expertise. The overwhelming evidence for this, and for the concomitant male tenure of virtually all things technological, including the computer systems design process, makes a powerful argument for specific forms of organisation which enable women to become active in the decision-making around technology. At the same time, the evidence already reviewed in our introductory sections indicates that women's exclusion from things technological is not so much a blanket exclusion as a failure of technological decision-making either to take their concerns into account, or to build on the positive aspects of their experience in ways which they can relate to. So, rather than seeking to devise ways of getting women into what are essentially male ways of organising computer systems design, forms of organisation for women must be based on, and appropriate to, women's particular concerns, experience and requirements.

The adapted Study Circle method which we have used in the library has tried to incorporate all of these aspects. Each of the five Study Circle groups of seven library assistants have been run broadly along the same lines, although specific inputs and discussion have varied somewhat between groups. The format of the groups' meetings has involved a mixture of exercises designed to get group members talking and exchanging information and experience, to get them to set priorities as far as working with the new computer system is concerned, and to get them to learn about library computer systems in ways which are directly relevant to their learning needs (for an outline of a Study Circle's programme of work see Appendix 1 to this chapter). The exercises have included 'homework' in which individuals find out more about some current aspect of library computer use which interests them, and group visits to other public libraries where integrated systems are in operation. In addition, the groups have requested sessions which provide them with the opportunity to discuss particular issues, such as training, health and safety, job design, and so forth, in more detail. At the end of each Study Circle, the group has compiled its own summary report outlining the particular concerns and the issues which had emerged. As a result, the groups have had an influence on the way the systems design process is being conducted and on the kinds of issues which are being raised.

First, the Study Circles have enabled the women involved to take initiatives themselves, rather than simply respond to other people's ideas, by providing them with a network of support within the organisation, a base from which to organise. The women have been able to identify issues of particular concern to library assistants as a group, and these shared concerns and awareness provide a basis for building the kind of confidence necessary to make demands. So, for example, several of the groups have compiled 'charters' for computer training and have approached those responsible for training within the organisation. Library assistants from the Study Circles are now involved in design groups drawing up the specification for the new system, and have been able to raise job design issues as part of those discussions. In addition, design group representatives have been vocal in arguing for, and achieving, greater library assistant representation within these groups than that originally conceded by management.

Second, the Study Circles have allowed the library assistants' skills and experience to be recognised as relevant within the context of systems design. The Study Circles aimed to analyse the actual work processes and skills of clerical workers, both in order to feed these into the systems design process and in order to legitimate and value these skills in the eyes of the women themselves. This entailed not simply taking the concept of 'skill' as a given, but exploring the gender and 'professional' issues which impinge on it. The Study Circle groups have been able to explore ways in which these skills and experience may be undermined by technological developments, but they have also, and perhaps more crucially, been able to be more explicit about their current contribution to the work of the library and therefore to the assistants' central role within it. One Study Circle report advises management to 'respect library assistants and recognise the value of their contribution'. This awareness provides both a basis on which to judge the effects of a given aspect of computerisation, and an increased sense of bargaining-power within the decision-making process.

The third way in which the Study Circles have influenced the systems design process has been through their ability to show how technical and non-technical issues affecting the library assistants' work are interconnected. The points that emerge from the Study Circle proceedings illustrate the fact that the library assistants' experience of technology cannot be separated from their experience as workers, and that strategies for improving their experience of technology have to be strategies which take on issues of inequality within the organisation, specifically those based on gender and those based on professional status. System requirements are related to wider social issues such as the need for good relations with borrowers, the need for time to develop less routine and more interesting areas of work, and the need for greater understanding of the work of the library as a whole, for example. Because the groups' starting-point in the discussions is their own experience, and this experience is defined as 'non-expert' as far as computers are concerned, then inevitably an analysis of their requirements from a computer system raises issues of job design, equal opportunities, health and safety, and so forth, as part and parcel of the discussion.

We would argue, therefore, that the Study Circles have provided a basis for the women clerical workers to play an active role in the process of office systems design. They have facilitated an understanding of clerical workers' experience of technology, and of the support and learning needs of women. We also argue that the results of the Study Circles present a challenge to the process of systems design itself, in that they raised issues which cannot be dealt with by a technology-led exercise alone. This challenge is inevitable, given women workers' subordinate position and the way in which male tenure of technology, including the traditional process of systems development, operates to maintain, or at least not to challenge, that position. Once women clerical workers find themselves able to raise their own concerns in relation to technology in ways which are relevant to them, then the implications of their position become visible and therefore open to challenge.

While the Study Circle process has placed the library assistants' concerns firmly on the agenda, and made their interests visible, this initial success is very vulnerable. Difficulties have already begun to emerge. These relate partly to the threat which the library assistants' strengthened position poses to established interests in the organisation, and partly to library assistants' continued lack of access to information and concomitant need for a high level of support.

The threat posed by the library assistants' new position can be seen in the responses of both management and union to their continued involvement in the systems development process. Although ostensibly this involvement has been welcomed by both sides, in practice it has been made very difficult by the failure of both to concede the need for forms of involvement which enable the women to operate effectively. To take an example: although Study Circle members sit on the library's systems design team alongside management, this team and its functional sub-groups are controlled by management with the assistants playing a subsidiary, consultative role. Management recognises the value of the women's contribution, but has resisted the tentative attempts by the assistants to organise autonomously, not by vetoing this idea but in failing to recognise the need for it. In practical terms, the provision of stand-by relief to cover the work of the assistants who are involved in the design team has been difficult to arrange with assistants being left to argue on an individual basis with reluctant middle managers about releasing them from other duties. For the union's part, although in theory supportive of the Study Circle experiment, it has made no move to follow up either the specific issues raised by the women, or the increased interest in becoming active around workplace issues manifest in many of the Study Circle members. The union appears wary of workers becoming involved and hence implicated in management decision, but does not appear to recognise that the assistants' enthusiasm for such involvement may in part stem from their lack of involvement in union affairs which they see as less relevant to their concerns. The danger for the women concerned is that they may be seen by some union activists as undermining the union's ultimate ability to negotiate around the new system; if the union fails to act on the issues raised by the Study Circles, this may well in time prove to be the case.

Related to this situation is the library assistants' lack of access to information on the options which may be open to management and which would serve their interests. Because they are struggling to represent themselves in the absence of representation within the library's decision-making structure, they have no accumulated knowledge of the kinds of solutions which may be available to solve the problems that they have identified. They are therefore very dependent on management's identification of potential solutions, and find it difficult to establish a bargaining position which would challenge these.

CONCLUSION

The theoretical basis of our case-study work, described in the introductory section of this chapter, involves a critique of deterministic views of technology in which women clerical workers feature as passive victims. Although acknowledging that such workers are vulnerable to job loss, deskilling, and deteriorating working conditions during periods of technological change, we would argue that an overly deterministic view allows little scope for discussion of the forms of intervention women can use to gain some control over the results of such processes. Such views assume the only hope of worker resistance and control to reside in conventional forms of negotiation and industrial action developed from a tradition of male craftworker organisation, in which women clerical workers feature hardly at all. These conventional union responses to technology are essentially reactive, and therefore rely for their effectiveness on the presence of a powerful, well-organised group of workers, able and willing to take action in support of their collective interests. Not only do women clerical workers clearly not conform to this model, but their experience of technology is by no means a passive and entirely negative one.

In addition, our analysis of trends in computer systems development indicates that there are areas of uncertainty and contradiction, and therefore potential choice, within the process of office systems design which women clerical workers may be able to use to their advantage. A major focus of our case-study work involves an analysis of the relationship between the experience of women clerical workers and the real process of office systems design, in order to reach an understanding of the kind of action women can take in order to resist the worst effects of technology on their working lives.

Our case-study work in the local authority shows that, far from being neutral, the office systems design process is a major arena for the perpetuation of gender inequalities. This is partly because of the exclusion of women from decision-making about new systems, and also because of the failure to acknowledge clerical end-users as having a role within the process. It is also related to the dominant technicist view of systems design, in which only things defined as 'technological' – the storage and flow of data, the hardware and software of the system – are formally considered. This dominant view acts as a means of excluding women workers' interests from consideration. At the same time, we have observed that the systems design process is by no means the super-efficient, logical, coherent, and rational exercise, controlled by systems analysts, portrayed in the textbooks. The textbook concept is founded on the notion of a rational and coherent management strategy, which was not apparent in our examples. In addition, we would argue that this model underestimates the potential role of users, however they may be defined. In the real systems design situation, organisational realities and conflicts bring about a situation where control is by no means clear-cut, but constantly open to informal redefinition and renegotiation. Within this scenario, it is possible to envisage a more active role for women clerical workers.

Defining and activating such a role is not straightforward, however. In order to achieve this, change needs to occur on a number of levels: on the level of the consciousness and confidence of women clerical workers themselves; on the level of the form taken by the process of systems design; and on the level of the response to inequality and conflict within the organisation. We would see the library Study Circles not simply in the context of enabling women clerical workers to become involved in a more or less established process, but in the context of a much wider debate about the nature of that process and of women's ability to exercise control over its results. In other words the Study Circle example should be viewed as an attempt to clarify some issues in relation to women's collective action around technology, rather than simply as another version of user-centred systems design.

The three facets of such action which the Study Circle work reveal as of crucial importance are first, a group-based approach; second, the need to discuss technology in the context of women's real experience; and third, the need for a design or decision-making process which deals with both technical and non-technical issues as part and parcel of the same process. We have described in our account of this case-study the value of the group both as a way of overcoming women's sense of ignorance about technology, and as a way of providing them with support in a context where they tend not to draw support either from management or from the union. We have shown how an initial sense of 'knowing nothing about computers' can be overcome by an approach which takes women's own experience as its starting-point, rather than processes to be automated, information flows, and so forth. We have also indicated that the issues around technology that women define as important to them are as much to do with job design and organisational issues as with 'technological' ones. We would argue that any kind of collective action which enables women clerical workers to make gains as a result of technological innovation must take these lessons on board.

We have noted in our description of the library case-study the apparent resistance of established interest groups to continued initiative-taking and collective action by the women concerned, and the difficulty of providing continued support for the women to overcome this. Such support needs to be forthcoming from the trade unions themselves, but in order to provide it, union policies need to reflect a broader view of collective worker response to technological change that they have done to date.

At a national level, there is evidence of a recognition by some, especially public sector, trade unions of the need for a shift away from the emphasis on formal New Technology Agreements (NTA's) as the sole response to technological change. The proliferation of NTA's in the late 1970s and early 1980s seemed at first to herald an era when unions would gain enough control over technological innovation to bring considerable benefits to their members. In practice, these benefits have not been forthcoming, especially in relation to women clerical workers (Murray, 1987). Massively widespread and intensive use of VDUs and keyboards are causing growing concern about health and safety problems such as eyestrain and repetitive strain injury (RSI). In our own experience of the local authority, we have observed the difficulty women workers have in keeping to limits on VDU use, and that in a workplace, where, on paper, such restrictions are formally agreed between management and union. The clerical unions are increasingly aware that these difficulties will not be resolved solely by formal agreements, but require some form of workplace action on job design. The recent teaching pack on job design developed collaboratively by NALGO, Civil and Public Services Association (CPSA) and the Association of Professional Executive, Clerical and Computer Staff (APEX) who represent large numbers of women clerical workers in the public sector, is evidence of this (NALGO, 1988). We would argue that this welcome shift also needs to incorporate specific forms of workplace organisation for women clerical workers, and to include consideration of other equal opportunities issues, such as skill acquisition and career development, as well as job design.

As far as the specific local authority context is concerned, we have already indicated its importance to women's clerical employment, even in a time of relative contraction. We have observed in our local authority example that the current financial constraints are pushing managers towards increased computerisation. If this is a national trend, there will be increasing pressure on the large numbers of women clerical workers who use the resulting systems, pressure made worse by widespread non-filling of vacancies or staff cuts. The current local authority climate also appears to be bringing about a contraction of political support for women's initiatives (note the recent abolition of local authority women's committees in Birmingham, Bradford, and the London Borough of Lewisham, for example), which indicates that the expansion of local authority equal opportunities work, characteristic of the 1980s, may be faltering. Furthermore, recent analyses of the outcomes of equal opportunities policies, which have largely been based on the formalisation of personnel procedures as the prime strategy, indicate that these have not been at all effective in changing the widespread pattern of segregation by sex (Gibbon, in press). Webb and Liff (1988) argue that this pattern will only be challenged by an equal opportunities approach which uses job design and skill acquisition for lower-grade women workers as its prime strategy. The involvement of NALGO in recent union initiatives on job redesign in relation to new technology may signal a new approach in response to the needs of women clerical workers in the public sector.

APPENDIX 1

Study Circle 5 – Draft Programme

This programme is based on previous Study Circles and our ideas about what was useful to people attending. However, it's open to the whole group to modify the programme if you find it doesn't meet your needs.

(1) Tuesday, 20th September, 2–4.30
    (i) Introduction and background to Study Circles
    (ii) Getting to know you and brainstorming
    (iii) Discussion of 'homework' on use of new technology at group members' worksites, covering:
- what systems are in use
- how they were introduced
- who uses it and how
- how it works/doesn't work
- health and safety issues
- training

(2) (i) Reports-back on 'homework'
    (ii) Formulation of questions about new technology
    (iii) Arrangements for visit to computerised library
(3) Computerised Library Visit
(4) (i) Report-back on visit
    (ii) Talk on specific aspect of new technology identified by group (e.g. health and safety, training, job design, etc.)
(5) (i) Talk on aspect of new technology (to be decided)
    (ii) Initial discussion of content of final report
(6) Visit to Computer Services Division, Libraries Computer Room
(7) Finalisation of Study Circle Report

6 Young Women, Sexual Harassment and Heterosexuality: Violence, Power Relations and Mixed-Sex Schooling
Jacqui Halson

INTRODUCTION

At first sight it might seem absurd to compare the behaviour of a young man who 'got really vicious' trying repeatedly to force a young woman to 'gob him off', that is, to fellate him, with that of another boy who 'merely' shouts 'Wiggle yer bum, then! Go on! Wiggle yer bum!' repeatedly to a teenage girl whilst they walked down a street *en route* from school one afternoon. One of the things they have in common is that both the young men in question were 'doing masculinity' in such a way that both the young women were, minimally, humiliated. What I hope to demonstrate in this chapter is, first, that the humiliations and oppressions which young women experience in their day-to-day and public lives are to be found also in their most intimate encounters with boys/men. That is, there are links between verbal sexual harassment and what has variously been called 'conquest sex' (Wyre, 1987) and 'pressurised' or 'coercive' sex forming a continuum of sexual violence (Kelly, 1987, 1988).

I do not intend to describe the full range of behaviours which constitute sexual harassment, however (see Farley, 1978; C. Jones 1984; Hadjipotiou, 1983), nor to document fully the diverse, and in some respect pleasurable, heterosexual encounters which young women describe. Rather, using illustrative examples, my aim is to explore the ways in which young women perceive or understand and negotiate their social world, some of them, sometimes in ways which, passively and actively, reproduce rather than challenge existing power relations. In the second section, I will locate the young women's experiences and perceptions within the structural contexts of their school and this society. I shall focus on the extent to which 'schools are reflections of society' (as the Headmaster once commented during an interview with me), assess the impact and limitations of one illustrative intervention on 'gender issues' and comment briefly on whether talking about gender and sexual violence in interviews with me had much of an effect on the young women's perceptions.

The discussion is based on information gathered as part of a graduate research project on gender, sexuality and power, a project which involved researching both girls/young women and boys/young men. I am not here concerned with what boys have to say for themselves (see Wood, 1984) nor with how they might be encouraged/forced, where appropriate, to behave differently. The paper focuses on how young women might empower themselves to act on their own behalves. The young women whose experiences are described were between thirteen and fourteen years old at the time of the study. They were white, working- and lower-middle-class students attending a coeducational school which I call Henry James Comprehensive (this and all other names are pseudonyms). I spent nine months in the school as a researcher, attending classes with students and conducting in-depth and focused tape-recorded interviews with some 29 'key characters' (16 girls, 13 boys). I also spent time 'just chatting' with them and observing them at leisure and in school and, of course, making copious notes.

SEXUAL HARASSMENT AND (HETERO)SEX-AS-VIOLENCE; SOME DEFINITIONS, SOME ILLUSTRATIONS AND SOME CONTINUITIES

Of the young women whom I interviewed more than once, *all* 16 of them had experienced some form of sexual harassment – whether verbal or non-verbal, in public or in private, by known and unknown boys/men according to my definition of the problem.

In analysing and writing up the young women's experiences I have tried to work with a definition of sexual harassment derived from my reading and thinking about the subject *and* to respect their definitions of acceptable or harmless and unacceptable or harmful behaviour. This has not been an easy task simply because their and my definitions of 'acceptable' and 'unacceptable' behaviour are so different. Despite Sue Wise and Liz Stanley's (1987) assertion that 'all women know about men', I would argue that it is eminently more sensible to accept that, whilst women 'know, consciously and unconsciously, what it means to be vulnerable to sexual and/or physical male intimidation and violence' (Stanko, 1985, p. 1), women *interpret* their experiences in different ways and, therefore, 'know' differently. It also seems sensible to me to think that 'sexual harassment' blurs into 'normal' or routine interactions between heterosexual women and men and is thus not 'known' or 'named' by all women in the same way (see Schneider, 1982; Herbert, 1989).

Initially, my working definition of sexual harassment was simply a paraphrase of Lin Farley's definition: 'non-reciprocal, unsolicited, (usually) masculine behaviour which asserts (usually) a girl's or woman's sexual identity over her identity as a person' (1978, p. 14). This covers a range of behaviour, some of it more subtle and commonplace, some of it more brutal and less commonplace. Whatever its particular form, the behaviour in question is experienced as humiliating, embarrassing, threatening rather than as pleasurable. It offends, it objectifies, it denies autonomy, it controls. However, defining sexual harassment thus still leaves us with the problem of 'drawing lines'. To illustrate: several girls' accounts of 'flirting' with Mr Newsom, his jokes about 'round bottoms' and other sexual innuendos are hard to include under the heading of sexual harassment because, although they clearly illustrate the way in which men teachers may relate to young women students as sexual beings, the young women concerned unambiguously asserted that they enjoyed this banter, welcomed it from this teacher and argued that it was reciprocated ('we tease him'). If such or similar behaviour is 'taken as a joke', does it then *not* constitute sexual harassment?

More recently I have adopted Liz Kelly's broader definition of sexual violence as a useful way of refocusing the questions somewhat. Kelly argues: 'Sexual violence includes any physical, visual, verbal or sexual act that is experienced by the woman or girl, at the time or later, as a threat, invasion or assault, that has the effect of degrading or hurting her and/or *takes away her ability to control intimate contact*' (Kelly, 1988, p. 41; my emphasis). This, more radical, definition allows us to redirect our queries *from* 'how did the young woman concerned experience the behaviour?' *to* 'how did the young woman concerned evaluate the behaviour?' *and* 'did it have the effect of degrading her in the view of others?' *and* 'did it take away her ability to control intimate contact?' It also allows for *changes* in women's perceptions of our experiences. Things which one 'takes as a joke' or 'doesn't mind' can be, and often *are*, subsequently re-evaluated.

When is a 'Joke' not a 'Joke'?

Using elements from both the above definitions allows us to see the wood despite the trees as it were. Consider the boy quoted at the beginning of the chapter. His 'joke', 'Wiggle yer bum then!', elicited no laughter from the young woman in the street (a joke is, by definition, 'something said or done to cause laughter'). His companion, another boy aged about 14, was highly amused at 'the joke'. She was stony-faced, as was another young woman on the receiving end of a comment shouted from the back of a crowded bus: 'drop your drawers and ten p's yours!', his friend 'correcting' him, and therefore reinforcing the comment, equally loudly: 'drop your drawers and ten *bob's* yours!' Also on a bus, I observed and overheard a conversation between another young woman, offering the last third of her cigarette to one of her school 'mates'. 'Peter', she said, 'do you want this?', to which he replied, 'I don't mind, Marianne, seeing as you're not going to give me your virginity', and, shortly afterwards, 'Play your cards right and you can have your clothes off tonight.' None of the three young women observed made an obvious response to these comments. They 'ignored' them but their fixed expressions and their tight lips suggested that they were offended and embarrassed by these 'jokes' which publicly drew attention to their gendered bodies, to their sexual identities. As Stanko has argued, 'silence, contrary to popular belief, does not mean tacit acceptance' (Stanko, 1985, p. 19). The 'jokes' had the effect of degrading the young women and of taking away their ability to control intimate contact; in this instance, removing their right to control with whom, where and when (if ever) they wish to 'discuss' their bodies, their underclothes, their sexuality.

The above illustrations are commonplace and of limited duration. This does not mean that they are trivial and of limited importance however. As I have argued elsewhere, such sexual harassment creates for women a hostile and intimidating environment and can, when perpetrated by men teachers and/or boys in classes, have the effect of reproducing girls' marginalisation from 'traditionally male' subjects, for example (Halson, 1989a).

What I came to record in my notes as 'the Polo "joke"' was a more prolonged affair. Lindsey, one of the young women I interviewed, became the butt of the Polo 'joke', widespread in the school, after the Xmas vacation when a young man, whom I call 'Wanker', had attempted, unsuccessfully, to have penetrative sex with her. As Janet explains:

Janet: But y'know he couldn't get a hard on ... an' he couldn't get up her ... so that's why he called her 'Polo hole'. But it ain't her fault because he never got a hard on so they were all takin' the piss out of her ... Wanker started it off cos he *said* he couldn't get it up ... he was incapable. Y'know what I mean? It was *his* fault.
Jacqui: So *she* got called names because *he* couldn't?

Instead of replying 'Yes', Janet idiosyncratically responded: 'Well he's a loudmouthed cunt anyway'. Noting the use of the perjorative term 'cunt' rather than the more appropriate though less frequently used terms 'wanker' and 'prick', I continued:

Jacqui: What does Lindsey think about the Polo 'joke'?
Janet: She don't mind. She takes it as a laugh. Cos she knows it ain't true.

The 'joke' was, from Lindsey's position, unsolicited and non-reciprocal. It publicly asserted her sexual identity over her identity as a person, had the effect of degrading her and took away her ability to control intimate contact. Lindsey, some time later, confirmed the details of her own story: Wanker tried to penetrate her, couldn't do it and called her names. I asked whether she called him any names:

Lindsey: No. He didn't like it in front of his mates so he called me it. An' every time I go down the street he shouted it in front of his mates ... I just stood there and didn't say anything. It don't bother me though. All his mates call me it.
Tracy: You get used to it.
Lindsey: Yeah. It don't bother me.

The 'joke' mockingly holds her responsible for a young man's failure to achieve an erection. Thus, to save him from ridicule, he and his mates, in support, called her 'Polo hole': she was too small; it's her failure, her fault. Further, Lindsey, according to her own testimony, isn't bothered; according to Janet she 'don't mind' and 'takes it as a laugh'. The girls, as Tracy said 'get used to it'. Before I explore these 'negative coping strategies' (Kelly and Scott, 1989), the sense of hopelessness or inevitability and the issue of self/woman-blaming, I want now to explore some of the links between verbal sexual harassment and heterosex.

Not so Much a Mystery, More a Form of Patriarchy

This subtitle is unashamedly pinched from Judy Lown's (1983) article and reflects my reaction upon reading Lynda Measor's comment that for 'adolescents . . . the sexual world was covert and mysterious . . . its rules had to be discovered and negotiated' (Measor, 1989, p. 42). For several of the young women I worked with, much of 'the mystery' had gone. Of 'my' 16 young women, eight had had some intimate heterosexual experience at the age of 14; of these, five had had penetrative heterosex; I knew two to be heterosexually inexperienced; the nature and extent of the remaining six young women's experience was unknown to me. (I discussed issues which were volunteered. I did not probe into matters which the girls were unwilling to share with me.)

Many of 'the rules', they had discovered from their experiences of 'going with boys', were patriarchal. In analysing how young women negotiate their heterosexual relationships and encounters, I have used Wendy Hollway's (1984) concepts of 'investments' and 'contradictions' (Halson, 1989b). It is important to be conscious of the investments which young and older women have in heterosex (pleasure sometimes and status) and not to dismiss 'sex with men' as 'violence against women' or as 'false consciousness' whilst at the same time being conscious of separatist critiques of the institution of heterosexuality and of the specific oppressions and struggles of lesbian women (see, for example, Hoagland and Penelope, 1988).

One of the 'obvious contradictions' is that women's sexual encounters and relationships with men are also all too often characterised by non-reciprocity, humiliation, the denial of autonomy, in short, by sexual violence. It would, however, be erroneous to assume that women are 'the passive objects (or victims) of male sexuality' (Holly, 1989, pp. 6 and 14). Rather, as evidenced by Liz, Mandy and several other young women of Henry James School, young women are first required to take an *active* part in servicing (young) men's sexual requirements. When they don't wish to, they may be forced. Second, and importantly, (young) women *resist*.

Mandy's account of her evening with Baz aptly illustrates the servicing aspect of heterosexual encounters. Mandy had fancied Baz for some time. Just before Xmas:

Mandy: ... he comes up to me. He goes, 'You comin' down my house?' I goes, 'Yeah. All right then' ... an' I thought, 'Oh god! This is my big chance!'

At the house Baz said, 'Come upstairs'. Mandy went upstairs. He put his arms round her and started kissing her. She took her pants ('Whatever you call 'em! We call 'em trollies or grundies or undercrackers!') off:

Mandy: (laughing) He got on top of me an' just did it! An' then we went downstairs. I gobbed him off down stairs in the front room ... he wanted to fuck me again but I had to go an' he wouldn't let me go. He goes, 'gob me off just once more an' I'll let you go ... you ain't goin' yet'. I thought, 'Fuckin' hell!' (This is twenty to twelve at night. I'm supposed to be in for half ten. Me dad went mad at that.) Anyway I went in the end ... an' it was me an' Christine cos Murph had just been fucked – I mean Chris had just been fucked by Murph.

There are innumerable things one could say about this account. For example, one could argue that there is a certain absence of reciprocity in this heterosexual encounter: it is an account of what Baz and Murph do *to* Mandy and Chris and of what the young women do *for* the young men. Although Mandy in some ways interprets her relationship as 'reciprocal' or 'mutual' (it was her 'big chance'), she also indicates that, in her world, boys do not 'get fucked' (passive). She 'slips up' when she says 'Murph had just been fucked', immediately 'correcting herself'.

Mandy seemingly engages in the non-reciprocated activity of oral sex with 'gay abandon'; she is an active participant. We cannot assume though that Mandy initiates or controls her sexual practices with complete autonomy. Sex does not take place in an ideological or political vacuum: it is socially constructed, albeit on a biological base, and it is constructed in terms which largely, though not inevitably, reproduce existing and systematic power relations between women and men. This power may be exercised in a variety of ways: for example, by brutal/physical coercion, by mild, if repeated, verbal pressure, and/or by strong expectations. Mandy's expectations about what constitutes 'appropriate' sexual behaviour are constructed in terms of giving pleasure to boys/men or of 'servicing' them. Thus she seemingly 'spontaneously' 'gobs him off'. However, Mandy's willingness to do this is reinforced by Baz's verbal commands and by *his* expectations. His assertion of his 'right' to control both the 'contours' and the duration of this sexual encounter limited, even removed, *Mandy*'s ability to control intimate contact. Other girls confirmed that such commands were common, that the boys expect the girls to 'gob them off' and that 'the girls *don't* expect it'.

Sometimes, there is more obvious sexual violence. Liz, amidst great and uncharacteristic embarrassment and with the assistance of two friends, eventually described how she had gone to the house of a boy she knew who:

> asked me to go out with him ... he said 'come round the next day'. And he wanted me to gob him off an' I kept sayin', 'no'. He goes, 'wank me off'. An' what he did, he got really vicious then cos I wouldn't gob him off. He kept tryin' to put me head down an' I wouldn't do it. So I pushed him off and that was it.

This incident was unambiguously experienced by Liz at the time as an invasion or an assault and as a denial of her right to control intimate contact, a right which she repeatedly asserted by saying 'no' and by pushing the young man off. Liz and other young women both feel and are coerced by and individually survive and resist sexual violence rather than, as Holly asserts, 'quietly living with passive femininity for an easy life' (Holly, 1989, p. 5). Meeting with this small group of young women over a period of nine months, and reading their transcribed accounts later, I was struck by their resilience and by their sense of humour as, for example, when Janet, cited earlier, told me that she had told the originator of the Polo 'joke', in front of all his friends, that it was *his* fault in order 'to embarrass him'. I don't know for certain whether Janet actually did so. Nevertheless, the girls' joking and laughing about it reaffirmed a sense of collective identity and a condemnation of his behaviour. Such 'woman-talk', involving heavy and sometimes riotously funny sarcasm, is not uncommon: through humour, young women challenge masculine norms and resist men's definitions of them. Young women resist sexual violence in other ways too. Liz said of the young man who had sexually assaulted her, 'I reckon he's a right bastard'. Thus, she condemns his behaviour, challenges his assertion of power over her and survives his sexually violent acts. On another occasion she screamed and kicked out at a group of boys who were, for a 'joke', trying to take her pants down; another girl slapped her little brother to stop him putting his hand up her skirt (see Halson 1989a). In addition to hearing their individual survival strategies, I was also struck by other features of the young women's narratives, in particular, by the number of times they said, 'You can't do nothin' about it', 'I ain't bothered', 'I don't mind', 'I don't care any more', 'you get used to it'. Not one of the young women ever said, 'How *dare* they do this to us!'

The Despair of the Oppressed

The young women I have been describing are lively, likeable, sometimes assertive, sometimes animated and amusing. Get them talking about what their boyfriends and other men/boys say to them and do to them and they become 'uncharacteristically subdued'. In her chapter 'I'll challenge it now wherever I see it'; from individual survival to collective resistance', Liz Kelly records the transformation of a group of women who identified as survivors of sexual violence:

> the transformation of the group accompanied the transformation in the members. Women recalled 'the despair of the oppressed' – feelings of hopelessness, self-blame, negative coping strategies – being overtaken by the possibility of change when someone showed they cared, when they were able to name and talk about sexual violence, when they placed responsibility for the abuse on the abusive man and when they recognized and validated actions they took whilst being abused which were based on hope and self-respect (Kelly, 1988, pp. 235–6).

Kelly notes the importance of several (interrelated) factors which affect the likelihood of such transformations occurring:

(a) talking (expressing anger, sharing experiences, giving and receiving support);
(b) personal and relevant contact with feminists;
(c) time;
(d) participating in the research;
(e) support from voluntary and other organisations (Kelly, 1988, ch. 9).

Given their age and the *absence* (relative and absolute) of their contact with feminists and support at Henry James School, it is not surprising that what I heard alongside, or often instead of, their expressions of survival, was 'the despair of the oppressed'.

Prior to Liz's disclosure about her experience of sexual violence, her friends, Wendy and Linda, had been 'prompting' her to tell me what had happened. Linda, who knew the details, said, 'She done summat naughty with him! In the kitchen!' (Note: she did something *with* him rather than he did something (violent) *to* her.) Wendy suggested: 'wanked him off?' Liz shook her head, laughing but embarrassed. Wendy: 'Gobbed him off?' Liz nodded, said 'right' and then immediately turned to me and said, '*don't hate me*'. Shocked, I replied, 'Why should I hate you?', whereupon she told me what had happened. Afterwards I asked:

> Jacqui: Why did you say, 'Don't hate me for it?' Is gobbing him off something that you think is dirty or –
>
> Liz: Well it is afterwards. You regret it, d'you know what I mean? ... Well [a little more defiantly], there's loads of girls that've done it. Have *you* done it? [Linda nods] See! *She's* done it ... but ... [becoming more subdued] I don't know, I'm just embarrassed about it. If people ask me I normally just say that I ain't. Unless it's me mates. [subdued] I've got over it now ... I ain't bothered. I don't care any more.

Initially shocked that Liz would feel for a moment that I would think badly of her (I thought she 'knew' I liked her and respected her), I later appreciated that it is entirely consistent with her, and the other girls', 'world view' that (even?) I should condemn her. That is, blaming and stigmatising women is part of Liz's and the other girls' 'normality'. The following accounts or 'cases' will illustrate this argument.

During an interview with four young women, the conversation turned into one about rape as one of the young women told us that she had been raped by three boys whom she knew at one of their homes. They then described the sexual assault of another girl:

> A: ... anyway they had 'X' – spread her legs open and tried to ram a ... cider bottle, weren't it?, up her.
>
> B: Yeah.
>
> Jacqui: Jesus Christ! Did *she* tell you about this?
>
> B: What gets me was her brother was there, weren't he? Was 'X' screamin'? What was she doing?
>
> A: I reckon she was enjoyin' it meself!
>
> B: Yeah. Cos she came and told everyone, didn't she?
>
> A: Yeah.

Notice how quick the young women are to focus on what 'X' was doing rather than on the boy's behaviour. Notice how quick they are to condemn 'X': they reckoned she was enjoying it; they imply that she should not have told everyone – she should have kept quiet about it. Later in the same interview, Lindsey asserted that some girls 'ask for trouble':

Jacqui: Why do you say that?
Lindsey: Well, because some people *do* ask for trouble don't they though, really?
Jacqui: I don't know. Do they?
Lindsey: Yeah!
Jacqui: If you're walking around at night are *you* askin' to be raped?
A: [quietly] No.
Lindsey: Depends how I walk! [laughter]
Jacqui: Does it? Really?
Lindsey: I don't know! If you walk with your hips swinging ... I'd say I should be in before dark – I'd expect it (otherwise) wouldn't I?

During another interview with three different young women, similar self/women-blaming assertions are made and defended. Wendy gave a long account of how she and her friend, Mary, had verbally berated and physically assaulted another young woman 'Y' who, they asserted, had had sex with two boys, one of whom was Mary's boyfriend, the other was Wendy's. They shouted at her: 'You're the biggest slag that I've ever fucking known and I know quite a few slags.' They hit her and they continued to call her a slag:

Wendy: ... and I was telling everyone just to get it around to show what a fucking old cow she was.
Jacqui: I understand the story and I understand why you were cross with 'Y'. Well I think I do anyway. Why erm ... how did you feel about [your boyfriend] and the other lad?
Wendy: ... I asked them why they'd done it and he [Wendy's boyfriend] says ... I mean, *be fair*, what would you say if a girl's stood there stripped naked and she wanted you to fuck her and you was a lad? You wouldn't turn it down would you? Not if you was a lad?
Jacqui: So you don't blame the boys at all?
Wendy: No!

'Being fair' means *not* blaming the boys. In particular, I asked why no-one seemed to be blaming the boyfriends for 'cheating on' Wendy and Mary. Liz said, 'it's hard to mouth it at your own boyfriend', then, 'she'd hate to lose him', suggesting that fear of losing their boyfriends is one of the factors which circumscribes young women's option to challenge their behaviour. Wendy asked her boyfriend whether he'd been drunk, 'and he said yes so I couldn't really do a lot about that, I mean, if he were drunk', she said, by way of excusing his infidelity. 'The point that got me,' she said, was that 'Y' had been 'trying to split Mary and [her boyfriend] up for ages ... that's why we had *her*.'

Rather than 'giving and receiving support' and 'naming and talking about sexual violence', these young women name each other and talk about 'slags', thus reproducing rather than challenging the power these labels have to define who they are and what they may and may not do. They blame young women for actions which they do not consider reprehensible in boys. The unselfconsciously assert the legitimacy of 'the sexual double standard'. They do not consider that the boys have any responsibility, accepting as inevitable their infidelity, their sexual promiscuity *and* their sexual violence. As I said earlier, when they are verbally sexually harassed and when they are assaulted, they are more likely to say, 'you can't do nothin' about it' or 'I don't care' than they are to say, 'How *dare* they call us slags/ make us the butt of their sexual jokes/assault us/rape us.'

Their ideas and practices in part constitute 'negative coping strategies' which themselves reflect the ideas which mythologise sexual violence, which 'deny the violence, normalise it or pathologise the offender and/or the abused woman, resulting in both the deflection of responsibility and the denial of women's (including their own) experience' (Kelly and Scott, 1989, pp. 34–38).

Let me be quite clear that in offering an account which describes – even highlights – young women's 'collusion' in 'patriarchal practices' and adherence to 'patriarchal ideals', I am doing so, first, because I sense their feelings of powerlessness and their despair and I do them no justice if I produce an account which glosses over this. Second, for pragmatic or tactical reasons, I emphasise where the young women are 'at' politically, so that interventions, initiatives and support can be 'pitched' appropriately. Third, I consider it important to comment on the extent to which girls do verbal and sometimes physical violence toward one another in order to counter accusations that 'girls are as bad as boys' (or, as Kelly and Scott (1989) comment, feminists' refusal (with a few important exceptions) to honestly explore the issue of violence *by* women has left us vulnerable to the 'women do it too' attack on our analysis). Such assertions neglect both the form and the context of the abusive labels: both the girls and the boys blame and 'punish' *women* (or 'types of women'), not each other equally; when the boys are called 'queer' or one of its equivalents by either boys or girls, it is femininity which is being derided and dominant (i.e. heterosexual and sexist) forms of masculinity which are being condoned and reproduced. They also neglect the fact that sexual violence is overwhelmingly directed towards women by men. In short, I am arguing that it is important to understand the ideologies which inhibit young women's options, in particular their option to resist and to challenge oppression. In Liz Kelly's words, women's choices are 'circumscribed by an ideology which encourages women to feel responsible for men's violence' and by 'the failure of social agencies to support abused women and act in their interests' (Kelly, 1988, pp. 217–8). It is to this latter point, the role of the school, that I now turn.

'SCHOOLS ARE REFLECTIONS OF SOCIETY'?

I do not have the space here to document the structural features of the school nor the different and competing ideologies of gender within the school. Suffice it to say that Henry James School has a gendered division of labour and gendered patterns of authority (see, for example, Mahoney, 1985, on 'who does what in schools?') and that the range of ideologies represented include reactionary/naturalistic ('boys will be boys'), liberal/humanitarian and liberal feminist. The Headmaster's view is that 'schools are reflections of society' and cannot, nor should, 'act as agents of deliberate social change'. Thus there are no official policies or interventions on the issue of sexual violence. The school largely fails either to support young women or to challenge young men's sexual violence. It therefore reinforces men's relative power and women's relative powerlessness. Indeed, some of the men teachers exercise their own power in relation to both women colleagues and women students in ways which have continuities with the masculine behaviour under consideration (see Mahoney, 1985; Kitzinger, 1988; Herbert, 1989; Halson, 1989a)

Even within this liberal/hostile (masculine) environment, there are, as one might expect, feminist teachers. One teacher who identified as a feminist to the extent that she felt 'sex discrimination issues' were 'close to [her] heart', raised some of the issues I have been discussing in one of a series of classes which were designed to develop the students' debating skills. The teacher, Ms Jay, had focused the students' attention on contemporary issues such as 'blood sports', 'the nuclear issue' and 'sex discrimination'. In each case, some 'stimulus material' was presented (video, a written account) before the students were asked to discuss the topic. The 'sex discrimination' debate followed a video about two sisters, one of whom was 'stereotypically feminine' – unassertive and coy with men. About to marry she initially accepts the sexual division of labour in the home and does not drive her boyfriend's car despite the fact that she is a competent driver. The other sister is, in Ms Jay's words, 'a bit of a rebel'. The video charts 'a day in the life' of these two women as the rebellious sister persuades the other to pinch the prospective husband's car for a 'joy ride' to the seaside. On the trip, the car breaks down and they encounter a group of young men. According to Ms Jay:

> the girl who's engaged uses her feminine wiles – looking helpless to get help (which) the other one completely quashes by being quite aggressive towards the boys which doesn't suit them at all so they drive off ... During the day they're sort of pursued by the same boys (who) try to chat them up. And it's the same sort of thing: the one girl is quite flattered; the other one just finds it completely obnoxious and makes it clear. It's quite amusing as well. And then ... because she's quite, probably, *anti*-male ... she's probably too extreme ... but towards the end she mellows a little because she meets a boy who actually apologises for his behaviour ... she sort of realises that the men are human, y'know.

The discussion which followed covered a range of issues raised by or alluded to in the video. These included: the sexual double standard; the sexual division of labour; whether it is flattering or offensive to be 'wolf whistled' at; whether it's all right for boys to express emotions/ cry; whether girls feel safe walking home at night; whether rapists should be hung. Again, there are a number of observations one could make about all this. I begin with the question of 'impact' before considering the 'pitch' of the intervention and whether it goes far enough.

Briefly, there was *some* impact on the young women's ideas arising both from this teacher's classwork and from my 'interventions' in the form of informal interviews and 'chats'. Young women 'noticed' or named things they had not noticed or named before.

For example following Ms Jay's class and during a group interview with me, one young woman declared that boys calling girls slags 'isn't fair' and that she was 'going to call *them* slags now!' Another young woman reflected on a comment that Lindsey had made during the discussion in Ms Jay's class about (not) feeling safe on the streets. Lindsey had said to one of the other girls, 'you'd be alright', meaning that the girl in question was 'unattractive' and would be an 'unlikely victim'. Linda said: 'that's not the point though . . . say there's a rapist on the street . . . he's gonna get the *next* gal that walks by on her own ain't he? And that could be anybody – whether they look stupid or not'. The subsequent discussion, transcribing onto eight sheets of A4, was *all* about their fears on the streets and at home (how their brothers 'play on' their fears), more experiences of 'ordinary violence' (being followed, being flashed, being 'cruised' by men in cars, being shouted at and commented upon) and 'normal precautions' (see Stanko, 1985).

Thus, for some girls, both the 'space' Ms Jay and myself helped to create for them had the positive effect both of 'breaking the silence' (see Herbert, 1989) and of validating their sense of 'unfairness'. There is, then, evidence of resistance and change. However, many of the young women's views recorded earlier in this chapter were expressed after Ms Jay's class and after I had been in the school for several months suggesting that in many respects, for many young women, the impact had been limited. I will discuss *my* failings at greater length elsewhere, limiting myself here to commenting on the limitations of the 'sex discrimination' debate.

The 'sex discrimination' issues were pitched at a level the students could 'relate to', the video resonated with their experiences and the teacher was one to whom the kids could relate, and so a space was provided for them to explore some gender issues. However, the time provided was limited to a few hours, the space was mixed and the 'pitch' was one which, although it resonated with *some* of the kids' experiences (of wolf whistles, 'sex roles'/the division of labour, 'boys crying'), it excluded other experiences of sexual violence. 'Wolf whistling' was 'on the agenda' and the young women were able to explore their feelings about how they felt (some 'objectified'; others 'flattered'). Nothing was said about, for example: the way the young women in the video and in the classroom risk rejection from men if they challenge rather than go along with their behaviour; the way in which the young women are stereotyped ('good girls'/'bad girls'/ 'slags') and how this constrains their options and denies their autonomy whilst lads' sexual behaviour is not only condoned but often encouraged (see Lees, 1986). The discussion about rape was almost exclusively about whether (stereotypical) rapists should be hanged rather than about how ordinary women like themselves are raped by ordinary lads/men whom they know (see Warshaw, 1988); how other forms of sexual violence, like coerced and non-reciprocal heterosex and 'being got' (see Halson, 1989a) and being the butt of jokes and being on the receiving end of sexual innuendoes which intimidate and offend, form a continuum which daily oppresses women and which some women collectively resist as well as individually survive.

This intervention, then, only approximates three of the factors which Kelly emphasised as important for women in making the transition from 'individual survival' to 'collective resistance': talking with women, time, and personal and relevant contact with feminists (Kelly 1988, pp. 224–6). It is not fair to judge Ms Jay's intentions harshly for falling short of a more radical feminist agenda. Her work (and mine) had *some* impact as I have mentioned above and her intentions were not primarily to raise issues of sexual violence. What her work illustrates is that much more – and special – time is required, for women to talk with women and about sexual violence, about the power of labels and of men, about their own strength and independence of spirit as well as about their despair and about the possibilities for resistance and for change. Kelly argues that the process of development of an oppositional political consciousness and organised resistance involves at least three stages of understanding and action:

> Individuals must see that the cause of their personal experiences is oppressive social relations. This understanding must be accompanied by a belief that social change is both necessary and possible. Individuals must then come together in some form of collective organization which is directed towards achieving the necessary change. (Kelly, 1988, p. 228).

Unlike the older women whom Liz Kelly interviewed, most of whom saw their experiences as being caused by oppressive social relations, the young women I interviewed, for the most part, drew on the dominant 'commonsense' (woman-blaming/man-exonerating) explanations of sexual violence, 'buried' rather than validated their experiences and felt hopeless or relatively powerless to challenge men's behaviour. The 'despair of the oppressed' was much in evidence. This is not very surprising since they were 14 years old and had not, therefore, had much time to reflect, to name and talk about sexual violence, to express anger and to compare their own and other women's experiences of oppression, survival and resistance. When space was made available, some impact was observed: young women talked about the power of labels and shared some of their own strength and independence of spirit as well as their despair.

The young women also feel and are rendered relatively powerless because the school – one potentially important social agency which could act in their interests – does not support them by challenging ideologies which circumscribe their choices. On the contrary, it (often unselfconsciously) reproduces them. Whilst schools assert through silence and non-intervention that they 'don't care', young women will perhaps continue to assert that they 'don't care', 'get used to it' and 'have to make the best of it'. They deserve better.

7 Gender Issues in Inter-Agency Relations: Police, Probation and Social Services

Alice Sampson, David Smith, Geoffrey Pearson, Harry Blagg and Paul Stubbs

INTRODUCTION

This paper is based on a two-year research project entitled 'Crime, Community and the Inter-Agency Dimension' and funded by the Economic and Social Research Council. The key agencies chosen for our research were the police, social services and the probation service. Our overall objective was to study patterns of agency cooperation within the criminal justice system and to identify important areas of policy tension and potential conflict between these state agencies (cf. Blagg *et al.*, 1988; Sampson *et al.*, 1988; Pearson *et al.*, 1989).

The sites on which these state agencies attempt to establish effective means of inter-agency working include local crime prevention initiatives, juvenile liaison panels, joint investigations into child abuse and child sexual abuse, and the courts. In this particular paper we set out to show that the 'systems approach' towards organisational behaviour, and its neglect of gender as an organisational issue, is unable to offer an adequate account of a number of key aspects of inter-agency work. Equally, the approach based on 'occupational cultures' and 'professional ideologies', which has been particularly influential in attempts to understand police work, fails in much the same way.

The difficulty, as we describe it here, is that gender relations and sexual divisions have important (and often unforeseen) implications for the criminal justice system. From an inter-agency perspective an important consideration to emerge from our research is that the experiences of women workers, who are often marginalised by discriminatory practices within their own organisations and by other agencies, have a significant impact on the nature of inter-agency cooperation and inter-agency tensions. These experiences mean not only that some forms of inter-agency work are severely limited by the avoiding action taken by women workers in order to minimise potentially discriminatory encounters, but also that as a means of countering their marginalisation women workers will establish different types of alliances with workers in other organisations.

Reflecting the general neglect of gender issues in organisational theory, and more specifically in the criminal justice system, we had not specifically identified them in our initial formulation of the research project. However, from an early stage in our research fieldwork it became clear that the question of gender was to play a central part in our understanding of inter-agency relations between police, probation officers and social workers. We found that not only is gender a means by which differential power is exercised between agencies, but that gender issues also help to explain some types of inter-agency tensions and some innovative joint inter-agency practices. For these reasons gender became, in its own right, a fundamental issue in our research project.

In order to substantiate these arguments this paper is structured in the following way: first we briefly review some of the literature on organisational theory; we then discuss how, through our gender-sensitive fieldwork approach, we were able to reach some understanding of how women's experience of working within their own organisation, and of working with men from other agencies, influences women's attitudes and behaviour towards their own work, and has discernible effects on inter-agency relations.

THE SYSTEMS APPROACH TO ORGANISATIONAL BEHAVIOUR

Hearn and Parkin (1987) have argued that systems thinking 'has become a new orthodoxy of management thought and theory', and that while it may take various forms and emphases, these have one thing in common – their neglect of issues of gender and sexuality in organisations: 'technology theory, contingency theory, open systems theory, inter-organisation theories and the rest are usually genuinely sexless' (p. 33). This is certainly true of much work in the field of direct relevance to this paper, that of 'inter-organisation theory'. The work of the Inter-Organisational Relations Group at the Tavistock Institute in the late 1970s, for instance, generated useful and sensitive concepts such as that of 'cultural gradient' to describe the differences in organisational cultures which anyone attempting to relate across the inter-agency boundary must take account of (for example, Friend, Noad and Norris, 1978); but, perhaps ironically in view of its point of origin, such work was indifferent to what might seem a major and obvious factor in many cultural gradients, that of gender. Systems theories, however open, have largely ignored the emphasis on the personal and indeed the sexual elements of organisational life which had been central to the thinking of an earlier generation of Tavistock researchers, such as Bion and Menzies. (For a recent evaluation of their contribution, see Pearson, Treseder and Yelloly, 1988.)

As Hearn and Parkin (1987) acknowledge, systems theories, although becoming dominant, did not entirely sweep the board. A more critical strand in organisation studies developed from the 1970s, in which the concern of feminist writers with gender divisions and with sexual harassment at work was an important influence (see, for example, Dex, 1985; Knights and Willmott, 1986; Walby, 1986); and some writing at least was concerned not only with gender but also with sexuality (Gutek, 1985). Nevertheless, the claim that this is a neglected field, frequently made by writers trying to draw attention to the importance of these issues in understanding organisations, seems justifiable. It has been argued that this suppression of sexuality is a central and essential element in all formal organisations – that they necessarily entail 'de-sexualisation' (Burrell, 1984). Taking a long historical view, and relating his analysis to that of Elias on the 'civilising process' and to Foucault's history of sexuality, Burrell argues that 'sexuality and labour power are not compatible'. In another version of this argument Burrell (1987) has also suggested that 'accounting and de-sexualisation go hand in hand' (pp. 91–2) and that 'desire ... is everything (at least potentially) that accounting is not' (p. 99). The organisational effort to suppress sexuality, according to Burrell, is however often resisted: desire reasserts itself, against the odds, in the form of sexual liaisons in the workplace.

The image of clandestine love behind the filing cabinets which Burrell's work tends to summon up is, as Hearn and Parkin (1987) suggest, more frequently found in magazine stories and the like than in formal organisational sociology; but this need not make it any less valid as a representation of one way in which sexuality is expressed and experienced in organisations. A very different expression of it is of course found in the surveys of sexual harassment listed by Hearn and Parkin. While acknowledging the interest of Burrell's broad historical sweep, they suggest that Burrell's opposition of organisation and sexuality is mistaken; sexuality, according to Hearn and Parkin, is in reality deeply embedded in organisational structure and experience. Organisations both construct sexuality – through, for example, the division of labour on gender lines – and are constructed by it, as they respond to the sometimes overt, sometimes hidden sexual behaviour and practices of their members. Although managements (and the organisational literature) may seek to deny it, sexuality is a pervasive organisational reality.

GENDER ISSUES IN THE CRIMINAL JUSTICE SYSTEM

Even if this radical rethinking of the relationship between organisations and sexuality is not accepted in its entirety, the neglect of such questions in the literature of most immediate concern to us, that on inter-agency relations in criminal justice, would still be striking if not surprising. To a naive outsider, the most obvious difference between the police and a social service department might well be that the first is predominantly male (about 90 per cent), while the second is predominantly female. At one level, the importance of this distinction is often recognised clearly enough: it is difficult to write about the police, for example, without stressing the importance of 'masculine' values (for example, Smith and Gray, 1983; Holdaway, 1983; Reiner, 1985). But while there has been some attention to the implications of this dominant ethos of 'masculinity' for women recruits within the police force (for example, S. Jones, 1986; Fielding, 1988), these have been hardly followed through in considering the relations which policemen have with, for instance, social work agencies. In recent discussions of police-social work relations, both Holdaway (1986) and Thomas (1986) completely neglect issues of gender. In these accounts, while it is acknowledged that the 'occupational culture' of the police is a rich repository of both racist and sexist prejudice, the approach to understanding the ways in which conflicts between occupational cultures and professional ideologies reproduce themselves remains as ungendered and desexualised as in the most abstract versions of 'systems theory'.

The study of Jones (1986), focusing on the discrepancies between formal statements of equality between policemen and policewomen as against the actual differences in deployment, promotion prospects and job satisfaction, is exceptional in that it does take the issue of gender seriously. While sexuality is tangential to Jones's study, it does nevertheless emerge clearly at some points. For instance, her account of the case of *De Launay* v *The Metropolitan Police* reveals the kinds of beliefs among senior police officers (men) which underpin discriminatory practices. WPC De Launay had been banned from working on traffic patrol with her married male partner because a supervisor suspected a sexual liaison. A chief superintendant, explaining the decision to her, is alleged to have said: 'Of course, if you were a man I would not have to make this decision. If you had a face like a back of a bus it would be better. But you are both attractive people' (quoted in Jones, 1986, p. 147).

WPC Launay won her case for sexual discrimination, but was criticised by the chairman of the industrial tribunal, on the grounds that she should have recognised that there was a 'problem' that would be a matter of 'genuine concern' to the chief superintendant responsible for 'discipline' at the garage (Jones, 1986, p. 147).

One increasingly important element of police work, the investigation of child sexual abuse, is an aspect of inter-agency work that in some areas at least has been 'feminised', in the sense that the work is largely done by women, and the shared experience of social workers and police officers can lead to the development of open and constructive informal channels of communication between the women and across agency boundaries. Our research also revealed some areas of joint work in which a parallel process of 'masculinisation' could be detected; this was the case, for instance, in the informal network which existed in one of our research locations, Milltown, between a probation officer (regarded as something of a maverick by his own management for his interest in informal approaches to crime prevention) and some policemen who were particularly involved in work with young people. Elsewhere, Hudson (1988) has noted a similar and more generalised tendency for intermediate treatment work to become a male domain. It would be an exaggeration to claim that the informal inter-agency networks which emerged in our own research were always gender-specific; but there was certainly a tendency in this direction, perhaps not surprisingly since the networks depended on a sense of camaraderie and shared understandings.

The importance of gender in inter-agency contacts is stressed in

Campbell's (1988) account of the child sexual abuse crisis in Cleveland. The policemen involved seemed to have had particular difficulty in dealing with the women who became the centre of mass media attention, Marietta Higgs, and the child abuse consultant in social services, Sue Richardson. Their 'forceful' and 'determined' characters (masculine qualities?) were repeatedly stressed by the police officers who dealt with them, and were part of the justification given by the police for their withdrawal from the process of inter-agency consultation. In an ironic reversal of stereotypical gender roles, the police relied on masculine intuition (that there could not really be as much sexual abuse as was being diagnosed), while the women were presented, by the police and the mass media, as cool, detached, impersonal professionals. Campbell's account shows how the meaning of an adjective like 'forceful' shifts when it is applied by men to a man as opposed to a woman; the word cannot convey a lack of masculinity, but may well imply a deviation from norms of feminity.

The examples which we have given of how gender issues and sexual divisions expressed themselves within organisations and through inter-organisational relations within the criminal justice system are by no means intended to be exhaustive. Nor is it implied that these always, or even most commonly, assume highly dramatic forms in terms of discrimination and prejudice. Even such commonplace matters of dress, presentation and appearance (implying gender-specific imageries) acquire a significance of their own, especially in inter-agency work which involves contact with powerful institutions such as the courts: it is still commonplace for women student probation officers to be told that they must wear a skirt when attending court, lending an odd twist to the adage about 'women wearing the trousers'. Hearn and Parkin (1987) also comment on the evaluation of appropriate dress in selection processes for women-dominated professions such as midwifery, health visiting and social work, and remark that only ten years ago at least one social work qualifying course listed 'appearance' among its criteria for selection. Its disappearance as a formal selection criterion does not, of course mean that it does not continue to operate informally.

RESEARCH METHODOLOGY

Our research over the two years took place in six localities, three in Milltown which is situated in the North of England, and three in inner

London. In all of these places we found instances of women workers who had been sexually harassed and who claimed that the attitude and behaviour of men workers influenced their own working practices. Although in general terms our research looked at a number of ways in which inter-agency relations operated at different points within organisational hierarchies, most of our research with women workers was at the grassroots level of each organisation. In part, this was because there were notably few senior women managers; but it was also because as our research developed it became clear that an important and neglected aspect of inter-agency relations involved the responses of women as workers at the frontline level of their organisations.

Early on in the fieldwork, when we began negotiating access to the state agencies, we found that, particularly in the police force, the two research fellows (one woman and one man) encountered sharply differing experiences in carrying through these negotiations. Similarly, we were made forcibly aware of the fact that women's experiences within the police, social services and probation service could also markedly differ from men's experiences within these same agencies. These differences also required some adjustment to the fieldwork strategies which were adopted, in that we found that women's experiences surfaced most of all in very informal settings, usually outside their workplace and when the interview had formally ended; for example, catching a bus together, walking to meetings, or chatting over a cup of coffee. In these ways it became increasingly clear that less formal strategies were required to 'rescue' the dimension of gender relations in the research.

The issue of gender and gender-sensitive methodologies, therefore, took on a central importance in our research. This, of course, is not a novel recognition, and in common with other researchers in the field of gender relations we tried to develop methodologies to give women genuine space to express themselves (Graham, 1983, 1984; Oakley, 1981; Finch, 1984; Stanley and Wise, 1983). Through informal semi-structured conversations we began to understand the dynamics of the differential power relations between women and men workers, and to explore their implications in terms of actual working practices and their effect on the position of women. To facilitate this process we encouraged the women to participate actively in discussions that were influenced by the interviewee's own attitudes and experiences and which therefore demanded a reflexivity on the part of the researcher (Cain, 1986).

Not all our research strategies were necessarily feminist in orientation. However, through our gender-sensitive approach to the research, some of the findings and some of the subsequent recommendations for changes in practice have, we feel, enabled us to contribute 'towards a transformative understanding of women's condition' (Cain, 1986, p. 256).

THE PARAMETERS OF THE RESEARCH

One of the consequences of adopting a gender-sensitive methodology, whereby the women themselves tended to structure the fieldwork interview, was to focus our attention on some of the differences between the police, social services and the probation service. We found that, for example, the women police officers frequently recounted recurring personal experiences of sexual harassment and discrimination within their own organisation, whereas probation officers and social workers tended to be much more silent on this issue. The recurring preoccupations of these workers were more likely to be about their experiences of abuse by workers in *other* agencies during the daily course of their working lives, together with their fears of being assaulted by their clients.

This paper does not specifically cover worker–client relations and the issue of gender, either from the point of view of the worker or the client. Even so, although our research was primarily about inter-agency relations, we picked up some information about worker–client relations, and this, together with sexual harassment and their position at the sharp edge of their organisation, seemed to contribute to the mutually supportive networks of women working together which we found in various of the offices. Where the women were 'political' and sensitive to feminist arguments around the oppression of women, it is possible that these types of working relationship have stronger bonds.

Due to the salience of women police officers' experiences of discrimination within their own organisation this paper might appear to be about how policemen interact with women workers from their own organisation and from other agencies. This, however, is not what the paper is about. Rather, we are seeking to show how we need a better theoretical understanding of gender in organisational theories and how gender plays a central part in inter-agency work within criminal justice. Essentially, our point is that gender relations and sexual discrimination have unintended consequences which reach beyond the domain of equal opportunities, as understood in some narrow formal sense. On the one hand, and quite fundamentally, women's experience of discriminatory practices and routine harassment often marginalises them as workers. Women workers are not merely passive recipients, however, who are simply moulded by these experiences. In response to various forms of discrimination and harassment, women workers either form new alliances across agency boundaries with other women workers who share and understand their experience of marginalisation, or they are resistant to inter-agency cooperation and devise avoidance strategies.

In stressing the importance of gender in inter-agency relations, and the effect of sexual harassment on intra- and inter-agency relations, the question is raised about how far these findings, based on two different geographical locations in Milltown and inner London, are applicable to all types of inter-agency forums and settings. Given that these two localities have experienced quite contrasting histories of relations between the police, social work and probation services – together with other differences in terms of urban development, demography and cultures – we would argue that, amidst clear evidence of constancy in these experiences in both British and North American research, what did nevertheless vary in our own research was the intensity and frequency of sexual harassment between locations and between different situations. Where sexual harassment was raised, every worker had her own story (or stories) to tell, but they usually stressed somewhere in the conversation that some male workers were much more insulting and abusive than others.

THE POSITION OF WOMEN WORKERS WITHIN THEIR OWN ORGANISATION

The existence of sexual discrimination and sexual harassment in all types of organisations as part of women's everyday lives and the recognition of sexual harassment as a social problem in its own right have been documented by other research studies (Evans, 1978; Stanley and Wise, 1983; Hanmer and Saunders, 1984). Broadly speaking, the experiences of the women workers whom we encountered in our research concur with these types of findings, although the extent and effect of sexual harassment was greater in the police force than in social and probation services.

Discrimination in the police occurs at several different levels and has a number of different implications for inter-agency relations. As Reiner (1985, p. 216) has expressed it, 'the police world remains aggressively a man's world'. This occupational world reproduces expectations and structures work practices which require 'masculine qualities' and 'masculine traits', from which the men police officers obtain central aspects of their status. This predominance of the 'cult of masculinity' immediately places women officers in an ambiguous position within their own organisation and it is unclear where police women get their status and respect from within their own organisation, except by playing the role of an 'honorary man'. A number of women officers commented on how this was unacceptable for them, and one succinctly summed up this point of view by saying, 'they are female men, not women'.

Our findings lend support to Jones's (1986) argument that women in the police may settle for one of two options as a 'working solution': de-feminisation or de-professionalisation. That is, drawing upon a position originally formulated by Ehrlich-Martin (1979), they can become either *police*women or police*women* (Jones, 1986, pp. 171–2). If they choose the first route, Jones suggests, they may win acceptance as equals by male officers, but only by being better at the job than their male counterparts. The second option is less threatening to men, but encourages the criticism that women are unable or unwilling to engage in all aspects of police work. For example, a woman police sergeant who said that she joined the police (after training as a teacher) because she wanted a job which would satisfy her enthusiasm for fast driving might well be expected to have to struggle to avoid being placed in one of the branches of policing – community relations, juvenile liaison and the like – traditionally considered particularly suitable for women. It is also notable that activities such as juvenile liaison are disparaged within the occupation slang of policemen as 'Playschool' policing, the 'Toy Squad', 'Care Bear' and the 'Teeny Sweeny' (Blagg et al., 1988).

The prejudice of their male colleagues, with which women officers have to cope, manifests itself in a number of ways (Southgate, 1981; Bloch and Anderson, 1974; Ehrlich-Martin, 1981). This might extend from stereotypical notions of 'women's work' – as when a male police sergeant said to a woman officer during an interview, 'Make us a cup of tea, Mrs Woman' – to the exclusion of women officers from the sharing of informal information. Women officers said they were often reminded that their place was 'at home' and commented on the fact that the prejudice they encountered prevented them from being as effective as some men officers. Bloch and Anderson (1974) and Ehrlich-Martin (1981) found in their studies on police women in North America that women officers were marginalised at this informal level and that this was an obstacle to the effectiveness of woman police officers; and Ehrich-Martin notes 'in particular sexuality which serves to keep women police officers in their place'. In another North American study on the sources of stress and dissatisfaction among women police officers, the most commonly mentioned source of individual stress was found to be 'the negative attitudes of male officers', with 'questions about sexual orientation' featuring prominently within this category (Wexler and Logan, 1983). 'If you are sleeping with someone you are a slut,' said one of Wexley and Logan's women police informants, 'if you are not, you are a dyke.'

The findings of the Policy Studies Institute survey of the Metropolitan Police, as these relate to women police officers, struck many notes of comparison with this dismal evidence from North America – relating to discrimination in recruitment procedures, promotion prospects, and selection for specialist and elite operational units – as well as indicating considerable areas of tension between men and women officers. 'Women face substantial prejudice', is how D. J. Smith (1983, p. 163) tersely summarised this aspect of the PSI survey. Fielding's (1988) study of the training and socialisation of police recruits has also provided ample evidence of the ways in which women officers are either vilified or patronised, often tending to internalise these male-dominated views of police competence.

During the course of our own interviews and visits to police stations and canteens our fieldwork experiences have borne out these findings of the ways in which women officers are controlled through comments and jokes and gossip. For example:

> If you are even-tempered you take most of the teasing and joking ...
> Most of it you don't get upset about and let it pass, but if you let rip then they stand back and say not to mind her. Usually they say 'Oh, it must be the wrong time of the month'. (Woman police constable)

Jokes and comments that stereotyped women by playing on derogatory images were reinforced by the way in which, from the perceptions of women officers, senior male officers treated them differentially. We can take the example of a woman sergeant in Mill town who led an all-women team specialising in the joint investigation (with women social workers) of allegations of child sexual abuse. The existence of this team, concerned with an area of work likely to arouse anxiety and suspicion among men (Campbell, 1988), was apparently seen as threatening by a number of male officers; and the sergeant spoke of how she had to deal with allegations and innuendoes which implied that to have achieved her relatively powerful and autonomous position she must have slept with important men in the organisation. In our experience, and in the experience of women police officers, the perceptions held of them by male officers were not infrequently sexualised:

> You know, they don't treat men and women the same. If you argue or answer back they say you're nutters or you're a lesbian. When I go up for my... Roger Sutton [male chief superintendant] asks me what I do in my spare time. Why aren't I married? Have I got any boyfriends? They never say that to a man and he knows he can get away with it as a woman won't say anything. They treat women as objects. (Woman police constable)

A question must arise at this point, as to whether or not these experiences of women police officers merely reflect a generalised tendency within our society to discriminate against women, or whether the police service reproduces these systems of prejudice and discrimination in a more active and intensified form. A directly similar line of questioning is, of course, necessary when addressing prejudice and discrimination on the basis of race and ethnicity (see Pearson *et al.*, 1989).

On several grounds, including observation in the course of the research, it seems likely that there is less room for manoeuvre within the gender role for policewomen than for, say, social workers or probation officers. Unless women in the police become, in Jones's terms, *police*women, and thus gain honorary admission to the men's club, they are likely to be quite firmly fixed in a particular mould of stereotypical femininity. The hierarchical domination of the police by men is more clear-cut than in the social work agencies; there is a far stronger emphasis on the virtues of toughness and discipline; and there are fewer women colleagues who might support an alternative interpretation of feminine identity.

Even so, Jones's distinction between *police*women and police-*women* might be applicable to the social work services as well. In one social services department a woman maingrade worker, who did not want promotion, gave the following account:

Traditionally social work was a caring and supportive job which due to these traditional women's tasks attracted mainly women. During the last 10 years or so men have become social workers and have chosen this profession mainly with a clear idea of becoming managers, whereas women remained ground workers, i.e. as the carers. Gradually women have become more involved in lower/middle management ... the women who have reached higher management, Assistant Director/Director level have done so by adopting male values and attitudes and are often very hard, aggressive people. (Woman social worker)

Our research did not explore how these views of women in senior management as 'female men' held out in practice. We were more concerned with how gender divisions influenced the grassroots level of inter-agency relations. Nevertheless, it must be acknowledged that there are substantial differences between the form and nature of inter-agency work between senior management as against grassroots relations; that it can be sometimes difficult to negotiate and implement inter-agency agreements struck between managers at the frontline level of service delivery; and that these variations might be related to differences between the attitudes and behaviour of women at these different levels.

However, there are equally important differences between the state agencies, at all levels of the hierarchy, in the relationships between men and women workers. The treatment of women police officers by male police officers stands in comparison with the relationships between male and female social workers and probation officers. Within the social services and the probation service we found that social workers and probation officers talked more about 'one-off' examples of sexual harassment from male colleagues. But while they did not appear to suffer from discrimination and sexual harassment to the same extent as women police officers, the preoccupations of both social workers and probation officers centred, as suggested above, on their experiences and worries about assaults and harassment by their clients. We found that women workers in some areas were trying to organise self-defence classes, were demanding more security on the entrances to their offices, while also making sure they were not alone in the office if a male client was making a visit, or cancelling visits if they were alone. On these issues they also felt that their male managers were dragging their feet and not taking the situation seriously enough.

By contrast, social workers and probation officers had quite a different perspective when it came to their relations with other agencies. When probation officers and social workers were talking about inter-agency relations, in fact, it was not uncommon for the women workers spontaneously to recount their experiences and feelings about sexual harassment from both the police and prison officers. It is to these accounts that we now turn.

THE COURT SETTING: SILENCE IN COURT?

The public image of the criminal courts is of a setting where procedures are governed by decorum and rationality. Social research has not always supported this view, of course, in that the courts are also characterised by their own distinctive system of politics and prejudice (Carlen, 1976; McBarnet, 1981; Parker et al., 1981), including those organised around questions of gender and sexuality as these apply to women defendants (R. Pearson, 1976; Carlen and Worrall, 1987; Morris, 1987). Even so, the court setting might seem an unlikely location within which to find sexual prejudice and discriminatory practices, particularly when these are directed against women professionals within the criminal justice system itself. However, the actually existing inter-agency relations between the police, social services and probation service in a court setting provide particularly clear evidence of how sexual discrimination and harassment can accentuate the differential power relations between these state agencies, while also inhibiting certain forms of inter-agency contact and promoting others.

In so far as power differentials are concerned, we have argued elsewhere (Blagg et al., 1988; Sampson et al., 1988) that in a variety of contexts involving inter-agency working the police continuously renegotiate a dominant position in relation to social services and the probation service. Where there are women workers from these services and a male police officer, the differential power of gender might be expected to compound the more powerful position of the police. How are these gender divisions negotiated in practice?

Anecdotal and research evidence has consistently documented the tensions and conflicts between the police, social workers and probation officers and illustrated how the different tasks and responsibilities of these state agencies account for areas of tensions between them (Thomas, 1986; Holdaway, 1986). We aim to show that the experiences of sexual harassment of women workers in the court setting, as well as widening the relative power differentials between the workers and between state agencies, indicate that inter-agency tensions are more than just differences between differen types of work and 'professional ideologies': they are also related to the gender of workers in a manner that goes beyond any boundaries of 'occupational culture', and indeed cuts across these boundaries.

One common response which comes across from the women workers is the way in which they feel in a powerless position to respond to sexual abuse, despite their anger and humiliation. They feel caught between fighting back on the one hand, and protecting their client on the other. In other words, through sexual harassment their credibility as a social worker or probation officer is challenged, and challenged moreover in a way that their male colleagues would not encounter. We can offer a few examples of such experiences:

> At court women are treated as second-class citizens and that's how they [the police] treat us. It's most difficult when getting access to the cells. River Court can be sexist. The problem with sexual harassment is, if you don't cooperate your client loses out. I've had some bad experiences. (Women probation officer)

> The problem with sexual harassment is that a working relationship is at issue, and it's that working relationship which gets abused. You have to restrain yourself and you know you mustn't blow it for that reason. It can be a simple matter of certain comments. (Woman probation officer)

> The police have much greater power than we do. We rely on their cooperation. In fact we're dependent on it and when they are obstructive it makes it very difficult for us ... I have been, and do get harassed by the police ... some do give you a lot of sexual harassment and don't take you seriously. It can make a difference to working relationships. I try and sort it out with the individual officer concerned. I was once locked in a cell by a police officer and he wouldn't let me out and made sexual jokes about me in front of my client and all the other prisoners. On that occasion I complained to the Inspector. (Woman court officer, social services department)

Experiences such as these appear to be entirely commonplace. Another probation officer talked about how she had frequently encountered unacceptable comments in the police canteen which was attached to the court, and how these prevented her from using the canteen which might otherwise have offered an informal context in which to foster inter-agency relations:

> When I'm in the canteen I can't argue back as it might hinder my working relations with them, so I don't go into the police canteen. (Woman probation officer)

These findings confirm the obvious point that workers' first allegiances are to their clients and to their own agency, and that where their relations with their client and their professional work are threatened, then workers react strongly and try to minimise the risks and dangers – which, in effect, means to withdraw from and avoid these situations. In some circumstances sexual harassment and verbal abuse might be thought of as a channel through which conflicts of professional orientation, which might otherwise be discussed and negotiated, are brought to an impasse:

> You know the kind of thing. We call them 'clients'. They [the police] call them 'villains'. Well, you could talk about that . . . it's a difference in perception, we have different jobs to do . . . it would be silly to expect probation officers and the police to see eye-to-eye about everything. So it's not that that worries me. It's just their attitude, the way they're always so patronising. They say it's a 'typical woman's attitude'. You'd be 'better off bringing up babies'. Women are 'soft' and 'sentimental', and that kind of thing. Either that, or they're trying to chat you up, 'Never mind dear, fancy going to the pictures tonight?' And that's quite unacceptable. I will not tolerate that. Either way, they just don't treat you as a professional, and they're sometimes downright insulting. But you can't answer back because then they've dragged you down to their level. So I just avoid those kinds of situations, do my job and that's that. (Woman probation officer)

Of course, there are always alternative strategies for dealing with this type of situation:

> Me? I just play the game. Put on a nice skirt, wear higher heels than I normally would, and flirt with them a bit. I don't particularly like it, but I usually get what I want. They're like little boys most of them. I suppose it's manipulation. In fact, it is. I can understand why some people would say it was unprofessional. (Woman senior social worker)

Here, in fact, we see a mirror-image of the kinds of anxieties which the presence of women officers in the police service can provoke in male colleagues:

> A lot of blokes, when they're out working with a policewoman, their motivation's not to do the job well, but to impress this female. (Police constable, quoted in Fielding, 1988, p. 161)

Given that cooperation in the court setting, as in any other, depends upon mutual trust and openness, it is rather obvious that this kind of defensive cooperation which results in women workers keeping themselves at arm's length from the personnel of other agencies (or 'playing the game') is a very flimsy and unstable basis for developing a strategy of inter-agency cooperation.

WOMEN WORKING TOGETHER: UNINTENDED EFFECTS OF SEXUAL HARASSMENT ON INTER-AGENCY RELATIONS

The final part of this argument is that, as well as withdrawing defensively from situations where they feel that they can neither defend their integrity as women and as professionals nor continue to act in a way that is compatible with their responsibilities towards their clients, women workers will also sometimes form new kinds of alliances and informal networks which transcend inter-agency boundaries. While it remains true that women workers in the police, probation and social services can be devalued and undermined by men – not only within their own organisation, but also outside their organisation whether within the 'community' or by other agencies – this should not be understood as a universal aspect of inter-agency conflict, whether in terms of a 'systems analysis' or a clash between 'occupational cultures'.

We have already alluded to the fact that in a particularly influential account of police–social worker relations, Holdaway (1986) describes difficulties in these relations as essentially deriving from divergences between the occupational cultures and professional ideologies of the two agencies. However, a major flaw in Holdaway's analysis is that while he acknowledges the masculine emphasis of the police culture, his analysis fails to address either the different gender compositions of the police and social work services, or gender divisions as these reproduce themselves in inter-agency work.

The key point, however, is that although these kinds of conflict are undoubtedly quite common, they are neither universal nor inevitable. Quite crucially for our own analysis in this paper, where inter-agency linkages involve women workers on both sides of the inter-agency divide, we sometimes found quite a different story. It was particularly interesting to find that when social workers and probation officers talked about their relations with their local police, if there was a local woman constable, she was often singled out as being the exception to the rest of the police force. Moreover, workers in these other agencies could name the women police officers, whereas few men officers are named by any of the workers whom we interviewed. For example:

> The police are racist and sexist . . . it's the way they see women and say things like 'I wouldn't let my wife do things like that' . . . it's their scathing attitude that gets to you . . . It helps so much knowing Sandra Tower [woman police sergeant in a Youth and Community section], it's not just a strange voice on the other end of the phone. We have a good relationship because we understand the roles of each other, we liaise on an informal basis, it's very important as we don't get the wrong expectations. (Woman social worker)

> I'm of the generation that would go to the police. But that's changed now, ever since my daughter has been a punk, the experiences she's had have been awful. It's made me anti-police. But on the other hand I have worked well with the police – Lynne Taylor [local Home Beat Officer] is very helpful. (Woman social worker)

> I particularly admired the techniques of the policewoman, she was very skilled and I learnt from her . . . I was very struck by how close we were on the moral issues involved . . . [We had] a philosophical discussion . . . so we could understand where each person came from and it was very close. I was impressed. (Woman social worker, talking about a joint child sexual abuse investigation in which she had been involved)

These quotations illustrate how social workers have identified with some women police officers as being 'different' from the police force as a whole, and that when they isolate these policewomen for special mention it is because of a confidence in working and cooperating with them. These allegiances are formed between women workers as 'professional' relationships, based on mutual respect. We would argue that such examples of inter-agency cooperation are symptomatic of situations where there is a narrowing of power differentials between the workers. But it is not that the agencies themselves have changed, with all the differences in power and preoccupations which separate them. Nor that the formal 'systems' of inter-organisational linkage have been altered. Nor that the 'occupational cultures' and 'professional ideologies' which distinguish different groups of workers have been transformed. What has been changed is that those aspects of inter-agency work which organisational theories based on the 'systems approach', 'occupational cultures' or 'professional ideologies', either ignore or deny – namely, gender divisions – have been effectively equalised. Gender is, of course, only one among many sources of power. We would nevertheless argue its centrality in understanding inter-agency relations in the sphere of criminal justice, and in any attempts to bring about improved approaches to multi-agency work.

CONCLUSIONS

(1) Sexual harassment is not an inevitable product of our society (Wise and Stanley, 1987, p. 79). Therefore an intra-agency self-examination of equal opportunities policies and other strategies to combat discrimination, particularly by the police, is a necessary first step before inter-agency policies can ever really take effective form.

(2) Cooperation between women workers in different agencies which comes about as a consequence of sexual harassment, and as a consequence the subordination and marginalisation of women in their own agency, has nevertheless only a narrow base amongst a small group of women workers. So that, although we have identified some pockets of mutually supportive inter-agency relations among women workers, this should not be assumed to have widespread implications.

(3) The crucial determinant of effective inter-agency relations is power. It is the power differentials running between different state agencies which influence other symptomatic forms of inter-agency conflict, such as struggles over confidentiality and privileged access information. Gender divisions have been identified as a crucial aspect of difficulties in inter-agency working; and if it is true as asserted by some theorists that organisational bureaucracies have denied and sought to eliminate issues of gender and sexuality, then what has been identified here might be called a return of the repressed.

8 Policing 'Domestic Violence'
Susan Edwards

INTRODUCTION

'Domestic violence' – wife assault or 'spousal violence' – has been discussed for the past twenty years. The medical and psychiatric professions have focused attention on why men batter, explaining male violence in terms of poor child-rearing practices, the cycle of violence, unemployment and drink problems, thereby generating a checklist of risk factors and abuse indicators. Such theorisations have informed the procedures and practices of the various helping agencies, shaping practitioners' perceptions of the cause of the violence and their solutions to and remedies for the problem. Often women have been blamed for their own victimisation. Susan Brownmiller's book *Waverly Place* (1989) testifies to the persistence of this victim-blaming model, and is the more surprising given Brownmiller's hitherto feminist stance. *Waverly Place* is based on the real-life case of Hedda Nussbaum, who is blamed for the death of her daughter Lisa, murdered by Joel Steinberg, the 'live-in boyfriend'. Brownmiller blames Hedda, and what she cannot understand she pathologises. She describes Hedda as just standing by because of cocaine addiction. Brownmiller has little to say about the ways in which woman are rendered helpless, powerless and terrified in such situations. Such 'ways of seeing' have contributed to repeated abuse and the escalation of assault by supporting a climate of opinion which promulgates the view that violence is an individual family matter where intervention is inappropriate and ineffective and resolution is to be sought by the parties involved. In turn, the pathologisation of domestic assault has facilitated the absence of public and community support, allowing the trivialisation of the abuse in and by the legal system to continue unchallenged. Given this individualistic interpretation, arguments about the patriarchal family and the distribution of power within it has often been regarded as inconsequential. Similarly, the subordination of women and the institutionalisation of powerlessness through enforced economic dependency have traditionally been considered secondary in discussions about why women stay on in relationships where men continue to use violence towards them and their children.

This chapter seeks to examine the current state of debate in the United Kingdom and internationally on the policing of domestic violence. This is examined through an exploration of policing, the courts and the author's own police study in Holloway and Hounslow in 1984 and 1988 and Streatham in 1989 in the light of recent legislative developments. The research findings are presented against the backdrop of the current status of the problem of 'spousal violence' within academic criminology and the problems faced by feminist jurisprudence in engaging with the law to bring about reform.

A CRITIQUE OF CONCEPTIONS OF 'DOMESTIC VIOLENCE'

Feminist sociologists and criminologists have deliberately made explicit the nature of the economic and ideological structures which make physical violence against women possible, and criticised the social climate in which it becomes normalised. In doing so they have attempted to construct alternative explanations for male violence. Research and debate on the deconstruction process has revealed both conventional attitudes to wife assault and the condoning of violence within the family by the institutions of policing and the courts. A major focus of this exploration has involved a consideration of the civil and criminal justice system (McCann, 1985; Parker, 1985; Edwards, 1989a, 1989b; Hanmer, Radford and Stanko, 1989; Walker, 1989); social work and helping agencies (Dobash and Dobash, 1985); and medical, social, probation and housing services.

Freeman (1980) has argued that the law itself constitutes the problem. He diverts attention away from the explanation of violent outbursts as some kind of inner pathology, to examine the way in which the juridical process condones violence and in so doing reinforces the prevailing ethos that violence against wives is of a different species from violence in public and violence against non-family members. However, feminist sociologists and criminologists have attempted to reconstruct the understanding of and the meaning inherent in spousal violence in our culture through an explication of how such meanings are given signification in law. This has involved an exposition of the way in which law is saturated with particular assumptions about violence and its victims and an attempt for some to reconstruct meanings and definitions through challenging the law and through feminist jurisprudence. The objective is to ensure greater protection for women through these critical exposés, and the accountability of law-makers, practitioners and the police within the legal process.

How this reconstruction should develop, the direction and extent of legal change required, and especially how far women should engage with the law – if at all – are issues that have divided any collective feminist response to domestic violence. If the battered women's movement was bitterly divided in the seventies over the interpretation of violence in the family (Erin Pizzey v. the National Women's Aid Federation), it is now divided over how far engaging with the law, the police and the legal process in the search for more effective protection for women is appropriate and how far it can really be effective. For some, to tangle with the effects of patriarchy through efforts to change the legal response is not going to alter the way men perceive women, nor the cultural climate within which men perceive themselves and their rights (Hanmer, Radford and Stanko, 1989; Smart, 1989). The law itself is the embodiment of patriarchal attitudes and inequality in power relationships. Experience has shown that it not only fails to confer rights on women but indeed has disempowered women in several ways and empowered men. Changing the law, its interpretation and legal application does not necessarily challenge the cultural iconography in which women as victims are perceived. Yet, in reply to these reservations, there is also a case to make regarding the symbolic function of law, where the law and policing educate and change wider cultural attitudes by setting the boundaries of acceptable behaviour and by making violence against women illegal through determined law enforcement (O'Donovan, 1985; Dworkin, 1981).

Within criminology, feminist criminologists have researched, written and spoken out alone. A major problem within the mainstream academic debate on crime and policing is that the issue of spousal violence has been relegated to the periphery. In order that the problem receive proper consideration and attention it must be rescued from the margins and placed in its reconstructed form within the mainstream debate. There are two immediate problems which have so far obstructed this assimilation. First, divisions persist within feminist criminology as to how far men should be involved in the research, articulation and redefinition of this crime. Some women, reacting to the history of colonisation and articulation by men of the experiences of women, argue that male criminologists, *inter alia*, have no place at all in these debates (for example, Donnerstein, 1980). Other feminist criminologists attack the apparent lack of interest of male criminologists and researchers in either feminist criminology or crimes which are specific in their commission and effects on women. Whatever the reason, the criminological enterprise, whether traditional criminology, radical criminology or left realist criminology, has steered well clear of the issue of violence against women in its various forms. (It is significant, however, that the 1988 edition of *Understanding Deviance*, by Downes and Rock, actually addresses both developments within feminist criminology and crimes against women.) So when we ask why a proper informed debate about spouse abuse has been suffocated, emerging only in feminist discussions which have continually been marginalised, it is not enough to hold legal and cultural institutions solely responsible; we must look to the institutions of knowledge and the zealously guarded empires of male academia, for they too have a case to answer.

THE NATURE AND EXTENT OF 'DOMESTIC VIOLENCE'

The extent of 'domestic violence', which ranges through assault, grevious bodily harm, threats to kill and attempted murder, remains unknown. Women are reluctant to report it not only to the police (Binney *et al.*, 1981; Montgomery and Bell, 1986) but also to victimisation survey interviewers (Hough and Mayhew, 1983; Hanmer and Stanko, 1985). Studies have shown that only 50 per cent of women in refuges contacted the police (Binney *et al.*, 1981; Edwards, 1989a). When women report domestic violence, police often do not regard such incidents as sufficiently serious to warrant police action, and even where they are considered serious, police forces lack any coherent policy regarding the arrest, detention and charging of such offenders. Finally, police action may be thwarted by prosecutors, who do not alway prosecute those cases the police report to them (Moody and Tombs, 1982; McLeod, 1983; Sanders, 1988; Edwards, 1989a). In describing the criminal justice process Stephen Box (1971) has used the analogy of a 'corridor of connected rooms'. This analogy can be used to understand the several possible exits through which cases disappear. Reported incidents of domestic violence often disappear at the onset because police recording practices continue to be determined not by prima facie evidence but by police discretion founded on a judgement of the prospective likelihood of complainants' withdrawal and on prosecutorial decision-making. McGillivray (1987) has referred to this element in the police process as 'precognition'. The police make an a priori assessment of the prosecutability of a particular case, frequently preferring not to set in motion what they see as the redundant process of 'criming' and subsequent prosecution if the case is unlikely to succeed. In consequence, crime figures on the extent of 'domestic violence' – from assault up to threats to kill – are incomplete, an artifact of police recording practice rather than any reflection of the number of women who reported violence to the police. Criminologists regard all crime figures as artifacts of policing, but it is important to recognise that specific configurations of crimes and victimisations are subject to routine and specific distortions and require separate examination. Not all reported crimes are equally subject to the same degree of distortion; therefore it is wrong to see the under-recording of crime by the police as homogeneous. Such distortions may institutionalise sex, gender and racial prejudice where the crime involves exclusively women or a particular racial group as victims. It is important, therefore, to disaggregate crime configurations one from another in order to understand the nature of the processes which legitimate certain recording or evasion practices.

Given the enormous difficulty incumbent in researching recorded crime, it is important to turn at the outset to the only relatively 'hard' facts we have on domestic violence, provided in homicide figures broken down by the relationship of victim to suspect. Homicide figures are not so easily massaged or manipulated; consequently the under-reporting and under-recording of spousal homicide poses a less serious problem for comparative research than, say, in cases of prostitution or spousal violence. Turning to the evidence on spousal homicide, we can see that women were nine times more likely than men to be victims in 1982 (104 women to 12 men), nine times more likely in 1983 (87 to 10), seven times more likely in 1984 (97 to 14), in 1985 seven times (100 to 15) and in 1986 nine times more likely, at 109 female to 12 male victims. Homicide figures demonstrate the high incidence of husbands killing wives and boyfriends killing girlfriends, which leads us to question why police and public safety programmes continually remind women of their vulnerability on the streets but remain virtually silent about their vulnerability in the home. In

19.5 per cent of homicides, husbands/boyfriends were the principal suspects. Put another way, nearly half of all those killed since 1982 have been female, and where there was a suspect 47.5 per cent have been husbands, male cohabitants, boyfriends, or former spouses or cohabitants.

In 1986, 109 wives/cohabitees were victims of homicide. These women were kicked, punched, head-butted, battered, suffocated, strangled, shot or stabbed to death. A further 13 women were killed by boyfriends. Wives were more likely than any other group to have been strangled/asphyxiated, hit with a blunt instrument or stabbed. Some of these women had called the police on previous occasions, and some of the offenders had a criminal record for violent assault against wives. For example, on 9 August 1989, Lawrence Lucien was convicted of manslaughter and sentenced to four and a half years' imprisonment. He stabbed his wife in the stomach following an argument about his wife's friend Joe Murray. At the trial Lucien made out a case of provocation. Police records, however, show that he had been abusing her for eight years and that police had refused bail on an earlier occasion that same year (1988) when there had been violence. Magistrates granted bail, and Lucien killed his wife (*Islington Gazette*, 10 August 1989).

Spousal or partner assaults occur because women find themselves in the home, trapped, living in a relationship with the aggressor. While women living in the home with violent men are most at risk, however, it is also clear from other studies (Moore, 1979; Edwards, 1989a, 1989b) that women who have lived with men in the past – ex-wives, ex-girlfriends, ex-cohabitees – are still at some considerable risk of violence and homicide. As Daly and Wilson point out (1987; p. 219) among legal married cohabiting Canadian spouses in 1974–83 a man was almost four times as likely to kill his wife as to be killed by her (404 cases as against 107), among estranged couples he was more than nine times as likely to kill her as she to kill him (119 cases as against 13).

Edwards (1989a) found that in cases of 'wife' homicide recorded in England and Wales for 1986, 31 per cent of victims were not residing with the aggressor at the time of the homicide. Similarly, figures for spousal homicide in Northern Ireland showed that a third of all female spousal homicide victims were not cohabiting with the aggressor at the time. It is clear, then, that men continue to beat, batter and kill the women from whom they have been separated. Despite the wealth of all this evidence and the risk to women from spouse assault, it is only very recently that policing strategies have been revised in order that spousal violence may be regarded with greater seriousness.

TRADITIONAL POLICING POLICY

Traditional police policy has already been much criticised. It is characterised by giving advice to women regarding civil remedies, solicitors and women's shelter groups, but not by arrest and the criminalisation of male violence. Indeed, general police orders in some forces indicated that assaults between man and wife were not a crime. Consider, for example, a Liverpool Police Instruction of 1926 which stated that officers should not interfere between man and wife because 'you will find that both will turn on you' (Bourlet, 1988). Latterly, studies in North America, Europe and Australia have identified the lack of police intervention in these disputes as the main problem (McLeod, 1982; Scutt, 1982; Oppenlander, 1982; Bell, 1984a, 1984b, 1985a, 1985b; Ferraro, 1989; Hatty, 1989; Zoomer, 1989). However, it is important to acknowledge at the onset that police intervention is circumscribed by the substantive law regulating police conduct regarding arrest and violent conduct. Police inertia must therefore be analysed within the parameters of a criminal justice system where all agents minimise the problem of violence against wives and where decisions of sentencers and prosecutors affect the nature of the action police officers take.

American studies which have examined the police response to domestic violence have all echoed similar findings and drawn uniform conclusions. Bell (1984a, 1984b, 1985a, 1985b), Oppenlander (1982) and Ferraro (1989) all found that police were reluctant to arrest the offender, and when they did it was usually in respect of some offence other than the assault. Data for Bell's studies have been derived from domestic disputes and violence known to the police, made available annually in the Ohio Report, which collates all recorded incidents of family violence. Bell's work develops from his earlier exploratory study of Ohio's data for a twelve-month period in 1980 (1984a, p. 25) to a multi-year study of recorded violence from August 1979 to December 1981 (1985, p. 301). During 1980, 55933 incidents were recorded to Ohio police jurisdictions. Of these, in 13125 cases (24 per cent) criminal complaints were filed, while the police initiated action independently in 477 cases (3.6 per cent). In 5292 cases (10 per cent of the total) an arrest was made under the Domestic Violence Programme. In a further 2008 (4 per cent) an arrest was made under other Ohio Revised Code violations. In 8662 cases (15 per cent) there was a referral to other agencies, such as social services or women's shelters, or to the civil process. In an overwhelming proportion of cases (39 971 – 71 per cent) there was a total absence of any kind of action. The Ohio data indicated that the majority of assaults were spousal – 79 per cent of wives and 8 per cent of husbands.

Clearly, as Bell concludes from his 1984 exploratory study, the replication study in the same year and the multi-year studies published in 1985, the police were reluctant to arrest, to make reports or to take any kind of action, unless the victim initiated the complaint. In addition he concluded that police officers were inadequately trained in counselling and referral techniques. Attempts at mediation often exacerbated the situation. The distortion of crime figures was a product of police discretion and a police culture which traditionally recorded violence in the home as non-criminal. Violent assault against wives was not seen as part of the crime problem.

Oppenlander (1982) similarly examined the police investigatory process and the nature of the police response to domestic violence in three metropolitan areas – Rochester in New York State and Tampa and St Louis in Missouri – for an eleven-week period commencing in May 1977. The database included 596 police investigations of arguments (disputes without physical contact) and assaults (including threats), for both domestic incidents (including relatives, ex-spouses and cohabitees) and non-domestic ones (involving unrelated persons). From the onset, Oppenlander found, police discretion and procedural mechanisms facilitated the construction of domestic assaults as a non-crime problem by diverting cases away from the criminalisation process. First, less than half of the domestic cases where assaults were alleged were treated as such, the remainder being described as 'family trouble', while 60 per cent of disputes between non-relatives were dispatched as assaults. Second, patrol officers were slower in arriving at domestic disturbances than at arguments between unrelated disputants. Third, in few domestic cases did the police arrest, although there were clear legal grounds for doing so. Out of 180 domestic arguments the police arrested 8.9 per cent, while out of 110 non-domestic arguments only 4 per cent resulted in arrests. In cases of domestic assault, out of 79 cases, 22 per cent resulted in arrest; out of 227 non-domestic assaults, over 13 per cent resulted in arrest. Although more suspects were arrested in domestic than in non-domestic arguments, there were twice as many injured victims in domestic than in non-domestic cases and so the proportion of arrests in domestic cases might have been much higher. A central finding was that in spousal cases arrests were made not to protect the victim but to preserve public peace and order. Thus in a high proportion of domestic assaults where arrests *were* made, it was for drunkenness or for resisting an officer. The following case is an illustration:

> The domestic suspect was drunk and hostile. He referred to the officers as 'the law', taunted them and refused to leave the house of the girlfriend, who looked bruised and scraped. Though he finally did leave, he continued yelling at the officers in the street, threatening to 'beat their heads'. The primary officer then placed the man under arrest for public drunkenness. When the suspect threatened to kill the officer at the police station, he added the charge of simple assault (of the female victim). (Oppenlander, 1982, p. 456)

The work of Zoomer (1989) in the Netherlands and Hatty (1989) in Australia shows, similarly, that police are reluctant to arrest men for assaulting their wives or girlfriends.

Traditional British police practice has been characterised by poor recording practices which have served to underestimate the problem and its extent, and a free rein in the use of discretion which has facilitated a poor level of service to victims. As Chatterton has explained in a wider policing context: 'one of the most extensively documented facts about police work is that the police under-enforce certain laws and jealously protect the discretion which that implies' (1976, p. 113). Both these aspects have contributed to wide variations in police recording practice between forces. As the Home Office Statistical Department has stated, 'variations are bound to exist in recording practices between forces', and as long as police discretion allows officers to decide (a) whether a crime has been committed and (b) what charge is the most appropriate, wide differences between police forces will persist. But the differences in the recording of spousal violence present a unique and peculiar distortion of crime statistics. Crimes where the complainant has a good reason not to prosecute result in the greatest degree of distortion. Arguably, any crime where the victim fears retaliation is prone to a high rate of withdrawal of the original complaint – for example, rape and racial attack (Chambers and Millar, 1986). However, the greater the degree of relationship between the victim and offender, the greater the likelihood of withdrawl of the complaint, especially if they are co-resident, and the greater the police predilection for avoiding paperwork at the report stage or else, once the incident is recorded and crimed, for erasing the crime at a later date. This problem of 'cuffing' has been noted in the United Kingdom and the United States, where officers may decide not to record an incident at all. Skolnick (1966, p. 171) found that even when a domestic offence had occurred, the patrolman (usually with the advice of his sergeant) may decide not to write it up as a crime, even if the offence appears serious. Skolnick explains that typically a 'no offence' report is made out for incidents where the matter is 'within the family' and where typically there is no complainant. Such events are routinely diverted out of the criminal justice process with the compliance of patrolmen who record them in assignment reports (equivalent to Incident Book reports in the Metropolitan Police Area) and not in crime reports.

Once recorded as a crime, an offence may later be erased from record. This practice of 'no criming' is a legitimate classification, although it is not always used legitimately. The legitimate use is explained by a mistaken recording at the initial stage, where a crime has not in fact been committed – say the case of the 'stolen' pedal cycle which turns out to have been borrowed and later returned. (Another legitimate use is where a case is transferred to another police jurisdiction and appears in their records, so that it must be erased in the originating jurisdiction to avoid double-counting.) The 'no crime', however, is used most typically in crimes where the complainant no longer wishes to give evidence, thereby weakening the prosecution case where no other witnesses are present. McCabe and Sutcliffe (1978), Steer (1981), Sanders (1988) and Edwards (1986b, 1989a) have found that it is male violence against female partners or ex-partners which is more prone than any other crime category to the application of this 'no crime' classification. Edwards (1989a) found that wife violence cases were more 'withdrawn-prone' than other cases of personal violence and subsequently more likely to result in a 'no crime' classification. In addition, present cohabitation with the aggressor seemed to be the overriding factor influencing a victim's decision not to press charges and the subsequent police decision to assign a 'no crime' result. This use of the 'no crime' classification has an especially great impact on variations in policing figures on spousal violence between forces. It is the persistent use of the category which deprives official figures on reported violence of any claim to accuracy. The use of the 'no crime' discriminates particularly against women, since spousal violence cases prone to this practice overwhelmingly involve the commission of violence by males against female spouses. In addition to poor recording practices, the police attitude to this kind of work is usually to regard it as 'not real police work' (Reiner, 1985). Domestic disputes were considered otherwise normal arguments which had gone over the top, so the police role was to calm the situation down. Few officers considered arrest ever appropriate, and even where it was considered appropriate they still did not arrest. Many officers saw 'criming' as a complete waste of time, since women almost always withdrew charges later. As one male officer explained:

> A husband and wife case is treated exactly the same as any other assault. But with hindsight in my experience they lead to great difficulties due to the charge being dropped. You always have this on your mind when you go to a case. It doesn't prejudice you at the time, you treat it as any other assault, but if they won't persue the matter, you have to drop it. If you were walking in the street and someone smashed you in the eye, I would arrest. If you were walking in the street and husband hit you, I wouldn't.

CHANGING POLICE POLICY AND PRACTICE

Clearly, such findings on police attitudes and the disposition of domestic violence cases have indicated the urgent need for reform in policing practice. Developments in North America have taken the lead in changing policing policy. Over the last few years the police in the United States have been improving training programmes, reviewing policy and emphasising arrest. Policing policy reform together with legislative measures have emerged following research studies commissioned by the American Police Foundation among others. An American Police Foundation study published in 1976 established that men who seriously assaulted wives/cohabitees, or else were responsible for their murder, were already known to the police for such violence in the past. This major finding provided the mandate for more rigorous police intervention at the onset of incidents. It was discovered that intervention at an early stage could interrupt the escalating chain of violence the authors had uncovered as the norm in serious spousal assault and homicide. Following this and similar studies (see Jolin, 1983) it became generally accepted that police intervention at the onset could significantly deter repeated abuse and homicide.

The American Police Foundation study was unable to point to whether one particular form of police response was more effective than any other. It was to an analysis of this precise problem that Sherman and Berk (1986) turned in their study of policing spousal abuse in Minneapolis in 1981. The research design tested the efficacy of three responses to simple domestic assault: (i) arresting suspects, (ii) ordering suspects to leave for eight hours, or (iii) providing information and advice to the persons involved. The responses were randomly assigned, and their effectiveness assessed by monitoring offenders' subsequent conduct months later. Victims were also interviewed. In short, Sherman and Berk found that of a sample of 252 suspects, those who had been arrested were the least likely to abuse again compared with those who were ordered to leave the home or those who were merely advised. In only 10 per cent of cases where an arrest was made was there a recurrence of violence; violence recurred in 19 per cent of cases where the police had offered advice and in 24 per cent of cases where the police had told the suspect to leave. Of the 136 persons arrested only three were formally prosecuted. The authors concluded that 'booking has a bite', although, since most of the suspects arrested were kept in custody overnight, it is more likely that the subsequent detention – rather than the arrest *per se* – was what had the salutary effect. Sherman and Berk conceded that where a suspect was released shortly after arrest the deterrent effect might be reduced.

The Ontario Experiment in Canada set out to evaluate the effectiveness of the introduction of a new policing policy on reporting, criming and prosecution. In May 1981 the London Police Force in Ontario introduced a new policy requiring officers to press criminal charges in cases of wife assault. Jaffe *et al.* (1986) assessed the impact of the new Ontario policy. One year prior to the policy implementation (1979) police laid charges in 12 cases, wives laid charges in 92 cases, resulting in a total of 104 prosecutions arising out of 444 reported cases. Public reporting did not increase after the introduction of the new policy (there were 443 cases in 1983), but the proportion of reported cases resulting in prosecutions rose from 23 per cent in 1979 to 72 per cent in 1983. The police were much more likely to press charges where complainants supported such action, however, and in only nine per cent of cases did police press charges where the victim was reluctant to proceed and had subsequently withdrawn the allegation. A major finding was that when the police rather than the victim laid the charges, victims reported a reduction in or termination of the violence, and even in cases where victims were reluctant to prosecute a reduction in repeated violence was reported if the police preferred changes.

In Europe, police forces have also considered revisions to contemporary policy and practice. This revision has been generated by the impact of the feminist campaign and debate. Hedy d'Ancona, the Dutch socialist member of the European Parliament, demanded in a report to the Parliament entitled *Violence Against Wives* the provision of shelters for battered wives and urgent support for them including an improvement in current policing practice. D'Ancona argued that the present lack of regard for victims of domestic violence is incongruous with other legislation and in breach of Articles 100 and 235 of the Treaty of Rome (1957) and abrogates the Universal Declaration of Human Rights. D'Ancona's resolution was adopted by 197 votes to 66, with 50 abstentions, calling for (i) better training of police officers to deal with violence, (ii) detailed statistical records to be kept of all crimes of violence against women, (iii) refuges to be made available to women (Steinmetz and van Andel, 1986). Consequently, police organisations throughout Europe are currently revising policy and training with regard to the problem of spousal violence.

In April 1987 the Danish Association of Chiefs of Police set up a working party to investigate problems in the policing of domestic disputes. Three issues guided the working party. First, it examined the police response to domestic violence and criminal prosecution. Second, it examined the current working and application of the Danish Criminal Law (Penal Code), s. 265, which applies to the use of injunctions, and third it explored police cooperation with other social agencies. The following recommendations were made: a greater consistency in reporting and recording of domestic incidents; a greater consistency in decisions to initiate prosecution; a transfer of the onus to charge from the victim to the police; where criminal proceedings are initiated, that punishment should be more onerous, with a condition of treatment attached in some cases; that the use of custodial remand should be considered to ensure the protection of the victim; and improved cooperation between police and other agencies.

CHANGING POLICE POLICY AND PRACTICE IN ENGLAND AND WALES

Policing policy and practice must be seen in the context of the legal constraints binding police conduct and current developments in legislation. The major problem at present is that the introduction of new policing policy together with the new compellability provision in the Police and Criminal Evidence Act 1984 (Pt 8, s.80) is obstructed by later legislation. Especially significant in this respect is the Prosecution of Offences Act 1985, which established the Crown Prosecution Service, including the criteria for prosecution declared in the Act and especially s.23, which allows for the discontinuation of cases.

Following the American initiatives already detailed, in 1984 the Metropolitan Police set up their own internal working party on domestic violence, composed of seven officers from the Metropolitan Police and five outsiders – three representatives from Islington Social Services Department and two from COPE (a training consultancy for community group skills). Two years later they produced a final report on the state of policing, with some proposals for change. The recommendations contained in the report indicated the need to consider a series of changes with regard to statistics, policy, training, victim support, and information provision. The report indicated that the main classifications for identifying domestic cases – which are 'disturbance', 'assault' and 'criminal damage' – did not indicate the seriousness or the nature of the offence. The 'disturbance' category in particular seemed to be used almost invariably to identify any incident, including those involving violence between partners. The proposals also indicated the need for more detail about the relationship of victim to offender to be included in crime reports, and a system for the more effective retrieval of other police records relating to the same incident, including Incident Book reports and injunctions. With regard to police policy, consideration should be given to the implementation of the new legislation and, in the event of sufficient evidence of assault, guidelines on conducting a prosecution even when the witness is hostile. An emphasis was also placed on training, with a view to challenging entrenched attitudes. This was to be conducted at all levels – recruits, inspectors, management. With regard to victim support, the report stressed that all efforts should be made to establish a multi-agency approach, effectively facilitated by single referral points between police and supportive agencies. Finally, internal publicity should be given to prioritise domestic violence as an area of police work in order that its status in policing might be enhanced.

On 24 June 1987, the Metropolitan Police announced new guidelines to London's police on how to handle incidents involving domestic violence and disputes. Commander Walter Boreham of the Community Relations Branch said, 'Nothing is more insidious than the circumstances of a woman subjected to violence in the place where she expects to be safe – her own home. We have been carefully looking at this issue for some time now, and our new policy is designed to tackle the problem.' The Metropolitan Police also extended their working definition of violence to include threats and attempts: 'A domestic dispute is defined as any quarrel including violence between family or members of the same household. Domestic violence occurs when a person or persons causes, attempts to cause or threatens to cause physical harm to another family or household member' (Metropolitan Police Press Notice, 199/87).

THE LEGISLATIVE FRAMEWORK

In 1984 the Police and Criminal Evidence Act (Pt 8, s. 80) made spouses legally compellable. This means that legal wives are compellable to give evidence against physically abusive husbands. This provision promises to revolutionise the success of the prosecution of physically abusive husbands and, in theory at least, has the potential for influencing police to report cases even where the witness is reluctant to give evidence. It also has the potential for affecting the decision of the Crown Prosecutor, since if the complainant is reluctant to testify the prosecutor can compel her to do so. This legislation places a spouse on exactly the same footing as any other witness with regard to giving evidence for the prosecution. (Indeed, the wife is now placed in the same position as a cohabitee.) The removal of the unique treatment of the spouse in such cases is very important and serves to convey the message to police officers and those working within the criminal justice process that domestic assault committed against a wife is not different from other violent assaults. However, as far as is known there have so far been no cases where the compellability provision has been used in the courts.

With the introduction of the Crown Prosecution Service (CPS) in 1986, following the implementation of the compellability provision, the effects of compellability in practice might be compromised not only by police officers' discretion in such matters but also by the demands made upon Crown Prosecutors in consideration of the criteria for prosecution. The function of the CPS is to assess, *inter alia*, the strength of evidence in a given case, the likelihood of conviction, together with the degree of public interest involved and the credibility of the victim or witness. Here the overriding imperative of the CPS is to bring successful prosecutions, and where a witness although compellable may in fact be hostile and therefore not convincing before a jury the CPs are more than likely to discontinue proceedings. In addition, in the event of a guilty plea, the CPs may also consider a prosecution inappropriate if the likely outcome or sentence is a small fine (see Criminal Justice Act 1988). Proceedings may be discontinued at the outset if a case can be withdrawn, or the prosecution may decide to offer no evidence.

The Criminal Justice Act 1988, s.153, states that the court is to give reasons for granting bail to a person accused of a serious offence. The interpretation of the Bail Act 1976 in these cases has been over-generous, since section 4 (1) states that if there are grounds for believing that an offender might interfere with a witness then bail should be refused.

In March 1989 Michelle Renshaw became famous for refusing to give evidence because of fear of retaliation. Her boyfriend was charged with assault upon her. Her refusal to give evidence was treated as contempt of court and she was imprisoned initially for one week – a decision later overturned on appeal. In most cases where the victim is reluctant to give evidence the prosecution offers no evidence or withdraws the case.

The Criminal Justice Act 1988, s.23, provides for the first time for the admission of statements made to the police as evidence in the absence of witnesses who out of fear do not wish to give oral evidence. The first known case of domestic violence where this provision was used was heard before Southwark Crown Court in July 1989. The offender was convicted on documentary evidence and sentenced to six months' imprisonment. If the Southwark case proves to be a test case, it shows that section 23 may be a refuge for the vulnerable witness.

THE LONDON DOMESTIC VIOLENCE AND POLICING STUDIES

It was against this comparative and legal backdrop that the several studies on domestic violence by the author (1984/5, 1988, and 1989 ongoing) were conducted. The 1984/5 and 1988 studies were conducted in two divisional stations in the Metropolitan Police Area (which has some 70 divisional stations altogether). The first London Domestic Violence and Policing Study, conducted in 1984/5 (Edwards 1986a, 1986b, 1987, 1989a, 1989b) examined in detail 449 domestic incident calls made to the police at Holloway and 324 at Hounslow Police Station. Calls were included in which an argument, dispute or incident of assault or criminal damage involved family members or persons where some degree of intimacy in the past or present was evident. Worden and Pollitz's definition best sums up the field of enquiry: 'Domestic disturbances include disturbances in which principals were adults involved in heterosexual "romantic" or conjugal relationship prior to or at the time of the incident, involving not only physical violence and the threat of violence, but also property damage and verbal arguments' (1984, p. 107).

Police records were consulted at Holloway Police Station from August 1984 to January 1984. Of the 449 calls for assistance made by the public either via the 999 emergency services or direct to the station, 75 per cent were made by victim complainers and 25 per cent by neighbours or bystanders. The majority of incidents reported (85 per cent) involved spouses, cohabitees, girl/boyfriends, ex-spouses, ex-cohabitees or ex-girl/boyfriends. (The remaining 15 per cent involved brothers/sister, parents and children.) In 98 per cent of all incidents men were the offending parties; in the remaining 2 per cent, where women were the principal suspects, there was counter-allegations. Police attended all the 449 calls recorded and dealt with the majority (81 per cent) either at the scene or at the station following a complaint made in person. In all these 363 cases, officers gave advice about other remedies available to resolve the situation, referring parties to social service agencies or marriage guidance or else to legal remedies. In 40 of the cases, officers completed a further Incident Book entry (involving the completion of a report for internal police reference). The grounds distinguishing between a case to be written up in the Incident Book and one suitable for a Crime Report were not altogether clear. It was not always that the cases in Crime Reports were more serious in nature than cases recorded in Incident Book reports (IRBs). Consider, for example, that in 29 cases, or 72.5 per cent of cases recorded in IRBs, physical assault was evident, including bruising, cuts, swellings following choking, punching or the use of a weapon. Nevertheless these cases were recorded as common assaults (s.42 of the 1861 Act) rather than assaults occasioning actual bodily harm (s.47). Finally, a total of 57 cases out of 449 were recorded on Crime Sheets as 'assaults occasioning actual bodily harm'. A total of 37 cases were recorded as Beat Crimes (lesser offences) and 20 cases as Major Crimes. In both Beat and Major Crimes physical assault was alleged by the complainant, and evidence of its commission clearly satisfied both reporting and investigating officers. The difference between cases involving physical assault which resulted in an IRB and those which resulted in a Crime Report could not be established on the grounds of objective physical criteria alone; other factors intervened, such as the complainant's reluctance to press charges, or other remedies being currently pursued (for example, injunction, divorce/separation). Of the 37 cases crimed, only 11 proceeded to the prosecution stage. Of these 11, only eight were heard in the magistrates' or Crown Court.

In the Hounslow District (which also covers Feltham) a total of 324 incidents were reported to the police during a six-monthy period. Again victim complainants reported the incident in 75 per cent of cases and neighbours/bystanders in 25 per cent. A total of 89 per cent of cases were 'spousal' in accordance with the definition cited earlier. Of all calls attended, 229 (86 per cent) were dealt with either at the scene or at the front counter. Of these, a total of 33 incidents were further recorded in IRBs. Again as at Holloway, 57 per cent of IRBs involved cases where physical assault had occurred and where it was of a degree and nature similar to other cases which were crimed. A total of 36 cases were crimed, recorded either as Beat Crimes or Major Crimes. A total of 86 per cent of both Beat Crimes and Major Crimes were finally classified as 'no crime', and proceedings were formally instigated in the remaining five cases, four resulting in court appearances.

In 1988 an evaluation study was funded by the Police Foundation. The purpose was to discover how far the Force Order was being implemented, to evaluate any year-on-year change in reporting, recording and prosecution practice, and to examine how far the policy was responsible for any change detected.

It is important to emphasise certain problems in the research design. First, the recording and prosecution of domestic assaults were not compared with non-domestic assaults. Second, given the nature of police recording practices, some cases may have been lost from the original sample. Third, while a year-on-year profile was investigable for most records, this was not possible for 'at the scene' arrests, were data were not retrievable in 1984/5. Fourth, in the later study cases reported and direct arrests were derived from the Computer Aided Despatch system (CAD) rather than from station message pads, the source in the 1984/5 study.

At Holloway during a six-month period (March to August 1988), a total of 732 domestic incident calls were made. Of these, 25 per cent (180) were further recorded as crimes. Arrests, including direct 'at the scene' arrests and arrests resulting from enquiries, were executed in 14 per cent of all reported incidents. To put it another way, there were 41 arrests made where crime reports were instigated, constituting 23 per cent of all cases crimed. A total of 24 cases were finally reported for prosecution. This meant that in only 59 per cent of the cases where a result-of-enquiry arrest was made did a prosecution follow. Prosecutions constituted only 13 per cent of all cases initially crimed. Finally, 65 per cent of all cases crimed resulted in a 'no crime' classification.

At Hounslow during the same six-month period a total of 633 domestic incident calls were made. Of these, 103 or 16 per cent were further recorded as crimes. Arrests, including at-the-scene arrests and arrests resulting from enquiries were executed in 22 per cent of all reported incidents. In other words, there were 32 arrests made where crime reports were instigated, constituting 31 per cent of all cases crimed. A total of 22 cases were finally reported for prosecution. This meant that in only 69 per cent of the cases where a result-of-enquiry arrest was made did a prosecution follow. Prosecutions constituted only 21 per cent of all cases originally crimed. Finally, 63 per cent of all cases crimed resulted in a 'no crime' classification.

Where a 'no-crime' was recorded, the majority of these classifications arose because the complainant decided that she did not want to give evidence in court against her aggressor. This resulted in women withdrawing a prosecution and the police recording this decision as a withdrawal of the allegation, which of course is not strictly what the women intended. The 'no crime' classification was also used legitimately where cases were transferred to other stations and thus included in crime figures there. Excluding this legitimate use of the 'no crime' reduces the overall rate of 'no criming' to 56 per cent of all crimes initially recorded at the Hounslow station.

Examining both locations, it is clear that force policy has made a significant impact on the reporting, recording and criming of cases and on 'no crimes' (see Tables 8.1 and 8.2). At Holloway there was a 63 per cent increase in the number of cases reported, and an

Table 8.1 Evaluating police policy on domestic incidents – Holloway

	Number of incidents	Crimes as a % of incidents	Arrests as a % of incidents	Cases reported for prosecution as a % of crimes initially recorded	No crimes as a % of crimes	IRBs
1984–5 Aug–Jan	449	13 (57)	2 (11)	19 (11)	81 (46)	40
1988 Mar–Aug	732	∧25 (180)	∧14 (41)* (63)†	∨13 (24)	∨65 (118)	119

Key * result of enquiries arrest only
† direct arrest
( ) Showing the mortality of cases as a proportion of incidents and crimes in a given year

Table 8.2 Evaluating police policy on domestic incidents – Hounslow

	Number of incidents	Crimes as a % of incidents	Arrests as a % of incidents	Cases reported for prosecution as a % of crimes initially recorded	No crimes as a % of crimes	IRBs
1984–5 Aug–Jan	324	11 (36)	2 (5)	14 (5)	86 (31)	33
1988 Mar–Aug	633	ˆ16 (103)	ˆ22 (32)* (99)†	ˇ21 (22)	ˇ61 (63)	177

Key * result of enquiries arrest only
† direct arrest
( ) Showing the mortality of cases as a proportion of incidents and crimes in a given year

increase of 95 per cent at Hounslow. The number of crimes recorded was up by 215 per cent in Holloway and 186 per cent in Hounslow. It is not possible to say how the totals of arrests made changed, but result-of-enquiry arrests at Holloway went up by 272 per cent, and at Hounslow by 540 per cent. Cases reported for prosecution as a percentage of crimes initially recorded increased at Holloway by 118 per cent and at Hounslow by 340 per cent. However, statistics can sometimes be misleading, and while here we are concerned with the numerical increase in 1988 over 1984/5, criminal cases reported for prosecution increased only marginally at Hounslow as a proportion of all crimes initially recorded, and they actually fell at Holloway (see Tables 8.1 and 8.2).

While the force order is obviously having an impact on the public reporting and police recording practices, force policy is having very little effect on the final prosecution of cases. Given the significant increase in recording, criming and the use of arrests, prosecutions should follow in a far higher proportion of cases, and certainly in those cases where suspects were arrested. Where an arrest was made in respect of a crime, the low prosecution of these cases is due to the police decision not to report for prosecution and to prosecutors discontinuing cases.

It can be said, however, that in looking at the two profiles, officers at Hounslow are much more likely to make a direct arrest at the scene for breach of peace etc. than are officers at Holloway, and more likely to make an arrest overall. Officers at Hounslow are less likely to crime incidents and more likely to prosecute. The two stations have an almost equal record for use of the 'no crime'. Why Hounslow should be more eager to arrest, less eager to crime incidents initially and more likely to prosecute will be explored in a more detailed analysis of the findings. Prosecution of spousal offenders is not the only goal of the force order, but certainly where an arrest has been made such cases should go on to the prosecution stage. In addition, the stringent requirements of the CPS need to be examined closely, if the CPS is not to have a countervailing effect on the impact of the force order.

However, the differences between the two stations do not belie the general trend towards an improvement in recording practices. It is also to be noted that other stations' records examined at Streatham in 1988 and 1989 by the author and colleagues, while demonstrating the same general trend, again reveal individual differences. Edwards (1988) found that in 29 per cent of all cases of physical assaults against spouses/partners recorded at two London police divisional stations in 1988, the victim and suspect lived separately but had previously been involved in an intimate relationship. Furthermore, unpublished figures from Streatham Divisional Station in 1989 reveal that 52 per cent of physical assaults recorded involved couples residing separately. The difference in recording practices and case mortality at each of the locations may be a function of the differences of individual cases, or it may also be an artifact of policing.

CONCLUSIONS

Implementation of any new policy is as good as its communicators and implementers. At both stations senior officers were keen for the new policy to be implemented by patrol officers attending calls. The impact of the policy, however, was also shaped by priorities and goals of individual stations as much as by the discretion of individual officers. Following Police Order 11, individual police stations then issued their own instructions complying with the Order. At Holloway, supervising officers were called upon to report fully all such cases, and a tagged CAD report was made of each case (instruction of 25 June 1987). A further instruction was issued on 22 September which indicated that where arrests were not effected victims would be conveyed to a place of safety if they so wished. While emphasising that various arrangements could be made for the victim, the instruction stressed that the action should remain a matter of personal choice. Where victims chose to remain on the premises, follow-up visits were seen as a vital means of ensuring their future safety. Victims were asked whether they would like a Home Beat officer to visit at some later date. At Hounslow the problem of domestic violence was identified as one of the divisional goals for 1988. Here one woman sergeant and a woman police constable have set up a domestic assault unit where they are responsible for monitoring all incidents where violence, threat of violence or attempted violence in the home or between intimates is taking place, and for conducting follow-up visits. A tagging system on CAD was introduced in March 1987 so that incidents could more easily be identified. Home Beat officers together with the women officers from the domestic violence unit take on the responsibility of follow-up visits, and women are not merely assisted in filling up a summons but encouraged to take steps towards their own future protection. The Hounslow Community

Police Consultative Group has also identified the need for closer cooperation between the various agencies, and a Domestic Violence Working Group has been set up in conjunction with the local authority (Hounslow Divisional Report, 1988).

All these local initiatives have their impact on translating police policy into local practice. It is the job of academics, researchers and all who are concerned about protecting women victims and making police accountable to ensure that the deconstruction of the conventional orthodoxy continues and that policy-makers and implementers continue to maintain the present climate of awareness about this very grave social issue.

9 Penetrating Women's Bodies: The Problem of Law and Medical Technology
Carol Smart

INTRODUCTION

Women's bodies are a site of contested meanings. Feminist research has documented the extent to which women's bodies have been a focus of power struggles, but in this paper I want to build on these insights and ultimately to concentrate more on the question of how meanings are reproduced and sustained. We know, for example, that the medical profession has striven, with some success, to exercise what is now regarded by many as legitimate control over women's bodies (e.g., hospital rather than home births). We perhaps focus less on the meanings that have been produced in the process of exercising this control. Arguably we have paid less attention than we should to the production of deeply-held views about diseased, contagious and sexualised bodies and malfunctioning reproductive organs, all of which come in part to symbolise women – and even enter into women's consciousness.

In this paper I am interested in exploring how women's bodies have come to act as signifiers of negative attributes in the field of law. So I shall look at instances of the production of iconographies of negative difference with regard to the female body in legal discourse. It is of course essential to recognise the extent to which law and medicine interweave in this project, law often becoming extremely dependent upon medical discourse to fashion its own mode of regulation and imagery. However, I do not intend to look into origins. I am not suggesting that it all begins with law/medicine in the nineteenth century (which is my point of departure) because we know that misogynistic views of women's bodies predate this period. Indeed they are integral to a wide range of different cultural and religious beliefs. However, I want to begin to unravel the importance of the signification of women's bodies in law for contemporary feminism and I cannot do this without raising some historical pointers whilst necessarily avoiding a deeper historical analysis here.

I propose to explore a number of areas in which law has very specific things to say about women's bodies. However, first I need to consider two issues. The first is the significance of language structures to the understanding of difference and dominance. The second is the special place of law in the disqualification of alternative discourses like feminism. Basically I am interested in the power of law to define issues in a way contrary to feminist interests, but in addition to have its version of events given maximum credibility.

LANGUAGE: DIFFERENCE AND DOMINANCE

In this huge subject I only wish to highlight a few basic points. Feminism has consistently pointed to the place of language in women's oppression (Spender, 1980; Miller and Swift, 1980). However, as Cameron (1986) and Weedon (1987) have argued, the dominant feminist approach has been in the liberal humanist tradition. That is to say it has been assumed that language and reality are two separate entities, with language describing or representing the real. The main feminist critique is that the real has been misrepresented or misdescribed, rendering women invisible or attributing to women undesirable attributes. However, more recent feminist work has begun to explore language in terms of the construction of subjectivity (Cameron, 1985). This has led to a denial of the fixity of meaning. We are no longer positing a feminist truth against a patriarchal lie, but acknowledging how meaning has been produced (through language) and offering alternative meanings. It is the political potential of challenging meaning which has become recognised as crucial to the feminist project (one example being the challenge of the meaning of pornography).

If we consider the role of language in the production of meaning we need also to consider how language reproduces meanings of difference and domination. This has been identified in the basic linguistic structures of binary opposites. It is argued that nothing has an intrinsic meaning; we understand the meaning of a thing in relation to its constructed opposite. Hence we operate a binary system of meanings of which core concepts are culture/nature, man/woman, good/bad, mind/body, masculine/feminine, rational/emotional, objective/subjective. As feminists (Harding, 1986) and others (Cousins, 1986) have pointed out, these are not just indicators of difference, but a process by which positive or negative evaluation is attributed to each side of the oppositional poles. Hence culture, man, mind, rationality, objectivity and masculinity become associated with the good and desirable, whilst nature, woman, body, emotionality, subjectivity and femininity are associated with the bad. In entering the world of symbolic meanings we come to know that less value is attached to one side of the binary division.

These points are perhaps now very familiar in feminist scholarship; however, we are yet to follow through with more detailed work on how this system of meanings operates within different discourses. I shall now turn to consider legal discourse.

THE POWER OF LEGAL DISCOURSE

In this section I wish to use concepts which derive from the work of Foucault (Gordon, 1980). I am particularly interested in his discussion of the relationship between truth and power. First Foucault separates his meaning of truth from an idea of absolute or 'real' Truth. He states:

> by truth I do not mean the ensemble of truths which are to be discovered and accepted, but rather the ensemble of rules according to which the true and the false are separated and specific effects of power attached to the true. (Gordon, 1980, p. 132)

He goes on to state:

> 'Truth' is to be understood as a system of ordered procedures for the production, regulation, distribution, circulation, and operation of statements ... 'Truth' is linked in a circular relation with systems of power which produce and sustain it, and to effects of power which it induces and which extend it. A 'regime' of truth. (Gordon, 1980, p. 133)

I wish to argue that law is its own regime of truth, one which dominates and excludes alternative accounts based on different systems of knowledge. In turn law's claim to truth plays a major political and cultural part in forms of regulation which are detrimental to the lives of women (in their multiplicity).

Feminist scholarship in the field of law has recently turned its gaze to legal method and jurisprudence (Thornton, 1986, 1989; MacKinnon, 1987; Mossman, 1986; Bottomley, 1987; Smart, 1989). This interest grew out of an awareness that changing the content of law was not enough to achieve feminist aims. There is a parallel to developments in sociology here. As feminists within the discipline began to argue that women were excluded, they also began to realise that it was not enough to add women into the existing regime of knowledge, using the same tools, retaining the same framework etc. (Smith, 1974; Roberts, 1981, Harding, 1987). Feminist legal scholars have recognised this too. Catharine MacKinnon perhaps makes this most forcefully in the following passage:

> When [the state] is most ruthlessly neutral, it will be most male; when it is most sex blind, it will be most blind to the sex of the standard being applied . . . Once masculinity appears as a specific position, not just as the way things are, its judgements will be revealed in process and procedure, as well as adjudication and legislation. (MacKinnon, 1983, p. 658)

Margaret Thornton (1986) has referrred to the androcentric standard in law. This is a standard which applies not only to judgments (example of rape and incest cases are perhaps paramount here) but also in the very construction of what constitutes legal knowledge. It is here that the work of Mary Jane Mossman (1986) on traditional legal method is useful. She identifies three main elements in the construction of legal knowledge/truth; these are boundary definition, the definition of 'relevance', and case analysis. The first, boundary definition, is the process by which certain matters are identified as outside the realm of law, i.e. they may be defined as political or moral. The importance of this is not where the boundaries are drawn, but the way in which the drawing of boundaries confers neutrality on law. Hence judges are able to argue that it is their job to interpret the law, not to become enmeshed with politics etc. In so doing they can point to the boundaries which law creates and, in so doing, gain credibility. This works in two directions. It retains law as a field in which politics (i.e. feminism) should not be allowed to enter, and it appears to keep law out of subjectivity.

It is perhaps important to state at this stage that we know perfectly well that the boundary is not 'real'. I am most emphatically not trying to argue that law really does what it says it does, nor am I arguing that it says one thing but 'really' does another, and that I know the reality of law. That work has been done many times over (Griffith, 1977; Sachs and Wilson, 1978). I am however arguing that it is part of law's claim to truth; it is part of the regime of truth to which law makes claim. In so doing law positions itself in a political hierarchy and is better able to silence alternative discourses.

The second element identified by Mossman is the definition of relevance. Every law student learns what is relevant to particular cases. Hence what may be relevant to individuals involved in disputes is not relevant to law. This issue is not in itself solely one of gender, but it may have specific gender implications in certain types of cases. Again rape is a good example. A women's sexual history is relevant to a rape case and must be investigated (in spite of the 1976 Sexual Offences (Amendment) Act; see Adler, 1987); the accused's however is not. So when feminists complain about this process it is perhaps not enough to point to its oppressive nature in specific cases, but to consider how law can only 'hear' what is already defined as relevant to its interests.

The third element is case analysis or the rules of precedent. The study of previous cases is said to reveal an inexorable legal logic which always, ultimately, leads the good lawyer to the correct decision. Only the trained legal mind can fathom this logic and will know which cases are good law, and which are bad. The main point is that the accumulated history of individual legal decisions will throw up the answer to new legal conundrums. Again it is hardly necessary to refute this any more (see Sumner, 1979). The point is that these three elements go to make up what is called legal method, which in turn successfully separates law from other systems of knowledge. Arguably it also constitutes law's claim to truth and hence the power of law to disqualify alternative accounts.

This last point is important because, whilst we might make the same claims for sociological knowledge, legal knowledge is already part of the structure and institutions of the state. To put it simply, the law is more powerful; it is also far more resistant to any challenges made to the credibility of its claim to truth. Where feminist scholarship is concerned this means that law is far more resilient to its attempts to deconstruct legal method (one major exception being the Institute of Women's Law in Oslo; see Dahl, 1987).

It might be useful at this stage if I construct an example which combines the points I have made about meanings and systems of knowledge, and legal method.

THE POWER TO DISQUALIFY

The rape trial distils and epitomises all of the problems that feminists have identified in relation to law. It is here we find the problem of legal method, the problem of the 'maleness' of law (as identified by MacKinnon, 1983) and the power of law to impose its view on individual actors as well as on a wider audience in terms of cultural meanings. It is also where women's bodies become the primary site of conflict over definitions. The rape trial is a quintessential moment in which law provides a specific meaning to women's bodies, reproducing cultural beliefs about female sexuality, but also constructing its own legal lexicon of the female body and rehearsing its own very powerful mode of disqualification.

There is not space here to detail feminist work on female sexuality and the challenge to cultural stereotypes (see Suleiman, 1986; Caplan, 1987; Haug, 1987; Mitchell, 1974). I am, therefore, taking for granted a position which discounts naturalism and focuses expressly on the ways in which the female body has become saturated with (hetero)sex; has come to mean (hetero)sex. Bits of women's bodies have become encoded with quite specific meanings whilst, at the same time, women have been constructed as having a relationship to their sexuality which presumes (i) an objective, separate entity outside consciousness, (ii) with which they have not yet come to terms. What is interesting here is not whether women's bodies have been sexualised whilst men's have not (implying therefore that equal treatment would be the solution), but the way in which women's sexualised bodies are a point of entry for specific cultural values. Women's bodies carry a heavy burden in this respect. They are the site of sex, but also reproduction. Yet it would seem that women themselves are regarded as poor caretakers of what is most valuable – because women are the ones who are emotional, subjective, unreliable, impulsive etc. There is therefore a regime of meaning through which we construct female sexuality as naturally perverse and capricious.

Onto this foundation law projects its own narrow focus. The rape trial is interested in innocence and guilt (beyond all reasonable doubt), consent and non-consent, intent and lack of intent (*mens rea*). The core element would seem to be the issue of consent/non-consent. If a women consents there is no rape. But the state of mind of the woman is read in terms of a general understanding of the emotionality, subjectivity, and capriciousness of women in matters of sex. This is of course, not a particularly new insight so I want to add another dimension to this understanding. I have suggested that women's bodies are sexualised and that in a phallocentric culture women's sexuality and sexual pleasure remains something of a mystery. Because women are seen as out of touch with their sexuality they are regarded as unreliable witnesses in relation to their own feelings. This goes further than the consent/non-consent issue because pleasure is construed as even more subjective than consent. So whilst we presume the rape trial is about proving consent, at another level it is about pleasure. Moreover this pleasure is located within the female body which is always already constructed as mysterious, foreign and not amenable to rational argument. The question of pleasure need not be addressed directly – indeed its influence lies in its taken-for-grantedness. Precisely because it is so commonplace that women's bodies are capricious, law need not make an issue of it in the routine management of rape and sexual assault.

But the problem of pleasure is not just one of whether it can be established or not. Rather it poses the problem of trying to define what is not pleasure in the field of sex. Since activities which some might find repellent can be defined as someone else's perverted pleasure how can we ever be certain pleasure was not achieved?

It might be useful to consider the issues schematically:

innocence	guilt
lack of intent	intent
consent	non-consent
pleasure	?

In this scheme we can see that at least if non-consent can be shown there is a possibility of establishing guilt. However if we have no category of non-pleasure in the field of sex, then the imputation of pleasure always has the potential to undermine a women's version of events. The question which remains however, is how, within the specific parameters of the rape trial, women find it so difficult to disassociate themselves from the presumption of sexual pleasure. This inability would seem to materialise through a process of reducing women to bits of their bodies, or more correctly their sexual parts, in the recounting of the rape event.

Anna Clark (1987) has described how the evidence of assaulted women in rape trials has been treated since the eighteenth century. She points to the basic contradiction between the requirement for a woman to speak of her assault in public, and the shamefulness attached to any woman who could speak of such things in public. Moreover, she indicates that as the trial has become more forensic in nature, women have been required to tell in greater and greater detail. In the 1980s a woman may not experience the same mechanisms of shame experienced by the woman in the 1780s or 1880s; however, in the telling of her story which she must undertake in open court, she inevitably draws attention to her sexualised body which becomes a spectacle, the main focus of the trial (see MacKinnon, 1987). The more she becomes the sexualised part of her body, the more she can be discounted. In the context of the rape trial the women's body, on which all attention is focused, becomes both the site of the alleged offence and a *conduit of disqualification*. In speaking of her parts we are reminded of the capriciousness of women in sexual matters; her closeness to nature and her mendacity and irrationality are implied. It is her body which is presumed to reveal the truth of the event (despite the woman herself). How was it clothed, did she have an orgasm, did she cry, did she make noises of pleasure? It is her body that engendered the desire which was then enacted upon it. Thus the dilemma is constructed: as women are presumed not to know their own minds in relation to sex, can there ever be certainty that this particular body did not experience pleasure even if the woman herself cannot admit to it? The woman is split into three parts, her mind, her body and her sexuality. Her sexuality is locked inside her body, but her mind is locked out. If we focus on the body (as happens in the trial) it may be possible to find evidence of sexual pleasure; her mind is in any case unreliable. The words she speaks therefore operate at a number of levels. She gives a legally acceptable account of the rape, this is her story strained through the requirements of the law. At the same time she speaks 'pornographically' (MacKinnon, 1987) of vaginas, penises, breasts and buttocks and where and how they made contact. Simultaneously she invokes the unknown (unknowable?) quality of woman's sexuality and sexual response, of irrational desires and subterranean, perverse pleasures.

In entering the rape trial the woman's body becomes the focus of the legal event but, when spoken of, her body disqualifies her as it is cross-examined in the light of legal reasoning and conventional wisdoms. It would be mistaken to take the rape trial out of context however. The disqualification of women in law through the process of associating her with a chaotic or unreliable body is not new, nor is it peculiar to this legal issue. Moreover we cannot assume that the meanings attached to women's bodies are always, and inevitably the same. They may vary according to whether the issue is one of rape, birth, abortion, child custody, illegitimacy and so on. I will elaborate on this in relation to a few key issues which have focused on women's bodies in the nineteenth century and in the contemporary situation.

HISTORICAL PERSPECTIVES ON LAW AND WOMEN'S BODIES

There are a growing number of studies which explore historically the relationship between law and women's bodies (Walkowitz, 1980; S. Edwards, 1981; R. Smith, 1981). Their focus has tended to be on examining how and why women's bodies (in terms of their sexual and reproductive capacities) have constituted a particular mode of regulation in law. These studies are not simply ones that identify a physiological difference and enquire how law treats this difference differently; rather they include analyses of how law constitutes the bodies of women in discourse, and how in turn notions about women's bodies (for example, as diseased, hysterical, immoral) have figured in the construction and practice of law.

In his work on law and insanity Smith (1981) provides an excellent example of this. He argues that concepts of woman and of nature were to some extent interchangeable in scientific discourse in the nineteenth century. Women were closer to nature; were overdetermined by their natures. Hence he maintains that there was a network of correspondences between women, nature, passivity, emotion and irresponsibility. These linkages were dependent upon the presumption of a split between mind and body, rationality and emotion, culture and nature which I discussed above. Because women were endowed with reproductive capacity, it was argued that they remained closer to nature, by extension from this they were also less rational and less morally responsible for their behaviour. Smith develops these arguments in relation to infanticide which was an offence gradually distanced from murder, and which was essentially the legal expression of a medically-determined condition. The condition was puerperal insanity (now post-natal depression). The point Smith makes is that *all* women were deemed to be unstable, but especially so at times of childbirth. Although not all women were deemed to be completely without responsibility (i.e. mad), cases of infanticide have shown how the law has readily abandoned judicial criteria for judging guilt in preference for the medical discourse on insanity (see Allen, 1987). His argument is that the medical discourse was deemed to be more appropriate to women's lives with their menstrual cycles, pregnancies, menopauses, and parturitions. In effect this meant that women became subject to a less punitive penal regime – because of their chaotic reproductive organs. However, it would be a mistake to assume that the scientisation of hysterical and chaotic female bodies in the nineteenth century inevitably led to a benevolent outcome.

Judith Walkowitz's study of prostitution in Victorian England reveals a different outcome. Through an examination of the Contagious Diseases Acts of the 1860s, Walkowitz shows how women's bodies, particularly those of working-class women, came to be regarded as sites of dangerous sexuality. Their danger was not only moral, but also medical in that they were seen as carriers of disease. These views were translated into draconian legislative measures which allowed local magistrates' courts to imprison working-class women in lock hospitals and force punitive medical treatment upon them. The main contribution of this research for an understanding of law, is not that it reveals a double standard, an inequality in the treatment of women and men, but rather that it provides a more profound understanding of how medical knowledge and legal discourse formed an alliance to regulated behaviours which were interpreted as injurious to public and individual health (moral and social). The significance of women's bodies, and the reasons why female rather than male bodies became problematic, are clearly linked to gender domination, but also to the religious discourse of the moral crusades, superstition and medical knowledge about women's reproductive functions, the Victorian association of sex with disgust and guilt and the maintenance of male military morale. Walkowitz therefore reveals a complex and intricate web of associations between class, gender, medicine, law, sexuality and economics.

Edwards' (1981) work on law and sexual offences applies a similar approach to an understanding of the legal construction of, specifically, the female victim and, in general, women's culpability. Her focus differs from Walkowitz's in that she traces the inculcation of medical and commonsensical discourses on women's bodies into the practice of law in the forum of the rape trial. Hence she maps out how law silences women's complaints of sexual abuse and how law goes further to embrace notions of women's culpability in terms of false accusations or in inducing the 'seduction' in the first place. In

Edwards's work, women are their sex in legal discourse. Hence notions about women's frigidity, fantasies, medical disorders, menstrual cycles are what constitute women in trials of sexual assault. She reveals that in this area at least, women were indeed constructed from bits of their bodies. Women were their sexual organs because medical discourse of the nineteenth century, on which the rape trial was heavily dependent, reduced women to their biological function, and this function was perceived as disordered.

We can see that, in these key areas in law, women quite literally became their bodies, they were reduced to their reproductive functions. This is not to argue that women themselves do not acknowledge that their bodies (and changes in their bodies) are significant. But legal and medical discourses have tended to make women little more than their bodily functions and processes, or bits of bodies. Yet it would be an overstatement to argue that women were (and can be) only their bodies or bits of bodies in law. There are areas of law where this reduction of women to anatomical parts has diminished. For example women's bodies are no longer held to be a disqualification for entering professions, or entering into legal contracts. However, the linkage of the concepts women–bodies–nature which operated to deny women's responsibility (they can't help it) whilst ironically discovering them to be culpable (they bring it on themselves), remains a powerful element in the construction of women as legal subjects in the field of criminal law and, as I shall argue below, in the area of reproductive law. Having a female body becomes a *conduit of disqualification*, no less significant because it does not always have the same effect in all areas of law and legal activity.

CONTEMPORARY ISSUES

Historical approaches to this question reveal the centrality of women's bodies to law, but also the significance of law's definition of the nature of women's bodies in a more general sense. But modern law does not necessarily operate in exactly the same way, albeit that nineteenth-century conceptualisations of women's bodies are not entirely exorcised. Hence they may be seen to re-emerge in the modern rape trial, or in defence pleas when counsels raise the issue of Pre-Menstrual Tension (Luckhaus, 1986; Allen, 1984). They are also there when lawyers raise the standard of the reasonable man as a guide to judging behaviour under specific circumstances. Can women, with women's bodies, ever fit the category of reasonable man and if not, does using the standard of the reasonable woman reduce the law to a laughing stock? (Allen, 1988).

These issues remain important but they should not blind us to newer struggles on the site of women's bodies. Modern medical technologies are extending the potential scope of law to penetrate women's bodies and to construct different iconographies and regimes of meaning.

Modern technology has accumulated knowledge about women's bodies and reproductive capacities. Following from this it is now possible to extend legal regulation over the unborn foetus, indeed to protect the foetus against the mother in whose uterus it is developing (Gallagher, 1987). It is also possible to identify the biological parents of children through genetic 'fingerprinting' and hence it becomes possible to impose legal parental duties far more extensively. As technologies have developed, so different functions of the body, or elements of the body, become subject to new forms of legal regulation. For example, women's ova are now a matter of legal debate since they can be removed from one body and placed in another, while men's rights to children are becoming linked to genetic relationships (or simply sperm) rather than relying on legally-established marital ties (Smart, 1987).

Whilst acknowledging that law can extend regulation into more and more intimate areas of the body and private life, we should also acknowledge that the law does not stand in one position. The law does not have a completely unified policy in relation to women or women's bodies. Hence we have coexisting legislation in the UK which, on the one hand legalises medical abortions, and on the other seeks to protect foetal life. Moreover we can see that we have moved from a position where law simply acted punitively in relation to questions of bastardy or abortion, to a state of highly differentiated responses to new fields like adoption, in vitro fertilisation, surrogacy, contraception, AID, and the right of embryos. Some of these responses may appear more liberal than traditional legal strategies, but their power to intervene and inspect the private lives and lifestyles of women should warn us against assuming that these modes are automatically less oppressive because they, for the most part, avoid criminal sanctions. Hence we can see that the development of law is not one of simple linear progress. Rather it is possible to perceive that law has entry into minute aspects of the life of the body and has the potential to regulate women's activities whilst appearing most liberal and benevolent. It is to these issues I shall now turn.

REPRODUCTIVE LAW

There is not an established area of law called Reproductive Law in the UK although there is a growing body of legislation and quasi legislative measures which relate to biological reproduction. Under this heading I would include measures on surrogacy, IVF and related techniques, abortion, illegitimacy, parental rights, foetal rights, infanticide, embryo experimentation, genetic manipulation and some aspects of inheritance laws. It is important to stress that all I am doing here is gathering existing legislation/measures under one heading. I am not attempting to create a new form of law such as Birth Law as promoted by Tove Stang Dahl (1987) in Norway. Dahl's idea of Birth Law is based on a reconceptualisation of the nature of legislation so that it becomes more congruent with the material reality of women's lives and their needs. This is outside the scope of this paper; instead I shall concentrate on the existing situation arising from abortion, IVF and AID. I will attempt to argue that central to the development of legislation in these areas is an implicit understanding of women's bodies (as outlined above) but also the potential for creating new meanings and new conditions for regulation.

As in the field of rape, in the area of reproduction and law women are little more than their bodies or bits of bodies. In this respect law has relied very heavily on medical discourses which have construed women as prisoners of their own wombs. This form of disqualification sits alongside an admittedly diminishing legal form of disqualification of women. By the latter I mean the legal tradition of presuming that women cannot be responsible for their affairs. Hence women have had different legal rights in relation to the guardianship of legitimate children, in terms of disposing of property or the ownership of property, in terms of occupation they could follow and so on. Certainly in terms of formal law women have now reached the status of adulthood, but in the field of reproduction this is constantly threatened by the dominance of the medical model of women in the grip of their hormones. It is also being threatened by a changing definition of motherhood which is emerging from legal conflicts between 'mothers' and 'fathers' over child custody, surrogacy and abortion. This redefinition is challenging the modern twentieth-century legal tenet that mothers generally work for the best interests of their children and are the best caretakers of young children. Although this ideal of motherhood was always susceptible to the spectre of promiscuous sexuality (i.e., the adulterous wife could not be a good mother) this has diminished to be replaced with different kinds of disqualifications. For example the threat of the sexualised body of the mother has changed from the manifestation of heterosexual promiscuity to one of lesbianism. It is not the active heterosexual mother who is deemed to be the most harmful anymore. There are also other developments, or perhaps more correctly 'old' issues are being reappraised in the light of modern developments. The mere fact that women terminate pregnancies, enter into surrogacy arrangements, conceive babies outside their wombs, opt for autonomous motherhood, or try to claim the sole custody of children, has begun to shift the terms of the debate towards one in which mothers become the problem and fathers are redefined as the source of children's welfare. Ideas about women's bodies, and women's relationship to their bodies are crucial to this redefinition. The case of *C* v. *S* (*The Times Law Report*, 25 February 1987) provides an instance of what I mean.

The case of *C* v. *S* involved two university students. The woman, suspecting she might be pregnant, had taken the 'morning-after pill', and thereafter believed she could not be. She was depressed at the time and was taking medication, but she also underwent an X-ray in the course of a medical examination. She then discovered she was in fact pregnant and decided to have a termination. By this time she was between 18 and 21 weeks pregnant. At this point her former boyfriend enters the scene, being revealed as a Right-to-Lifer. He takes her to court to try to prevent the abortion taking place.

The woman's right to an abortion was enshrined in the 1967 Abortion Act and she had the support of doctors who argued that the medication and the X-ray would have damaged the foetus and that her health would be impaired by a continuation of the pregnancy. However, alongside this legislation exists the Infant Life Preservation Act 1929. Section 1 of this act provides that 'any person who, with intent to destroy the life of a child capable of being born alive, by any wilful act causes a child to die before it has an existence independent of its mother, shall be guilty of a felony' (see Kingdom, 1985a, 1985b).

This case was brought under this Act, it being argued that with the advances being made by medical science the 18- to 21-week-old foetus was capable of being born alive. The case was not one of fathers' rights as the press tended to report it – although clearly it had implications for fathers' rights. It was in fact much more complex and subtle than a clash of rights. The putative father was attempting to use shifts in medical science to challenge an established principle that no foetus under 28 weeks was capable of being born alive. He failed to do so because the judge decided that the weight of medical evidence was against him. However, the attempt marked an important shift in the debate about who should adjudicate on women's bodies.

THE WOMAN'S BODY

In *C* v. *S* the woman's body was fully regulated by the medical profession. They had prescribed her drugs and administered the X-ray. She is clearly depicted as a woman out of control of her body but fortunately under the tutelage of her doctors. She does not look like a good prospect as a mother anyway. Indeed in the event of a custody conflict over a child born to such a woman she would be in a very poor position. (This is in fact more or less what happened in this case, because she had the baby and the father now has *de facto* custody although to my knowledge this was not contested in court.) So we can construct a vision of the woman who may have an abortion but, by wanting it disqualifies herself as a mother. In seeking to control her reproductive function, she abdicates the right to care for its product.

There are other meanings to be derived from this case however. A crucial one is the separation of the foetus from the mother who is carrying it. This separation is of course the basis of the foetal rights movement and it is closely linked to the development of new medical technologies. We are increasingly able to conceptualise the foetus as separate from the mother through the (unreal) imagery of so-called test-tube babies (Stanworth, 1987), through ultrasound screening which allows direct access to the foetus, bypassing the mother (Farrant, 1985), and through the development of intensive care which does mean that (some) very premature babies can survive. The conceptualisation of the foetus as separate leads rapidly to the attempt to accord the foetus rights as a legal subject. The moral claim of a right to life becomes far more concrete and attaches itself to an identifiable being. The relationship between the mother and foetus is also rendered more tenuous. In IVF and GIFT, most particularly in instances of multiple pregnancies, the mother becomes the incubator rather than the active producer. She is also diminished in comparison to the doctors who become the central actors.

This separation of mother and foetus in turn leads to a reconceptualisation of the mother as a potential threat to the entity inside her. So, for example, while smoking may be seen as a habit which causes harm to the individual, it becomes a harm to another separate being if the women is pregnant. The next step becomes one of instituting legal protections against this kind of harm. So in North America there are moves to force women to have Caesarean births and to undergo other involuntary procedures; there also arises the possibility of imprisoning woman in hospitals and of allowing legal actions against mothers who have lifestyles detrimental to their unborn offspring (Gallagher, 1987). We begin to see the re-emergence of the nineteenth-century lock hospital which was used for women with suspected venereal diseases. In the nineteenth century they were introduced to protect men, in the twentieth century they may be introduced to protect foetuses against their mothers. The point is that such draconian measures can be justified by the redefinition of mothers as unreliable bodies.

In these developments we can see the return of the iconography of the chaotic female body – but now grounded in modern science and not quasi superstition. There are no wandering wombs here, nor erroneous beliefs that men catch VD whilst women spread it. Rather we have a science which fits with modern liberal thinking on healthy bodies. Smoking and the use of drugs are bad for the health of the body, they are clearly bad for the foetus – obviously we should have measures to protect the foetus! It can become very hard to argue against such benevolent-sounding thinking especially when it is grounded in a deep suspicion of women's unreliable bodies.

FURTHER PENETRATIONS

It is possible to begin to map the various ways in which reproductive technologies are creating new sites for legal intervention. The creation of legal relationships can increasingly be based on laboratory results, whilst medical access to human ova and conceptuses raises new questions of ownership. Although the question of the legal 'ownership' of children is now irrelevant, the question of who owns, or has the right to control, gametes is another matter.

I am particularly interested in the former question, namely that of the creation of legal relationships. It is often remarked that the new reproductive technologies (especially IVF or full surrogacy) threaten the established basis of the family in which the married parents are presumed to raise their genetic offspring. However, in law the primary issue has always been the legal contract of marriage (between husband and wife) and not the biological relationship (between father and child) (Hoggett, 1981). The latter was presumed to follow the former regardless of the realities of conception (Smart, 1987). The primacy of the legal relationships has diminished in recent years however with the rise in divorce and unwed motherhood. This has posed a major problem of how to attach men to children. In the area of illegitimacy there are currently provisions going through Parliament which will give unmarried fathers the right to share 'parental responsibility' for children with mothers (The Children Bill 1988). This is not an automatic right but if granted it will put the father in the same legal position as the mother. In effect this means the end of autonomous motherhood outside marriage. This has further ramifications where reproductive technologies are concerned. The sperm donor (and possibly the male commissioning parent in surrogacy cases) will be in the same position as the unmarried father. At present it is proposed that the married mother who uses AID will be protected from any future demands made by him via the device of registering her husband as the father of her child. So where there is a legitimate husband on the scene the biological father can be excluded. However, the unmarried mother has no such protection. The solution made explicit in the Warnock Committee Report (1984) is to make AID in infertility clinics unavailable to unmarried women, but AID can be obtained informally. Under such circumstances the mother, particularly if she breaks the code of the non-sexual maternal body by being lesbian, risks having to share legal rights with the donor. The ability of genetic fingerprinting to determine precisely who the genetic parents of a child are makes this almost inescapable. (Indeed the principle that an AID donor should be entitled to access to 'his' child was established in 1989 in The Netherlands. The case involved a lesbian mother.) Medical penetrations therefore carry the potential of new forms of regulation, of reorganising paternal rights in a fashion independent of marriage but where fathers still exercise some control over the produce of women's bodies. Indeed it is hard to escape the conclusion that law can tolerate biological reproduction only if it proceeds under the gaze and supervision of the rational authority of the father. Woman's bodies when unsupervised can generate chaos. They threaten to produce children without legally recognised fathers, they are subject to irrational emotions and they generate immoderate desires. Such bodies must clearly be confined.

REDEFINING WOMEN'S BODIES

Legal and medical discourses have set a specific agenda in which women's bodies become inevitably defined as problematic. The issue for feminism is how to redefine this definition. There have been strategies which have defied the idea of pregnancy as a disease, or which have insisted on a woman's right to choose. However, these strategies can be problematic when applied to law. The claim to rights is now quite counter-productive (Berer, 1988; Kingdom, 1985). Women's rights can be matched by the claim to foetal rights, and in any case women are now widely seen as having equal rights so that further claims are simply seen as unjust prerogatives and overindulged self-interest. It is also not entirely clear to me that the problem is one of rights or equality. I have not identified the centrality of women's bodies to law simply in order to argue that bodies should be ignored, or should be treated as if they are male bodies. I see no great benefit for women, for example, in having pregnancy treated as an illness in order for it to fit into the Sex Discrimination Act because this piece of legislation requires that a woman compares herself to a man in order to establish discrimination.

I am also uncertain that we can talk of a single strategy or practice as if a unified policy arises from our analysis. I have discussed law as a singular concept here to underline how it is constructed as if it were a unity. However, it is no such thing and so it is mistaken to presume a unified strategy will meet the various problems that law creates. It may also be important to consider strategies which avoid law altogether. Feminists have perhaps been too ready to turn to law, using rights discourse as if it were inherently progressive. More recently there have been attempts to go beyond a simple appeal to law to constructed an alternative feminist jurisprudence (MacKinnon, 1987) or a Women's Law (Dahl, 1987). Such measures challenge the form as well as the content of law suggesting a new basis for concepts of justice and equity to replace existing doctrines. These are interesting developments, but they leave unanswered the question of why *law*, even feminist law, should continue to regulate so many areas of civil or private life. In the UK the tendency to turn to law for a solution is less marked than in North America or Scandinavia, but the influence of feminist legal scholarship and legal campaigns may begin to alter this orientation. In the desire to do something, tackling and reformulating law feels tangible. However, this overlooks what I regard as the juridogenic nature of law. Just as medicine may be iatrogenic, so law may create unforeseen wrongs in the process of enforcing rights. Empowering law does not necessarily empower women.

In a sense we have gone as far as we can go with law perceived in traditional campaigning or reformist terms. Feminists have pursued the equality route and the rights route and these goals have largely been achieved – but with little major effect. However, what these attempts have revealed is a much deeper problem. This problem is the way law constitutes a site of the production of meanings, in particular problematic meanings for those of us with women's bodies. Yet in being a site of the production of meanings, law also provides a site for contesting meanings – often in a very public way. The outcry over outrageous judgements in sexual abuse or rape cases is one instance of a contest over meaning and a gradual redefinition of the meaning of having a female body. Other areas of law may be less visible and do not provide such public forums. Nonetheless it is the (often hidden) meanings which law constructs and reproduces which are most problematic. We need to challenge these meanings through language, most particularly we need to confront the problem of the law's claim to truth which disqualifies alternative visions and experiences which arise from the multiple subjectivities of inhabiting women's bodies.

Bibliography

ADLER, Z. (1987) *Rape on Trial* (London: Routledge & Kegan Paul).
ALLEN, H. (1984) 'At the Mercy of Her Hormones: Premenstrual Tension and the Law', *m/f*, vol. 9, pp. 19–44.
ALLEN, H. (1987) *Justice Unbalanced* (Milton Keynes: Open University Press).
ALLEN, H. (1988) 'One Law for All Reasonable Persons?', *International Journal of the Sociology of Law*, vol. 10, no. 4, pp. 419–32.
ARNOLD, E. and FAULKNER, W. (1985) *Smothered by Invention* (London: Pluto Press).
ATKINS S. and HOGGETT, B. (1984) *Women and the Law* (Oxford: Blackwell).
AVISON, D. E. and WOOD-HARPER, A. T. (1986) 'Multiview – An Exploitation of Information Systems Development', *The Australian Computer Journal*, vol. 18, no. 4, November 1986.
AYERS, P. and LAMBERTZ, J. (1986) 'Marriage Relations, Money and Domestic Violence in Working-Class Liverpool, 1919–1939', in J. Lewis (ed.), *Labour and Love* (Oxford: Blackwell).
BACON, W. (1978) *Public Accountability and the Schooling System* (London: Harper & Row).
BALLARD, B. (1984) 'Women Part-Time Workers: Evidence from the Women and Employment Survey', *Employment Gazette*, September.
BELL, D. GREEN, E., OWEN, J., PAIN, D. (1988) 'Human-Centred Design: A Methodology in Action' (European Conference on Information Technology for Organisational Systems, Athens, May 1988), in H. J. Bullinger, E. N. Protonotarios, D. Douwhuis and F. Rein, (eds), *Concepts for Increased Competitiveness* (Amsterdam: North-Holland)
BELL, D. J. (1984a) 'The Police Response to Domestic Violence: An Exploratory Study', *Police Studies*, vol. 7, no. 3, pp. 23–30.
BELL, D. J. (1984b) 'The Police Response to Domestic Violence: A Replication Study', *Police Studies*, vol 7, no. 3, pp. 136–44.
BELL, D. J. (1985a) 'The Police Response to Domestic Violence: A Multi year Study', *Police Studies*, vol. 8, no. 1, pp. 58–64.
BELL, D. J. (1985b) 'A Multi-Year Study of Ohio Urban, Suburban, and Rural Police Dispositions of Domestic Disputes Victimology', *An International Journal*, vol. 109, nos. 1–4, pp. 301–10.
BERER, M. (1988) 'Whatever happened to "A Woman's Right to Choose"?', *Feminist Review*, vol. 29, pp. 24–7.
BERK, R. A. and NEWTON, P. J. (1985) 'Does Arrest Really Deter Wife Battering? An Attempt to Replicate the Findings of the Minneapolis Spouse Abuse Experiment', *American Sociological Review*, vol. 50, April, pp. 253–62.
BILLINGTON-GREIG, T. (1911) *The Militant Suffrage Movement* (London: Frank Palmer).

BINNEY, V., HARKELL, G. and NIXON, J. (1981) *Leaving Violent Men* (England: Women's Aid Federation).
BIRDS EYE (1983) *Housekeeping Monitor 1983* (Public Relations Department: Birds Eye Ltd).
BLAGG, H., PEARSON, G., SAMPSON, A., SMITH, D. and STUBBS, P. (1988) 'Inter-Agency Cooperation: Rhetoric and Reality', in T. Hope and M. Shaw (eds), *Communities and Crime Reduction* (London: HMSO).
BLACKSTONE, W. (1974) *Commentaries on the Laws of England* (Oxford: Clarendon Press).
BLOCH, P. and ANDERSON, D. (1974) *Policewomen on Patrol: Final Report* (Washington: University of California Press).
BOGDANOR, V. (1979) 'Power and participation', *Oxford Review of Education*, vol. 5, no. 2, pp. 157–68.
BOTTOMLEY, A. (1987) 'Feminism in Law Schools' in S. McLaughlin (ed.), *Women and the Law* (University College London, Faculty of Law, *Working Papers*, no. 5).
BOURLET, A. (1988) *Police Intervention in Marital Violence* (University of Kent: M.Phil. Dissertation).
BOWER, M. (1986) 'Daring to Speak its Name', *Feminist Review*, no. 24, pp. 40–56.
BOX, S. (1971) *Deviance, Reality and Society* (New York: Holt, Reinhart & Winston).
BRAVERMAN, H. (1974) *Labour and Monopoly Capital* (New York: Monthly Review).
BREEN, D. (1975) *The Birth of a First Child* (London: Tavistock).
BREHONY, K. (1989) 'Neither Rhyme nor Reason – Primary Education and the National Curriculum' in M. Flude and M. Hammer (eds.), *The 1988 Education Act* (Barcombe, Sussex: Falmer Press).
BROWNMILLER, S. (1989) *Waverly Place* (London: Chatto & Windus).
BURNISTON, S., MORT, F., and WEEDON, C. (1978) 'Psychonanalysis and the Cultural Acquisition of Sexuality and Subjectivity' in Women's Study Group (eds.) *Women Take Issue* (Birmingham: Centre for Contemporary Cultural Studies).
BURRELL, G. (1984) 'Sex and Organisational Analysis', *Organisation Studies*, vol. 5, no. 2, pp. 97–118.
BURRELL, G. (1987) 'No Accounting for Sexuality', *Accounting, Organisations and Society*, vol. 12, no. 1, pp. 89–101.
CAIN, M. (1986) 'Realism, Feminism, Methodology and Law', *International Journal of the Sociology of Law*, vol. 14, pp. 255–67.
CAMERON, D. (1985) *Feminism and Linguistic Theory* (London: Macmillan).
CAMERON, D. (1986) 'What is the Nature of Women's Oppression in Language', *Oxford Literary Review*, vol. 8, nos. 1–2, pp. 79–87.
CAMPBELL, B. (1988) *Unofficial Secrets: Child Sexual Abuse – The Cleveland Case* (London: Virago).
CAPLAN, P. (1987) *The Cultural Construction of Sexuality* (London: Routledge & Kegan Paul).
CARLEN, P. (1976) *Magistrates' Justice* (London: Martin Robertson).

CARLEN, P. and WORRALL, A. (eds.) (1987) *Gender, Crime and Justice* (Milton Keynes: Open University Press).
CASSELL, J. (1977) *A Group Called Women* (New York: McKay).
CHAMBERS, G. and MILLAR, A. (1986) *Prosecuting Sexual Assault* (Scottish Home and Health Authority).
CHATTERTON, M. (1976) 'Police and Social Control', pp. 104–22 in Joan King (ed.), *Control Without Custody* (University of Cambridge, Cropwood Papers).
CHATTERTON, M. (1983) 'Police Work and Assault Charges', pp. 194–220 in M. Punch (ed.), *Control in the Police Organisation* (Cambridge: MIT Press).
CHECKLAND, P. (1981) *Systems Thinking, Systems Practice* (London: Wiley).
CHITTY, C. and LAWSON, D. (1988) *The National Curriculum* (London: Bedford Way Papers).
CHODOROW, N. (1978) *The Reproduction of Mothering* (Berkley, Los Angeles, London: University of California Press).
CLARK, A. (1987) *Men's Violence: Women's Silence* (London: Pandora).
COCKBURN, C. (1983) *Brothers: Male Dominance and Technological Change* (London: Pluto Press).
COCKBURN, C. (1985) *Machinery of Dominance: Women, Men and Technical Know-How* (London: Pluto Press).
COOLEY, M. (1980a) *Architect or Bee?* (Slough: Langley Technical Service).
COOLEY, M. (1980b) 'After the Lucas Plan', in Collective Design/Projects (ed.). *Very Nice Work if You Can Get It* (Nottingham: Spokesman).
COOPER and LYBRAND (1988) *Local Management of Schools* (London: HMSO).
COOTE, A. and CAMPBELL, B. (1987) *Sweet Freedom* (Oxford: Blackwell).
COUSINS, M. (1986) 'Men and Women as Polarity', *Oxford Literary Review*, vol. 8, nos. 1–2, pp. 164–9.
COWARD, R. (1983) *Patriarchal Precedents* (London: Routledge & Kegan Paul).
COX, C. and BOYSON, R. (1975) (eds), *The Black Papers* (London: Temple Smith).
COX, C. and BOYSON, R. (1977) (eds), *The Black Papers* (London: Temple Smith).
CROMPTON, R. and JONES, G. (1984) *White-Collar Proletariat: Deskilling and Gender in Clerical Work* (London: Macmillan).
CROMWELL, R. E. and OLSON, D. (1975) *Power in Families* (New York: Sage).
DAHL, T. S. (1987) *Women's Law* (Oxford University Press).
DAHLERUP, D. (1988) 'From a Small to a Large Minority: Women in Scandinavian Politics.' *Scandinavian Political Studies*, vol. 1, no. 4.
DAHLSTROM, E. (1967) *The Changing Roles of Men and Women* (London: Duckworth).
DALE, R. (1981) 'Control, Accountability and William Tyndale', in R. Dale *et al.* (eds.), *Education and the State; Politics, Patriarchy and Practice* (Barcombe, Sussex: Falmer Press).

DALTON, K. (1983) The Menstrual Cycle – Mitigating Circumstances: Familiar Rhetoric. *International Journal of Law*, vol. 11, pp. 285–400.
DALY, M. (1979) *Gyn/Ecology* (London: The Women's Press).
DALY, M. and WILSON, M. (1987) *Homicide* (New York: Aldine de Gruyter).
DAVID, M. and NEW, C. (1985) *For the Sake of the Children* (Harmondsworth: Penguin).
DAVIES, C. and ROSSER, J. (1986) 'Gendered Jobs in the Health Service: a Problem for Labour Process Analysis', in D. Knights and H. Willmott (eds) *Gender and the Labour Process*, (Aldershot: Gower).
DEEM, R. (1986) *All Work and No Play* (Milton Keynes: Open University Press).
DEEM, R. (1989) 'The Reform of School Governing Bodies: The Power of the Consumer Over the Producer?', in M. Flude and M. Hammer (eds.), *The 1988 Education Act* (Barcombe, Sussex: Falmer Press).
DEPARTMENT OF EDUCATION AND SCIENCE (1977) *A New Partnership for our Schools (the Taylor Report)* (London: HMSO).
DEPARTMENT OF EVIRONMENT (1981) *Labour Force Survey* (London: HMSO).
DEX, S. (1985) *The Sexual Division of Work* (Brighton: Wheatsheaf Books).
DEX, S. (1987) *Women's Occupational Mobility: A Lifetime Perspective* (London: Macmillan).
DINNERSTEIN, D. (1987) *The Rocking of the Cradle* (London: Women's Press).
DOBASH, R. and DOBASH, R. E. (1984) 'The Nature and Antecedents of Violent Events', *British Journal of Criminology*, vol. 24, no. 39, pp. 269–88.
DOBASH, R. and DOBASH, R. E. (1985) 'The Contact Between Battered Woman and Social and Medical Agencies', pp. 142–65, in J. Pahl (ed.), *Private Violence and Public Policy* (London: Routledge & Kegan Paul).
DOBASH, R. and DOBASH, R. E. (1980) *Violence against Wives* (London: Open Books).
DONNERSTEIN, E. (1980) 'Aggression, Erotica and Violence Against Women', *Journal of Personality and Social Psychology*, 1980.
DOWNES, D. and ROCK, P. (1988) *Understanding Deviance* (Oxford: Clarendon Press).
DWORKIN, A. (1981) *Pornography; Men Possessing Women* (London: Women's Press).
EARLEY, P. (1988) *Governor's Reports and Annual Parents' Meetings* (Slough: National Foundation for Education Research).
EASLEA, B. (1981) *Science and Sexual Oppression* (London: Weidenfeld & Nicholson).
EDGELL, S. (1980) *Middle Class Couples* (London: Allen & Unwin).
EDWARDS, S. (1981) *Female Sexuality and the Law* (Oxford: Martin Robertson).
EDWARDS, S. S. M. (1985) 'A Socio-legal Evaluation of Gender Ideologies

in Domestic Violence Assault and Spousal Homicides' *Victimology: An International Journal*, vol. 10, nos 1–4, pp. 186–205.

EDWARDS, S. S. M. (1986a) *The Police Response to Domestic Violence in London* (Polytechnic of Central London) July.

EDWARDS, S. S. M. (1986b) 'Police Attitudes and Dispositions in Domestic Disputes', *The London Study Police Journal*, July, pp. 230–41.

EDWARDS, S. S. M. (1986c) 'The Real Risks of Violence Behind Closed Doors', *The New Law Journal*, 12 December.

EDWARDS, S. S. M. (1987) 'Sex Role and Family Ideologies in Policing Domestic Violence', *Victimology: An International Journal*.

EDWARDS, S. S. M. (1988) 'Change in Police Policy on Domestic Disputes: The Experience of the Metropolitan Police in London' (Paper presented to the Politizei Fürungsacademic, Munster, West Germany, September) 26–30.

EDWARDS, S. S. M. (1989a) *Policing Domestic Violence* (London and New York: Sage).

EDWARDS, S. S. M. (1989b) 'An Evaluation of the Impact of Police Policy on Police Response to Domestic Violence Calls' (A Final Report for the Police Foundation, London).

EHN, P. (1988) *Work-Oriented Design of Computer Artifacts* (Swedish Centre for Working Life).

EHN, P. and KYNG, M. (1987) 'The Collective Resource Approach to Systems Design' in G. Bjerknes *et al.* (eds) *Computers and Democracy – A Scandinavian Challenge* (Aldershot: Avebury).

EHRENREICH, B. and ENGLISH, D. (1978) 'The "Sick" Women of the Upper Classes', in J. Ehrenreich (ed.), *The Cultural Crisis of Modern Medicine* (New York: Monthly Review Press).

EHRENREICH, J. and ENGLISH, D. *For Her Own Good* (London: Pluto Press).

EHRLICH-MARTIN, S, (1979) 'Policewomen and Policewomen: Occupational Role Dilemmas and Choices of Female Officers', *Journal of Police Science and Administration*, vol. 7, no. 3.

EHRLICH-MARTIN, S. (1981) *Breaking and Entering: Policewomen on Patrol* (University of California Press).

EICHENBAUM, L. and ORBACH, S. (1985) *Understanding Women* (Harmondsworth: Penguin).

EICHENBAUM, L. and ORBACH, S. (1987) 'Separation and Intimacy', in Ernst and Maguire (1987)

EQUAL OPPORTUNITIES COMMISSION (1986) *Equal Opportunities and the School Governor* (Manchester: Equal Opportunities Commission).

EQUAL OPPORTUNITIES COMMISSION (1989) *Gender Issues: the Implications for Schools of the Education Reform Act* (Manchester: Equal Opportunities Commission).

ERNST, S. (1987), 'Can a Daughter be a Woman?', in Ernst and Maguire (1987).

ERNST, S. and MAQUIRE, M. (eds.), (1987) *Living With the Sphinx* (London: The Women's Press).

EVANS, L. (1978) 'Sexual Harassment: Women's Hidden Occupational

Hazard' in J. Chapman and M. Gates (eds.), *The Victimisation of Women* (Beverley Hills, California: Sage).
EVANS, T. (1988) *A Gender Agenda* (London and Sydney: Allen & Unwin).
EVASON, E. (1982) *Hidden Violence: a Study of Battered Women in Northern Ireland* (Belfast: Farset Press).
EXETER SOCIETY FOR CURRICULUM STUDIES RESEARCH GROUP (1987) *Parents as School Governors: Interim Report* (University of Exeter).
FARLEY, L. (1978) *Sexual Shakedown* (New York: McGraw Hill Book Company).
FARRANT, W. (1985) 'Who's for Amniocentesis? The Politics of Prenatal Screening' in H. Homans (ed.), *The Sexual Politics of Reproduction* (Aldershot: Gower).
FAWCETT, H. G. (1911) *Women's Suffrage* (London: T.C. & E.C. Jack).
FERRARO, K. J. (1989) 'The Legal Response to Woman Battering in the United States', pp. 115–84, in J. Hanmer, J. Radford and E. Stanko (eds.), *Policing Male Violence* (London: Routledge & Kegan Paul).
FIELDING, N. G. (1988) *Joining Forces: Police Training, Socialisation and Occupational Competence* (London: Routledge & Kegan Paul).
FINCH, J. (1984) '"It's Great to Have Someone to Talk To": The Ethics and Politics of Interviewing Women' in C. Bell and H. Roberts (eds.), *Social Researching* (London: Routledge & Kegan Paul).
FLUDE, M. and HAMMER, M. (eds.) (1989) *The 1988 Education Act* (Barcombe, Sussex: Falmer Press).
FOX-KELLER, E. (1985) *Reflections on Gender and Science* (New Haven: Yale University Press).
FREEMAN, M. D. A. (1980) 'Violence Against Wives: Does the Legal System Provide Solutions or Itself Constitute the Problem?' *British Journal of Law and Society*, vol. 7, pp. 215–41.
FREUD, S. (1955a) 'Analysis of a Phobia in a Five Year Old Boy (1909)', *Complete Works*, vol. X (London: Hogarth Press).
FREUD, S. (1955b) 'Totem and Taboo (1913)', *Complete Works*, vol. XIII (London: Hogarth Press).
FREUD, S. (1955c) 'Introductory Lectures (1916)', *Complete Works*, vol. XVI (London: Hogarth Press).
FREUD, S. (1955d) 'From the History of an Infantile Neurosis', *Complete Works*, vol. XVII (London: Hogarth Press).
FREUD, S. (1955e) 'New Introductory Lectures', *Complete Works*, vol. XXII (London: Hogarth Press).
FRIEDAN, B. (1963) *The Feminine Mystique* (Harmondsworth: Penguin).
FRIEDMAN, A. and CORNFORD, D. (1987) 'Strategies for Meeting User Demands – An International Perspective', in G. Bjerknes *et al.* (eds.), *Computers and Democracy – A Scandinavian Challenge* (Aldershot: Avebury).
FRIEDMAN, A. and GREENBAUM, J. (1984) 'Wanted: Renaissance People', *Datamation*, September, 1984.
FRIEND, J., NOAD, A. and NORRIS, M. (1978) 'Progress in Understanding Linkage: A Concluding View from the Research Team', *Linkage*, vol. 3, pp. 27–34.

FROSCH, S. (1987) *The Politics of Psychoanalysis* (London: Macmillan).
GALLAGHER, J. (1987) 'Prenatal Invasions and Interventions: What's Wrong with Fetal Rights', *Harvard Women's Law Journal*, vol. 10, pp. 9–58.
GALLOP, J. (1982) *Feminism and Psychoanalysis: The Daughter's Seduction* (London: Macmillan).
GANE, C. and SARSON, T. (1979) *Structured Systems Analysis: Tools and Techniques* (New Jersey: Prentice-Hall).
GASKELL, J. (1987) 'Conceptions of Skill and the Work of Women: Some Historical and Political Issues', in R. Hamilton and M. Barrett (eds.), *The Politics and Diversity* (London: Verso)
GIBBON, P. (in press) *Equal Opportunities in Sheffield Policies and Outcomes* (Sheffield City Council, Department of Employment and Economic Development).
GILLESPIE, D. (1972) 'Who has the power? The Marital Struggle', in H. P. Deitzel (ed.), *Marriage and the Struggle of the Sexes* (West Drayton: Collier Macmillan).
GLENDINNING, C. and MILLAR, J. (1987) *Women and Poverty in Britain* (Brighton: Wheatsheaf Books).
GLENN, E. and FELDBERG, R. (1979) 'Proletarianising Clerical Work: Technology and Organisational Control in the Office', in A. Zimbalist (ed.), *Case Studies in the Labour Process* (New York: Monthly Review Press).
GOLBY, M., BRIGLEY, S. and EXETER SOCIETY FOR CURRICULUM STUDIES (1989) *Parents as School Governors* (Tiverton, Devon: Fairway Publications).
GOODMAN, S. and PERBY, M. (1985) 'Computerization and the Skill in Women's Work', in Olerup *et al*, (eds), *Women, Work and Computerisation: Opportunities and Disadvantages* (Amsterdam: North-Holland).
GORDON, C. (1980) *Michel Foucault: Power/Knowledge* (Brighton: Harvester Press).
GORER, G. (1971) *Sex and Marriage in England Today* (London: Nelson).
GRAHAM, H. (1983) 'Do Her Answers Fit His Questions? Women and the Survey Method' in E. Garmarnikow, D. Morgan, J. Purvis and D. Taylorson (eds.), *The Public and the Private* (London: Heinemann).
GRAHAM, H. (1984) 'Surveying Through Stories', in C. Bell and H. Roberts (eds.), *Social Researching* (London: Routledge & Kegan Paul).
GREENBAUM, J. (1987) *The Head and the Heart: Using Gender Analysis to Study the Social Construction of Computer Systems* (Computer Science Department, Aarhus University, Denmark).
GRIFFITH, J. A. C. (1977) *The Politics of the Judiciary* (London: Fontana).
GRONFELDT, J. and KANDRUP, S. (1985) 'Still Dancing after All These Years', in A. Olerup, E. Sehmeider and E. Monod (1985).
GUTEK, B. A. (1985) *Sex and the Workplace* (San Francisco: Jossey-Bass).
HAAS, L. (1981) 'Domestic Role Sharing in Sweden', *Journal of Marriage and the Family*, vol. 43.
HAAS, L. (1982) 'Parental Sharing of Child-Care Tasks in Sweden', *Journal of Family Issues*, vol. 3, no. 3.
HAAS, L. (1986) 'Wives' Orientation Towards Breadwinning: Sweden and the U.S.', *Journal of Family Issues*, vol. 7, no. 4.

HADFIELD, G. (1989) 'Teachers Exploiting Parent Power Laws', *The Sunday Times*, 22 January.
HADJIPOTIOU, N. (1983) *Women and Sexual Harassment at Work* (London: Pluto Press).
HALL, V., MACKAY, H. and MORGAN, C. (1986) *Headteachers at Work* (Milton Keynes: Open University Press).
HALSON, J. (1989a) 'The Sexual Harassment of Young Women', in L. Holly (ed.), *Girls and Sexuality: Teaching and Learning* (Milton Keynes: Open University Press).
HALSON, J. (1989b) 'Going With Boys! The Form and Meaning of Heterosexuality for Young Women' (paper presented at a meeting of the British Sociological Association's Sexual Division Group, on *Young Women Living with Contradictions*, Cambridge College of Arts and Technology, 29 April 1989).
HANMER, J., RADFORD, J. and STANKO, E. (1989) *Policing Male Violence* (London: Routledge & Kegan Paul).
HAMNER, J. and SAUNDERS, S. (1984) *Well-Founded Fear: A Community Study of Violence to Woman* (London: Hutchinson).
HANMER, J. and STANKO, E. (1985) 'Stripping Away the Rhetoric of Protection: Violence to Women, Law and the State in Britain and the U.S.A.', *International Journal of the Sociology of Law*, vol. 13, no. 4, pp. 357–74.
HARDING, S. (1986) *The Science Question in Feminism* (Milton Keynes: Open University Press).
HARDING, S. (1987) *Feminism and Methodology* (Milton Keynes: Open University Press).
HATTY, M. (1989) 'Policing and Male Violence in Australia', pp. 70–89, in J. Hanmer, J. Radford and E. Stanko, *Policing Male Violence* (London: Routledge.
HAUG, F. (ed.) (1987) *Female Sexualization* (London: Verso).
HEARN, J. and PARKIN, W. (1987) *'Sex' at 'Work'* (Brighton: Wheatsheaf Books).
HENLEY, N. (1977) *Body Politics* (New Jersey: Prentice-Hall).
HERBERT, C. (1989) *Talking of Silence, the Sexual Harassment of School Girls* (London: Falmer Press).
HERNES, H. M. (1987) *Welfare State and Woman Power* (Oslo: Norwegian University Press).
HERNES, H. M. (1988a) 'Scandinavian Citizenship', *Acta Sociologica*, vol. 31, no. 3.
HERNES, H. M. (1988b) 'The Welfare State Citizenship of Scandinavian Women', in K. B. Jones and A. G. Jonasdottir (eds.), *The Political Interests of Gender* (London: Sage).
HIRSCHEIM, R. (1985) *Office Automation* (Reading, Mass.: Addison-Wesley).
HIRSCHEIM, R. (1987) 'User Participation in Practice' (Paper to the Conference on *Participation in Systems Design*, London Business School, April 1987).
HOAGLAND, S. and PENELOPE, J. (eds.) (1988) *For Lesbians Only: A Separatist Anthology* (London: Only Women Press).
HOBSON, B. M. (1986) 'Women, Work and the State: A Comparison of

Women's Labour Force Activity in Sweden and the U.S.' (paper presented to the Harvard University Center for European Studies International Conference on *The Feminisation of the Labour Force*).

HOGGETT, B. (1981) *Parents and Children* (London: Sweet & Maxwell).

HOLDAWAY, S. (1983) *Inside the British Police: A Force at Work* (Oxford: Blackwell).

HOLDAWAY, S. (1986) 'Police and Social Work Relations – Problems and Possibilities', *British Journal of Social Work*, vol. 16, pp. 137–60.

HOLLWAY, W. (1984) 'Gender Difference and the Production of Subjectivity', in J. Henriques, W. Hollway, C. Urwin, C. Venu, and V. Walkerdine (eds.), *Changing the Subject* (London: Methuen).

HOLLY, L. (1989) *Sexuality and Schooling* (Milton Keynes: Open University Press).

HOMER, M., LEONARD, A. and TAYLOR, P. (1985) 'The Burden of Dependency', in N. Johnson (ed.), *Marital Violence* (London: Routledge and Kegan Paul).

HORNEY, K. (1973a) 'The Flight From Womanhood (1926)', in Miller (1973).

HORNEY, K. (1973b) 'The Problem of Female Masochism (1935)', in Miller (1973).

HOUGH, M. and MAYHEW, P. (1983) *The British Crime Survey: First Report*, Home Office Research Study no. 76 (London: HMSO).

HUDSON, A. (1988) 'Boys will be Boys: Masculinism and the Juvenile Justice System', *Critical Social Policy*, vol. 21, pp. 30–48.

HUMPHRIES, J. (1981) 'Protective Legislation the Capitalist State and Working Class Men: The Case of the 1842 Miners Regulation Act, *Feminist Review*, vol. 7, pp. 1–29.

HUMPHRIES, J. and RUBERY, J. (1988) 'Recession and Exploitation; British Women in a Changing Workplace 1979–85', in J. Jenson, E. Hagen, and C. Reddy (eds.), *Feminisation of the Labour Force* (Cambridge: Polity Press).

HUNT, P. (1978) 'Cash transactions and household tasks', *Sociological Review*, vol. 26, no. 1, pp. 555–71.

HUNT, P. (1980) *Gender and Class Consciousness* (London: Macmillan).

HUWS, U. (1982) *Your Job in the Eighties* (London: Pluto Press).

IRAGARAY, L. (1974) *Speculum de l'autre Femme* (Paris, Editions de Minuit).

IT STRATEGY SERVICE (1988) *Women into I.T.*

JACKSON, M. (1982) 'The Nature of 'Soft' Systems Thinking: The Work of Churchman, Ackoff and Checkland', *Journal of Applied Systems Analysis*, vol 9.

JACKSON, M. (1985) 'Social Systems Theory and Practice: The Need for a Critical Approach', *International Journal of General Systems*, vol. 10.

JAFFE, P., WOLFE, D. A., TELFORD, A. and AUSTIN, G. (1986) 'The Impact of Police Laying Charges in Incidents of Wife Abuse', *Journal of Family Violence*, vol. 1, pp. 37–49.

JAYARANTA, N. (1986) 'Normative Information Model-Based Systems Analysis and Design (NIMSAD): A Framework for Understanding and Evaluating Methodologies', *Journal of Applied Systems Analysis*, vol. 13.

JEFFERIES, G. and STREATFIELD, D. (1989) *The Reconstruction of School Governing Bodies* (Slough: National Foundation for Education Research).

JENSON, J., HAGEN, E and REDDY, C. (eds.), *Feminisation of the Labour Force* (Cambridge: Polity Press).

JOLIN, A. (1983) 'Domestic Violence Legislation: An Impact Assessment', *Journal of Police Science and Administration*, vol. 11, pp. 451–6.

JONES, C. (1984) 'Sexual Tyranny in Mixed-Sex Schools: An In-Depth Study of Male Violence', G. Weiner (ed.), *Just a Bunch of Girls: Feminist Approaches to Schooling* (Milton Keynes: Open University Press).

JONES, K. B. and JONASDOTTIR, A. G. (1988) *The Political Interests of Gender* (London: Sage).

JONES, S. (1986) *Policewomen and Equality* (London: Macmillan).

JUDD, J. (1988) 'Parents Robbed of School Power', *The Observer*, 23 October.

KELLY, L. (1987) 'The Continuum of Sexual Violence', in J. Hanmer and M. Maynard (eds.), *Woman, Violence and Social Control* (London: Macmillan).

KELLY, L. (1988) *Surviving Sexual Violence* (Polity Press in association with Basil Blackwell).

KELLY, L. and SCOTT, S. (1989) 'With Our Own Hands: Violence Between and By Women', *Trouble and Strife*, no. 16.

KINGDOM, E. (1985) 'Law's recognition of a woman's right to choose', J. Brophy and C. Smart (eds.), *Women in Law* (London: Routledge & Kegan Paul).

KITZINGER, C. (1988) '"It's Not Fair on Girls": Young Women's Accounts of Unfairness in School' (Paper presented at the British Psychological Society Annual Conference, University of Leeds, 15–18 April).

KLEIN, M. (1988) 'The Oedipus Complex in the Light of Early Anxieties (1945)', in *Love, Guilt and Reparation* (London: Virago).

KNIGHTS, D. and WILMOTT, H. (eds.) (1986) *Gender and the Labour Process* (Aldershot: Gower).

KOGAN, M., JOHNSON, D., PACKWOOD, T. and WHITTAKER, T. (eds.) (1984) *School Governing Bodies* (London: Heinemann).

KRISTEVA, J. (1971) 'Le Lieu Semiotique', in Kristeva *et al.* (1971).

KRISTEVA, J., REY-DEBOVE, J. and UMIKER, D. J. (eds.) (1971) *Essays in Semiotics* (Paris: Mouton).

LABOUR PARTY (1986) *Equal Opportunities for Girls and Boys – What Every Labour Governor Needs to Know* (London).

LAND, F. BETJEJARUWAT, N., SMITH, C. (eds.) (1983) 'Factors Affecting Social Control: The Reasons and Values', in *Systems, Objectives, Solutions*, vol. 3.

LAND, H. (1969) *Large Families in London* (London: Bell).

LEARMOUTH AND BURCHETT MANAGEMENT SYSTEMS (1986) *Introduction to Learmouth and Burchett Management Systems Structured Development Methology.*

LEES, S. (1986) *Losing Out: Sexuality and Adolescent Girls* (London: Hutchinson).

LEIULSFRUD, H. and WOODWARD, A. (1987) 'Women at Class Crossroads; Repudiating Conventional Theories of Family Class', *Sociology*, vol. 21, no. 3.
LELLO, J. (1979) *Accountability in education* (London: Ward Lock).
LIDDINGTON, J. and NORRIS, J. (1978) *One Hand Tied Behind Us*. (London: Virago).
LIE, M. and RASMUSSEN, B. (1985) *Office Work and Skills* in Olerup *et al*. (1985).
LIFF, S. (1986) 'Technical Change and Occupational Sex-Typing', in Knights and Wilmott (1986).
LIFF, S. (1988) *Gender, Office Work and Technological Change* (Paper to the Programme on Information and Communications Technologies (PICT) Workshop, Bath University, 25–27 March, 1988).
LODGE, B. (1986) 'Poly Researchers Say Heads Are Still Far Too Autocratic', *The Times Educational Supplement*, 7 March 1986.
LODGE, B. (1987) 'Struggling to Cope With the Unfamiliar', *The Times Educational Supplement*, 2 May 1987, p. 7.
LONDON STRATEGIC POLICY UNIT (1988) *Women – the Key to I.T.*
LOWN, J. (1983) '"Not So Much a Factory, More a Form of Patriarchy": Gender and Class During Industrialisation', in E. Gamarnikow, D. Morgan, J. Purvis and D. Taylorson (eds.) *Gender, Class and Work* (London: Heinemann).
LUKES, S. (ed.) (1986) *Power* (Oxford, Blackwell).
LUCKHAUS, L. (1985) 'A Plea for PMT in the Criminal Law', S. Edwards (ed.), *Gender, Sex and the Law* (London: Croom Helm).
McBARNET, J. (1981) *Conviction: The Law, the State and the Construction of Justice* (London: Macmillan).
McCABE, S. and SUTCLIFFE, F. (1978) *Defining Crime: A Study of Police Discretion* (Oxford: Blackwell).
McCANN, K. (1985) 'Battered Women and the Law: the Limits of the Legislation', in J. Brophy and C. Smart (eds.), *Woman in Law* (London: Routledge & Kegan Paul).
McDONALD, G. W. (1980) 'Family Power: The Assessment of a Decade of Theory and Research, 1970–79', *Journal of Marriage and the Family*, pp. 841–54.
McGILLIVRAY, A, (1987) 'Battered Women: Definition Models and Prosecutorial Policy', *Canadian Journal of Family Law*, vol. 6, pp. 15–45.
MacKINNON, C. (1983) 'Feminism, Marxism, Method and the State: Toward Feminist Jurisprudence', *Signs*, vol. 8, no. 2, pp. 635–58.
MacKINNON, C. (1987) *Feminism Unmodified: Discourses on Life and Law* (London: Harvard University Press).
McLEOD, M. (1982) 'Victim Non-Cooperation in Domestic Disputes', *Criminology*, vol. 21, no. 3, pp. 396–416.
MACLURE, S. (1988) *Education Reformed: A Guide to the 1988 Education Act* (London: Hodder & Stoughton).
MACLURE, S. and BECHER, T. (eds.) (1978) *Accountability in Education* (Slough: National Foundation for Education Research).
McNEIL, M. (ed.) (1987) *Gender and Expertise* (London: Free Association Books).

McRAE, S. (1987) 'The Allocation of Money in Cross-Class Families', *Sociological Review*, vol. 35, no. 1, pp. 92–122.
MAHONEY, P. (1985) *Schools for the Boys? Co-education Reassessed* (London: Hutchinson).
MANN, M. (1987) 'Ruling Class Strategies and Citizenship', *Sociology*, vol. 21, no. 3.
MARSHALL, T, H. (1963) 'Citizenship and Social Class', in *Sociology at the Crossroads* (London: Heinemann).
MARTIN, J. and ROBERTS, C. (1984) 'Women's Employment in the 1980s', *Employment Gazette*, May.
MASSON, J. (1984) *Freud: The Assault on Truth* (London: Faber).
MEASOR, L. (1989) '"Are you coming to see dirty films today?" Sex Education and Adolescent Sexuality', in C. Holly (ed.), *Girls and Sexuality* (Milton Keynes: Open University Press).
MIES, M. (1983) 'Towards a Methodology for Feminist Research', in G. Bowles and R. Duelli Klein (eds.), *Theories of Women's Studies* (London: Routledge & Kegan Paul).
MILLER, A. (1981) *For Your Own Good* (London: Pluto Press).
MILLER, C. and SWIFT, K. (1980) *The Handbook of Non-Sexist Writing* (London: The Women's Press).
MILLER, J. B. (ed.) (1973) *Psychoanalysis and Women* (Harmondsworth: Penguin).
MILLER, J. B. (1978) *Towards a New Psychology of Women* (London: Allen Lane).
MILLETT, K. (1971) *Sexual Politics* (New York: Doubleday).
MITCHELL, J. (1974) *Psychoanalysis and Feminism* (Harmondsworth: Penguin).
MONTGOMERY, P. and BELL, V. (1986) *Police Response to Wife Assault* (A Northern Ireland Study).
MOODY, S. R. and TOMBS, J. (1982) *Constructing Prosecution Decision: The Case of the Procurator Fiscal* (Scottish Academic Press).
MOORE, D. N. (1979) *Battered Women* (Beverley Hills: Sage).
MORGAN, C., HALL, V. and MACKAY, H. (1983) *The Selection of Secondary School Headteachers* (Milton Keynes: Open University Press).
MORGAN, D. H. J. (1985) *The Family, Politics and Social Theory*, (London: Routledge & Kegan Paul).
MORRIS, A. (1987) *Women, Crime and Criminal Justice* (Oxford: Blackwell).
MOSSMAN, M. J. (1986) 'Feminism and Legal Method: The Difference it Makes', *Australian Journal of Law and Society*, vol. 3. pp. 30–52.
MUMFORD, E. (1985) 'Sociotechnical Systems Design' (Paper to the Conference on Development and Use of Computer-Based Tools, Aarhus University, Denmark, August, 1985).
MURRAY, F. (1987) 'Reconsidering Clerical Skills and Computerization of U.K. Retail Banking'. (Research Paper, Departments of Computer Studies and Applied Social Studies, Sheffield City Polytechnic.)
NATIONAL ASSOCIATION OF LOCAL GOVERNMENT OFFICERS (1988) *Training Pack on Job Design* (Video and written materials) (Produced jointly with APEX and CPSA).

OAKLEY, A. (1981) *Subject Woman* (London: Fontana).
O'CONNOR, M. (1987) 'Promotion for PC Plod', *The Guardian*, 9 June 1987, p. 17.
O'DONOVAN, K. (1985) *Sexual Divisions in Law* (London: Weidenfeld & Nicholson).
O'DONOVAN, K. and SZYZYCZAK, E. (1988) *Equality and Sex Discrimination* (Oxford: Blackwell).
OFFICE OF POPULATION CENSUSES AND SURVEYS (1984) *General Household Survey 1982* (London: HMSO).
OKIN, S. M. (1980) *Women in Western Political Thought* (London: Virago).
OLERUP, A., SEHMEIDER, E., MONOD, E. (eds.) (1985) *Women, Work and Computerisation: Opportunities and Disadvantages* (Amsterdam: North-Holland).
OPPENLANDER, N. (1982) 'Coping or Copping Out', *Criminology*, vol. 20, nos. 3–4, pp. 449–65.
OZGA, J. (1989) 'Studying Policy-Making Elites' (paper given to Journal of Educational Policy Seminar Series, Policy Studies Institute, February).
PAHL, J. (1980) 'Patterns of Money Management Within Marriage', *Journal of Social Policy*, vol. 9, no. 3, pp. 313–35.
PAHL, J. (1983) 'The Allocation of Money and the Structuring of Inequality Within Marriage', *Sociological Review*, vol. 31, no. 2, pp. 237–62.
PAHL, J. (1989) *Money and Marriage* (London: Macmillan).
PANKHURST, S. (1931 reprinted 1977) *The Suffragette Movement* (London: Virago).
PARKER, H. CASBURN, M. and TURNBULL, D. (1981) *Receiving Juvenile Justice* (Oxford: Blackwell).
PARKER, T. (1985) 'The Legal Background', pp. 97–109, in J. Pahl (ed.), *Private Violence and Public Policy* (London: Routledge & Kegan Paul).
PATEMAN, C (1983) 'Feminism and Democracy' in G. Duncan (ed.) *Democratic Theory and Practice* (Cambridge: Cambridge University Press).
PATEMAN, C. (1985) 'Women and Democratic Citizenship' (The Jefferson Memorial Lecture, University of California, Berkeley).
PAUKERT, L. (1984) *Employment and Unemployment of Women in OECD Countries* (Paris: OECD).
PEARSON, G., TRESEDER, J. and YELLOLY, M. (eds.) (1988) *Social Work and the Legacy of Freud* (London: Macmillan).
PEARSON, G., SAMPSON, A., BLAGG, H., SMITH, D. and STUBBS, P. (1989) 'Policing Racism', in R. Morgan and D. J. Smith (eds.), *Coming to Terms With Policing* (London: Routledge & Kegan Paul).
PEARSON, R. (1976) 'Women Defendents in Magistrates' Courts', *British Journal of Law and Society*, vol. 3, pp. 265–73.
PEMBERTON, P. (1986) *Management and Trade Union Response to the Perceived Implications of Microelectronic Technology in Selected Areas of the Service Sector* (Sheffield City Polytechnic).
PHILLIPS, A. and TAYLOR, B. (1980) 'Sex and Skill: Notes Towards a Feminist Economics', *Feminist Review*, vol. 6.
PRINGLE, R. (1988) *Secretary Talk* (London and Australia: Verso/Allen & Unwin).

Bibliography

RANDALL, V. (1988) *Women and Politics* (London: Macmillan).
REINER, R. (1985) *The Politics of the Police* (Brighton: Harvester).
RESSNER, U. and GUNNARSON, E. (1987) *Group Organised Work in the Public Sector* (Aldershot: Gower).
RICHARDS, M. (ed.) (1984) *The Integration of a Child into a Social World* (Cambridge: Cambridge University Press).
RILEY, D. (1983) *War in the Nursery* (Harmondsworth: Penguin).
ROBERTS, H. (ed.) (1981) *Doing Feminist Research* (London: Routledge & Kegan Paul).
ROBINSON, S. (1984) 'Parent to the Child', in Richards (1984).
ROLFE, H. (1986) 'Skill, Deskilling and New Technology in the Non-Manual Labour Process', *New Technology, Work and Employment*, vol. 1, Spring 1986.
ROSENBROCK, H. (1982) *Social and Engineering Design of an FMS* (Amsterdam: Cape 83).
RUBERY, J. (ed.) (1988) *Women and Recession* (London: Routledge & Kegan Paul).
RUGGIE, M. (1984) *The State and Working Women* (Princeton, NJ: Princeton University Press).
RUGGIE, M. (1988) 'Gender, Work and Social Progress', in J. Jenson *et al.* (eds.), *Feminization of the Labour Force* (Cambridge: Polity Press).
SACHS, A. and WILSON, J. H. (1978) *Sexism and the Law* (Oxford: Martin Robertson).
SAFILIOS ROTHSCHILD, C. (1970) 'The Study of Family Power Structure: A Review 1960–69', *Journal of Marriage and the Family*, vol. 32, pp. 539–52.
SALLIS, J. (1988) *Schools, Parents and Governors* (London: Routledge & Kegan Paul).
SAMPSON, A., STUBBS, P., SMITH, D., PEARSON, G. and BLAGG, H. (1988) 'Crime, Localities and the Multi-Agency Approach', *British Journal of Criminology*, vol. 28, no. 4, pp. 478–93.
SANDERS, A. (1988) 'Personal Violence and Public Order: The Prosecution of Domestic Violence in England and Wales', *International Journal of the Sociology of Law*, vol. 16, pp. 359–82.
SAYERS, J. (1981) *Biological Politics* (London: Tavistock).
SAYERS, J. (1986) *Sexual Contradictions* (London: Tavistock).
SCANZONI, J. (1979) 'Social Processes and Power in Families', in W. Burr, R. Hill, I. Nye and I. Reisa (eds.), *Contemporary Theories about the Family* (New York: The Free Press).
SCHNEIDER, B. (1982) 'Consciousness About Sexual Harassment Among Heterosexual and Lesbian Women Workers', *Journal of Social Issues*, vol. 38, no. 4.
SCHUBERT, J. (1988) Translation of Danish Police Chief Officers' Policy on Domestic Violence.
SCOTT, H. (1982) *Sweden's 'Right to be Human', Sex Role Equality; The Goal and the Reality* (New York: M. E. Sharpe).
SCUTT, J. (1982) 'Domestic Violence and the Police Response' in C. O'Donnell and J. Craney, *Family Violence in Australia* (Melbourne: Longman).
SECONDARY POWER 'Notebook; *School Governor*, March, p. 3.

SEGAL, H. (1984) *Introduction to the Work of Melanie Klein* (London: Heinemann).
SHERMAN, L.W. and BERK, R. A. (1984) 'The Specific Deterrent Effects of Arrest for Domestic Assault', *American Sociological Review*, vol. 49, no. 2, pp. 261–72.
SIIM, B. (1987) 'The Scandinavian Welfare States – Towards Sexual Equality of a New Kind of Male Domination?', *Acta Sociologica*, vol. 30, pp. 3–4.
SIIM, B. (1988) 'Towards a Feminist Rethinking of the Welfare State', in K. B. Jones and A. G. Jonasdottir (eds.), *The Political Interests of Gender* (London: Sage).
SILTANEN, J. (1986) 'Domestic Responsibilities and the Structuring of Employment', in R. Crompton and M. Mann (eds), *Gender and Stratification* (Cambridge: Polity Press).
SIMON, (1988) *Bending the Rules: The Baker Reform of Education* (London: Lawrence & Wishart).
SKOLNICK, J. (1966) *Justice Without Trial* (New York: John Wiley).
SMART, C. (1984) *The Ties That Bind* (London: Routledge & Kegan Paul).
SMART, C. (1987) '"There is of course the Distinction Dictated by Nature": Law and the Problem of Paternity', in M. Stanworth (ed.), *Reproductive Technologies* (Cambridge: Polity Press).
SMART, C. (1989) *Feminism and the Power of Law* (London: Routledge).
SMITH, D. (1974) 'Women's Perspective as a Radical Critique of Sociology', *Sociological Inquiry*, vol. 44, no. 1, pp. 7–14.
SMITH, D. J. (1983) 'A Survey of Police Officers', in *Police and People in London* (London: Policy Studies Institute).
SMITH, D. J. and GRAY, J. (1983) *Police and People in London* (London: Policy Studies Institute).
SMITH, R. (1981) *Trial by Medicine* (Edinburgh University Press).
SOCIAL TRENDS 1985 (London: HMSO).
SOCIALIST EDUCATION ASSOCIATION (1988) *Handbook for School and College Governors*, 3rd edn (London).
S.O.U. (1982) *Enklare Foraldraforsaking* (Stockholm: SOU)
SOUTHGATE, P. (1981) 'Women in the Police', *The Police Journal*, vol. 54, no. 2, pp. 157–67.
SPENDER, D. (1980) *Man Made Language* (London: Routledge & Kegan Paul).
SPENDER, D. (1982) *Women of Ideas (and what Men have done to Them)* (London: Ark).
STAMP, P. (1985) 'The balance of financial power in marriage', *Sociological Review*, vol. 33, no. 3, pp. 546–66.
STANKO, E. (1985) *Intimate Intrusions: Women's Experience of Male Violence* (London: Routledge & Kegan Paul).
STANLEY, L. and WISE, S. (1983) *Breaking Out: Feminist Consciousness and Feminist Research* (London: Routledge & Kegan Paul).
STANWORTH, M. (ed.) (1987) *Reproductive Technologies* (Cambridge: Polity Press).
STEER, D. (1980/1) *Uncovering Crime. The Police Role*. Royal Commission on Criminal Procedure. Research Study 7 (London: HMSO).

STEINMETZ, C. H. D. and VAN DANDEL, H. C. (1985) *Mishandleing en Hulpverleining* (The Hague: Staatsuitgeverij).
STONE, I. (1988) *Equal Opportunities in Local Authorities: Developing Effective Strategies for the Implementation of Policies for Women* (London: HMSO).
STRACHEY, R. (1928, reprinted 1979) *The Cause* (London: Virago).
STREATFIELD D. (1988) *School Governor Training and Information for Governors* (Slough: National Foundation for Education Research).
SULEIMAN, S. R. (1986) *The Female Body in Western Culture* (Cambridge: Harvard University Press).
SUMNER, C. (1979) *Reading Ideologies* (London: Academic Press).
TALBOT, M. and WIMBUSH, E. (eds.) (1989) *Relative Freedoms* (Milton Keynes: Open University Press).
THERBORN, G. (1980) *The Ideology of Power and the Power of Ideology* (London: New Left Books).
THOMAS, T. (1986) *The Police and Social Workers* (Aldershot: Gower).
THOMPSON, C. (1973) 'Cultural Pressures in the Psychology of Women (1942)', in Miller (1973).
THORNTON, M. (1986) 'Feminist Jurisprudence: Illusion or Reality?', *Australian Journal of Law and Society*, vol. 3, pp. 5–29.
THORNTON, M. (1989) 'Hegemonic Masculinity and the Academy', *International Journal of the Sociology of Law*, vol. 17, no. 1.
VEHVILAINEN, M. (1986) 'A Study Circle Approach as a Method for Women to Develop their Work and Computer Systems' (Paper to the IFIP Conference, *Women, Work and Computerisation*, Dublin, August 1986).
WAGNER, I. (1985) 'Women in the Automated Office', in Olerup *et al.* (1985).
WALBY, S. (1986) *Patriarchy at Work* (Cambridge: Policy Press).
WALBY, S. (1987) 'Flexibility and the Sexual Division of Labour' (Paper presented to the Conference, *Part-Time Work: Whose Flexibility?*, West Yorkshire Centre for Research on Women, (University of Bradford, September 1987).
WALKER, J. (1988) 'Women, the State and the Family in Britain; Thatcher Economics and the Experience of Women', in J. Rubery (ed.), *Women and Recession* (London: Routledge & Kegan Paul).
WALKER, L. (1989) *Terrifying Love* (New York: Harper & Row).
WALKOWITZ, J. (1980) *Prostitution and Victorian Society* (Cambridge University Press).
WARNOCK, M. (1984) *Report to the Committee of Inquiry Into Human Fertilisation and Embryology*, Cmnd 9314 (London: HMSO).
WARSHAW, R. (1988) *I Never Called it Rape* (New York: Harper & Row).
WEBB, J. and LIFF, S. (1988) 'Play the Whiteman: The Social Construction of Fairness and Competition in Equal Opportunities Policies', *Sociological Review*, vol. 36, no. 3.
WEBSTER, J. (1988) *Influencing the Content of Women's Work in Automated Offices* (paper presented to the International Federation for Information Processing Conference: *Women, Work and Computerisation*, Amsterdam, April 1988).

WEEDON, C. (1987) *Feminist Practice and Poststructuralist Theory* (Oxford: Blackwell).
WEST, J. (1982) *Work, Women and the Labour Market* (London: Routledge & Kegan Paul).
WEXLER, J. and LOGAN, D. (1983) 'Sources of Stress Among Women Police Officers', *Journal of Police Science and Administration*, vol. 11, no. 1, p. 46.
WILLIAMS, R. (1987) 'Democratising Systems Development – Technological and Organisational Constraints and Opportunities', in Bjerknes *et al.* (eds.), *Computers and Democracy – A Scandinavian Challenge* (Aldershot: Avebury).
WILLIAMS, R. and MOSELEY, R. (1982) 'The Trade Union Response to Information Technology: Technology Agreements', in Bjorn-Anderson *et al.* (eds.), *Information Society: For Richer or Poorer* (Amsterdam: North-Holland).
WILSON, E, (1981) 'Psychic Law and Order', *Feminist Review*, no. 9, pp. 63–78.
WILSON, G. (1987) *Money in the Family* (Aldershot: Avebury).
WISE, S. and STANLEY, L. (1987) *Georgie Porgie: Sexual Harassment in Everyday Life* (London: Pandora).
WOOD, J. (1984) 'Groping Towards Sexism: Boys' Sex-Talk', in A. McRobbie and M. Nava (eds.), *Gender and Generation* (London: Macmillan).
WOOD, S. (ed.) (1982) *The Degradation of Work: Skill, Deskilling and the Labour Process* (London: Hutchinson).
WORDEN, R. E. and POLLITZ, A. A. (1984) 'Police Arrests in Domestic Disturbances: A Further Look', *Law and Society Review*, vol. 18, pp. 105–19.
WYRE, R. (1987) 'Beware Collusion With "Conquest Sex"', *Community Care*, 25 June.
ZOOMER, O. (1989) 'Policing Woman Beating in the Netherlands', pp. 125–54, in J. Hanmer, J. Radford and E. Stanko, *Policing Male Violence* (London: Routledge).
ZWEIG, F. (1961) *The Worker in an Affluent Society* (London: Heinemann Educational Books).

Author Index

Adler, Z., 161
Allen, H., 166, 168
Anderson, D., 123, 124
Arnold, E., 82
Atkins, S., 22
Austin, G., 144
Avison, D. E., 79
Ayers, P., 55

Bacon, W., 60, 61
Becher, T., 61
Bell, D., 77
Bell, D. J., 139
Bell, V., 136
Berer, M., 139, 174
Berk, R. A., 144
Betjejaruwat, N., 78, 79
Billington-Greig, T., 23
Binney, V., 136
Blackstone, W., 23, 114
Blagg, H., 114, 123, 125, 127
Bloch, P., 123, 124
Bogdanor, V., 60
Bottomley, A., 160
Bourlet, A., 139
Bower, M., 13
Box, S., 136
Boyson, R., 61
Braverman, H., 79, 85
Brehony, K., 61
Brigley, S., 66, 70
Brownmiller, S., 133
Burniston, S., 18
Burrell, G., 116

Cain, M., 120, 121
Cameron, D., 158
Campbell, B., 1, 119, 125
Caplan, P., 162
Carlen, P., 127
Casburn, M., 127
Chambers, G., 141
Chatterton, M., 141
Checkland, P., 78

Chitty, C., 75
Clark, A., 163
Cooley, M., 78, 79, 85
Cooper & Lybrand, 64
Coote, A., 1
Cornford, D., 79
Cousins, M., 159
Coward, R., 17
Cox, C., 61
Cromwell, R. E., 46

Dahl, T. S., 161, 169, 174
Dahlerup, D., 38, 39
Dahlstrom, E., 25
Dale, R., 61
Daly, M., 6, 138
David, M., 66
Davies, C., 82
Deem, R., 74, 76
Department of Education and Science, 61
Department of the Environment, 42
Dex, S., 81, 116
Dinnerstein, D., 13
Dobash, R., and Dobash, R. E., 55, 134
Donnerstein, E., 136
Downes, D., 136
Dworkin, A., 135

Earley, P., 63
Easlea, B., 82
Edgell, S., 46
Edwards, S., 134, 136, 138, 142, 154, 165, 166
Ehn, P., 77, 78, 79, 82, 87
Ehrlich-Martin, S., 123, 124
Eichenbaum, L., 5, 6, 15
Equal Opportunities Commission, 58
Evans, L., 122
Evans, T., 68
Evason, E., 55
Exeter Society for Curriculum Studies Research, 66, 70

193

Fairley, L., 97, 99
Farrant, W., 170
Faulkner, W., 82
Fawcett, H. G., 23
Feldburg, R., 81
Ferraro, K. J., 139
Fielding, N. G., 117, 124, 129
Finch, J., 120
Flude, M., 64
Fox-Keller, E., 82
Freeman, M. D. A., 134
Freud, S., 2, 7, 8, 9
Freidan, B., 3
Friedman, A., 79
Friend, J., 114
Frosch, S., 15, 17

Gallagher, J., 168, 172
Gallop, J., 11
Gane, C., 31
Gaskell, J., 82
Gibbon, P., 95
Gillespie, D., 46
Glenn, E., 81
Golby, M., 66
Gordon, C., 159
Gorer, G., 55
Graham, H., 120
Green, E., 77
Greenbaum, J., 79, 80
Griffith, J. A. C., 161
Goodman, S., 82
Gronfeldt, J., 87
Gray, J., 117, 124
Gunnarson, E., 87
Gutek, B. A., 116

Haas, L., 88
Hadjipotiou, N., 97
Hall, V., 62
Halson, J., 100, 102, 104, 109, 112
Hammer, M., 64
Hamner, J., 122, 134, 135, 136
Harding, S., 159
Harknell, G., 139
Hatty, M., 141
Haug, F., 162
Hearn, J., 115, 116, 119

Herbert, C., 99, 109, 111
Hernes, H. M., 34, 35, 36
Hirscheim, R., 79, 81
Hoagland, S., 102
Hoggett, B., 22, 173
Holdaway, S., 117, 127, 130
Hollway, W., 102
Holly, L., 102, 104
Horney, K., 12
Hough, M., 118, 136
Humphries, J., 22
Hunt, P., 50
Huws, U., 81

Jackson, M., 78
Jaffe, P., 144
Jayaranta, N., 78
Jefferies, G., 58
Johnson, D., 62
Jolin, A., 143
Jones, C., 97
Jones, S., 117, 118, 123

Kelly, L., 97, 99, 101, 104, 108, 109, 112
Kanderup, S., 87
Kingdom, E., 170, 174
Kitzinger, C., 109
Klein, M., 13, 14
Knights, D., 116
Kogan, M., 62
Kyng, M., 79

Lambertz, J., 55
Land F., 78, 79
Land, H., 55
Lawson, D., 75
Leamouth and Burchett Management Systems, 78, 81
Lees, S., 112
Leiulsfrud, H., 33, 34, 38
Lello, J., 61
Lie, M., 82
Liddington, J., 23
Liff, S., 83, 95
Logan, D., 124
Lown, J., 102
Luckhaus, L., 167
Lukes, S., xi

Author Index

Mackay, H., 62
MacKinnon, C., 160, 162, 166, 174
Maclure, S., 61
Mahoney, P., 109
Mann, M., 19
McBarnet, J., 127
McCabe, S., 142
McCann, K., 134
McDonald, G. W., 46
McGillivray, A., 137
McLeod, M., 136, 137, 139
McNeil, M., 82
McRae, S., 50
Marshall, T. H., 19, 20, 21, 24
Mayhew, P., 118, 136
Measor, L., 102
Millar, A., 141
Miller, C., 158
Miller, J. D., 3, 10
Millett, K., 3
Mitchell, J., 9, 10, 11, 162
Montgomery, P., 136
Monod, E., 80
Moody, S. R., 136
Moore, F., 138
Morgan, C., 62
Morgan, D. A. J., 50
Morris, A., 127
Mort, F., 18
Moseley, R., 84
Mossman, M. J., 160
Mumford, E., 77, 78
Murray, F., 81, 82, 95

NALGO, 84, 95
New, C., 66
Nixon, J., 136
Noad, A., 114
Norris, J., 114
Norris, M., 23

Oakley, A., 8, 120
O'Donovan, K., 20, 22, 25, 135
Office of Population Censuses and Surveys, 42
Owen, J., 77
Okin, S. M., 23
Olerup, A., 80
Olsen, D., 46

Oppenlander, N., 139, 140, 141
Orbach, S., 5, 6, 15

Packwood, T., 62
Pahl, J., 41, 49
Pain, D., 77
Pankhurst, S., 23
Parker, H., 127
Parker, T., 134
Parkin, W., 115, 116, 119
Pateman, C., 19
Paukert, L., 32
Pearson, G., 114, 116, 123, 125, 127
Pearson, R., 127
Pemberton, J., 84
Penelope, J., 102
Perby, M., 82
Pollitiz, A. A., 149

Pringle, R., 73

Radford, J., 134, 135
Randall, V., 69
Rasmussen, B., 82
Reiner, R., 117, 123, 143
Ressner, U., 87
Riley, D., 3, 14, 15
Robinson, S., 13
Rock, P., 136
Rosenbrock, H., 77
Rosser, J., 82
Ruggie, M., 30, 36, 38

Sachs, A., 22, 161
Safilios Rothschild, C., 46
Sallis, J., 70
Sampson, A., 114, 125, 127
Sanders, A., 136, 142
Sarson, T., 81
Saunders, S., 122
Sayers, J., 4, 8, 11, 13, 16
Scanzoni, J., 46
Schmeider, E., 80
Schnieder, B., 99
Scott, H., 25, 37
Scott, S., 101, 108
Scutt, J., 139
Segal, H., 13, 14

Sherman, L. W., 144
Siim, B., 36
Skolnick, J., 142
Smart, C., 135, 160, 168, 173
Smith, C., 78, 79
Smith, D., 114, 125, 127
Smith, D. J., 117, 124
Smith, R., 165
Southgate, P., 123
Spender, D., 23, 71, 158
Stamp, P., 50
Stanko, E., 99, 100, 111, 134, 135, 136
Stanley, L., 99, 120, 122, 132
Stanworth, M., 171
Streatfield, D., 58
Steer, D., 142
Steinmetz, C. H. D., 145
Stone, L., 83
Strachey, R., 23
Stubbs, P., 114, 125, 127
Suleiman, S. R., 162
Sumner, C., 161
Sutcliffe, F., 142
Swift, K., 158
Szyzyczak, E., 20, 22, 25

Talbot, M., 74
Telford, A., 144
Therborn, G., 49
Thomas, T., 117, 127
Thornton, M., 160
Toombs, J., 136
Treseder, J., 116
Turnbull, D., 127

Van Dandell H. C., 145
Vehvilainin, M., 80, 87

Wagner, I., 83
Walby, S., 81, 82, 116
Walker, J., 29
Walkowitz, J., 165
Warshaw, R., 112
Webb, J., 95
Webster, J., 81
Weedon, C., 18, 158
West, J., 81
Wexler, J., 124
Whittaker, T., 62
Williams, R., 84
Willmott, H., 116
Wilson, E., 6
Wilson, G., 138
Wilson, J. H., 22, 161
Wimbush, E., 74
Wise, S., 99, 120, 122, 132
Wolfe, D. A., 144
Wood, J., 98
Woodward, A., 33, 34, 38
Wood-Harper, A. T., 79
Worden, R. E., 149
Worrall, A., 127
Wyre, R., 97

Yelloly, M., 116

Zoomer, O., 141
Zweig, F., 55

Subject Index

abortion, 165, 170
abuse of wives, 55, 133–56
agendas, 68, 69, 73
America (North), 79, 172, 174
American Police Foundation, 143
anti-racism, 75
anti-sexism, 76
arrest, 150–6
Asian, 59, 63, 73
assaults
  violent, 134–56
  sexual, 104, 106
Australia, 141

bisexuality, 12
black, 59, 62, 63, 66, 70, 72
black women, 5
Black Papers (Education), 61
breadwinner, 51

Canada, 144
carers, 26
castration, 7, 8, 19
child allowances/benefits, 30–3
child, care, 24–5, 28–30, 33
children/childhood, 6–16, 22, 63, 171, 172, 173
citizenship, xii, 19–40
clerical work, 81–96
clerking, 71, 73
clients, 35, 40, 121, 126, 129
clitoris/clitoral, 7, 12
computers, 77–96
consciousness, 162
consciousness-raising, 1, 5, 87
courts, xi, xii, xiii, 127, 134, 148, 159–66
crime, 137, 148–56
Criminal Justice Act, 148
criminal justice system, 114, 115, 117, 136
criminology, 134, 135, 136
culture, 158

Denmark, 145
Department of Education and Science, 60, 61
dependency, 54
discourse, xii, xiii
domestic violence, 133–56
Education Acts, 59, 62–3
Education Reform Act, 59, 63–5, 73, 75, 76
employment, 21, 26, 27, 32, 37, 40, 42, 48
equal opportunities policies, 83, 84, 86, 90
equality, 25–40, 118
ethnicity, 68, 69, 74
Europe, report to Euro-Parliament on violence against women, 145

familial ideology, 26
family, xi, xii, 3, 6, 10, 11, 26, 28, 31, 38, 50, 82
family policy, 25–40
fathers, 10, 14, 15, 33, 67, 169, 173
feminism/feminists, 6, 104, 111, 112, 158, 159, 160, 162, 175
feminist jurisprudence, 160, 174
feminist research, 121
foetus, 170–1
franchise, 20
free market, 26

governing bodies (schools), xi, 58–76

heterosexuality, 6, 7, 13, 14, 97, 98, 102, 103, 109, 162, 170
homicide, 137, 138, 144
household, 42–55
housework, 34, 50
humour, 104
husband, 42–55

ideology, 49, 51, 52, 53, 55, 66, 103, 109, 113

Subject Index

incest, 2, 7
industrial tribunal, 118
infantcide, 165
insane, 22
inter-agency relations, 114–32
intermediate treatment, 118
knowledge
  institutionalisation of, xiii
  systems of, 159, 160, 161
labour market, 28, 30, 32, 35, 37, 38, 54, 81
Lacanian 9–12
language, 10, 11, 158–9
law, 157, 159–75
legal discourse
lesbian, 102, 170
local authority, 83–96
local education authorities, 58–61, 69
local management schools policy, 64, 75

managers/management, 78, 86, 91, 92, 115, 117, 126
marriage, 23, 41–57, 173
masculinity, 97, 117, 119, 123, 136, 158, 159
medical profession, 133, 157, 171
mental health system, 3, 6, 12
middle class, 21, 61, 75
Muslim, 72
mothers/motherhood, 3, 7, 10, 14, 15, 16, 27, 32, 38, 67, 74, 169, 170, 172, 173

National Curriculum, 64
Netherlands, 141

occupational culture, 126, 128, 130, 131
organisations, theory, 115, 116, 117

parents, 30, 37
patient, 2
patriarchy, xi, xii, xiii, 1, 5, 9, 10, 11, 57, 75, 102
penis/phallus, 7–12, 14
police, xi, 114–32, 135, 137, 139–56
  Metropolitan Police, 147

Police and Criminal Evidence Act, 146
probation service, 114, 118, 120, 121, 122
professions, 21, 22, 86, 129
prostitution, 166
protective legislation, 21
provocation, 138
psychoanlysis, 1–18
psychology, 1, 3

Qualification of Women Act, 1918, 20

race, 125
racial attack, 141
racism, 117, 131, 137
rape, 106, 108, 112, 141, 162–6, 175
reproduction, 169–74
resistance, xii, 8, 20, 102, 104, 109
role theory, 3

Scandinavia, 80, 174
sexism, 117, 131, 137, 174
sex discrimination, 111, 118, 122, 124, 125
Sex Discrimination Removal Act, 1919, 20
sexual abuse, 119, 166, 175
sexual assault, *see* rape
sexual division of labour, 6
sexual identity, 99, 100, 101
sexual harassment, xi, 97–113, 120, 122, 127, 128, 130, 132
sexual violence, 99, 102, 104, 111 (*see also* rape)
sexuality, xii, 2, 100, 116, 117, 124, 162, 163, 164
schools, xiii, 58–71, 97–113
sisterhood, 5
skills, 79, 88, 110, 131
social class, 21, 66, 68, 69
social services, 114–32
social workers, 119
sociology/sociologists, xii, 3, 8, 116, 134
Sweden, 25–40

Taylor Committee/Report, 62
teachers, 99, 109, 110, 111

technology, 77, 91, 93, 94
trade unions, 35, 37, 83, 91, 94
truth, 159, 160, 161

unemployment, 133

vagina, 8, 13, 14
victim, 137, 140, 156

Warnock Committee Report, 173
welfare state, 24, 35, 38
white, 98
wife, 41–55
women's liberation movement/ women's movement, 3, 5, 13
work, 21
working class, 5, 22, 33, 63, 72, 73, 98